DEVELOPING WRITING TEACHERS

"A major strength is combining into one text teacher as writer and teacher as one skilled in pedagogy. The teacher stories about their own writing and their responses to the writing of their peers will inspire teachers in their own writing.
Ruie Pritchard, North Carolina State University, USA

"The strength of this book is in the way it draws together different perspectives and synthesizes research from a broad range of studies, but [is] located within a practical, professional context. It will be useful to pre-service and in-service teachers and any other practitioner with a professional interest in writing."
Debra Myhill, University of Exeter, UK

The premise of *Developing Writing Teachers* is this: When teachers of writing identify as writers, it adds a special dimension to their writing pedagogy. Practical and accessible while drawing on a range of relevant research and theory, this text is distinguished by its dual focus on teachers *as* writers and the teaching *of* writing. Part I addresses the question, What does it take for a teacher of writing to develop an identity as writer? Using case studies and teacher narratives, it guides readers to an understanding of the current status of writing at the beginning of the 21st century, the role of expressive writing in developing a writing identity, the relationship of writing to genre and rhetoric, writing and professional identity, and writing as design. Part II focuses on pedagogical practice and helping writer-teachers develop a toolkit to take into their classrooms. Coverage includes building a community of writing practice; the nature of writing as process; the place of grammar; the role of information, communication and representational technologies; and how assessment, properly used, can help develop writing.

Features

- *Research based*: Draws on academic and research literature that theorizes the nature of writing and proposes ways of enhancing writing pedagogy
- *Practical guide*: Invites readers to engage in a range of writing activities and reflect on them, and offers ways *in* to these tasks and activities which make them doable

- *Teacher stories*: Accounts of teachers who formed new identities as writers and changed their practices in ways that led to changes in their students' motivation to write and writing performance
- *Companion Website*: Additional readings/documents; PowerPoint presentations; Assessment resources, especially rubrics; Planning resources, including lesson and unit plans and planning guides

Terry Locke is Professor of Arts and Language Education, The University of Waikato, New Zealand.

DEVELOPING WRITING TEACHERS

Practical Ways for Teacher-Writers to Transform their Classroom Practice

Terry Locke

Routledge
Taylor & Francis Group

NEW YORK AND LONDON

First published 2015
by Routledge
711 Third Avenue, New York, NY 10017

and by Routledge
2 Park Square, Milton Park, Abingdon, Oxon OX14 4RN

Routledge is an imprint of the Taylor & Francis Group, an informa business

Library of Congress Cataloging in Publication Data
  Locke, Terry, 1946–
  Developing writing teachers : practical ways for teacher-writers to transform their classroom practice / by Terry Locke.
  pages cm
  Includes bibliographical references and index.
  1. English language—Rhetoric—Study and teaching. 2. Creative writing. I. Title.
  PE1404.L63 2014
  808'.042071—dc23

ISBN: 978–0–415–63183–9 (hbk)
ISBN: 978–0–415–63184–6 (pbk)
ISBN: 978–0–203–09645–1 (ebk)

Typeset in Bembo and Stone Sans
by Florence Production Ltd, Stoodleigh, Devon, UK

Printed and bound in the United States of America by Publishers Graphics, LLC on sustainably sourced paper.

To National Writing Projects around
the world and the teachers they have inspired

CONTENTS

PREFACE

This book had a number of prompts. One is the fact that in virtually all Anglophonic countries, student writing performance lags behind their reading. Not only do students underperform as writers; they appear to be progressively *less* motivated to write the further along they are in their compulsory schooling. If we shift our attention to teachers, we find widespread evidence that teachers don't write much either. Many teachers lack confidence in themselves as writers and certainly don't *identify* as writers.

Related to this first prompt is the ambiguity of the book's title. On the one hand, it could be read as "Developing the teacher of writing"; on the other hand, it could be read as "Developing the teacher who writes". In fact, the book is about both of these topics. In addition, it is premised on the conviction that teachers—not just teachers of English language arts—but all teachers need to see themselves as teachers of writing who write.

A second prompt was more positive. Research, particularly associated with Writing Project professional development in the United States and, more recently, New Zealand and the United Kingdom, has testified to the transformative effects which occur when teachers, through sustained engagement in acts of writing and reflection in communities of practice, assume identities as writers and enact this identity with their students. In general, this transformation in identity is accompanied by transformations in pedagogical practice. This is because such teachers have a newfound understanding of what pedagogical practices around writing actually *work*.

A third prompt was personal. In a tentative way, I saw myself as a writer before I became a college student and long before I found myself in a high school classroom. Over a period of 40 years, I have engaged in a variety of writing acts: writing reviews, poetry, press releases, prose fiction, academic articles and so on.

Despite this experience, the "terror of the blank page" is still something I grapple with. However, I have also developed a firm belief in ways in which all teachers can develop what I call the *disposition* to write. This book is aimed at helping teachers develop this disposition, so that they can truly experience what it means to write one's self, including one's professional self, into being.

I have written this book mostly for teachers and those learning to teach. The "you" I have in my head as I use the second-person mode of address is a composite of teachers in both primary school and high school settings that I have met over the years. Many of these teachers have been colleagues with whom I have served in a range of high schools. Many have been teachers whose professional formation I have played a role in. Others have been members of collaborative research projects, some focused on ways of exploring how certain kinds of professional learning for teachers can have positive spin-offs in their classrooms, especially in relation to the teaching of writing.

My second audience consists of teacher educators. Many of us doing this important work are currently operating in settings where the policy environment is constructing our "success" in terms of pre-specified standards and outcomes. Many of us are feeling the pressure to adopt an instrumental approach to initial teacher education by providing our students with simple "how to's," while finding we have few opportunities to engage these tertiary learners in the kind of sustained personal formation that will develop their confidence as writers and wide readers.

The two parts into which this book is divided reflect its dual preoccupation. The focus of the first part of the book is the teacher who writes. Here the word "writing" in the phrase "writing teacher" has a strong verbal sense, suggesting a teacher whose identity is in part constituted by writing as an activity which the teacher herself engages in. In this part of the book, I explore what it means to be a writer in the 21st century and reflect on ways in which the identity of "writer" can be claimed and developed by a teacher like yourself.

In the second part of the book, the word "writing" in the phrase "writing teacher" is a noun (gerund), where "writing" is a thing that teachers teach and learners learn. This part of the book focuses on a range of topics related to the practice of teaching writing, particularly in primary and high-school settings.

This Book Has a Number of Distinctive Features:

1. It directly addresses teachers who are asking themselves such questions as: What does it mean to identify as a writer? What kind of teacher of writing am I? How do I feel about myself as a writer? How might those feelings change and what relevance does this have to me as a teacher of writing? How do I feel about myself as a teacher of writing? What aspects of my teaching practice do I feel secure in? What aspects am I insecure about?

2. It is research-based, that is, it draws on current (and not so current) academic and research literature that both theorizes about the nature of writing and proposes ways of enhancing writing pedagogy. Where appropriate, I refer to research that backs up the claims I make. At the end of each chapter, you will find references to further reading that will help develop your understanding of themes that have been treated.

3. It has global reach in that it draws on the experiences of teachers and the findings of researchers from all parts of the English-speaking world. It is no surprise that teachers of writing in many parts of the world are facing the same issues and dilemmas in their classrooms in relation to the teaching of writing.

4. It serves as goad and guide, that is, it invites you as reader to engage in a range of writing activities, and reflective and inquiry tasks. In many instances, it also offers ways *in* to these tasks and activities, through process modeling, thus making these activities doable. I suggest strongly that you keep a reflective journal as you journey through this book. It is *not* a book to be read in one sitting! Rather, you might think of it as a traveling companion with whom you can take up conversations about writing and the teaching of writing as time in your busy life allows.

5. It shares stories about teachers who have assumed new identities as writers and who have changed their practices in ways which have led to changes in their students' writing performance and motivation.

Structure of the Book

Part I: The Teacher as Writer

After a scene-setting introduction (Chapter 1), the focus in the first part of the book is on you as writer rather than as *teacher* of writing. You might think of it as a guide taking you on a journey that helps you try out what it might mean for *you* to identify as a writer. Part 1 has five chapters:

Chapter 2: Writing in the 21st Century

This chapter examines what it means to call ourselves writers. I discuss the nature of writing itself, viewing it as a historically and culturally situated and constrained activity that has changed over time. I look at different ways of answering the question, "What does it mean to be a writer?" I then set the scene for what happens in the remainder of this book by discussing writing (like literacy) as technologized, as a product as well as a practice, as a mode of expression and representation, and as a socially and culturally framed rhetorical act.

Chapter 3: Writing the Self Through Storying

This focus in this chapter is on personal or expressive writing. It provides a range of prompts for writing that have been successful with teachers, in writing workshop (and other) settings, and examples of such writing. It shows how writing can be used for a range of personal purposes: writing for self-discovery; writing to learn; writing to establish one's voice; and writing as a way of constructing identity.

Chapter 4: "One's-self I Sing": The Democratic Self in Writing

This chapter begins by revisiting the ancient concept of rhetoric and the rhetor—the person with designs on an audience and who fashions his or her text accordingly using the resources at his or her disposal. It argues that all texts have a rhetorical purpose and are produced in order to get something done. Viewed this way, writing becomes the heart of the democratic forum, enabling speakers to develop, sustain, defend, negotiate and modify a position in dialogue with others. This chapter argues that texts are generally multifunctional—describing, narrating and arguing a case. It explores the concept of genre and argues that even literary genres can be thought of as having a persuasive force.

Chapter 5: Writing as Enacting the Professional Self

The setting for this chapter is the professional life of the teacher. I argue here that writing has a key role to play in a teacher's professionality and explore the relationship of professionality to writing. I raise questions around the teacher's voice—to whom or to what does this voice address itself and how? In particular, how can the professional self be sustained through writing in a context where teachers' voices can be silenced and where "audit" cultures operate to disempower and deprofessionalize teachers.

Chapter 6: Writing as Design

This chapter focuses on the written text as visual artifact. It enlarges the concept of "writer" to include such terms as "composer" and "designer" and explores the implications of this renaming for "writing" practice. It offers examples of teachers exploiting the affordances of digital technology to produce multimodal texts and hypertexts, but also confirms that the "visual" has always been with us.

Part II: The Teacher of Writing

The second part of the book addresses key issues you will want to engage with as a teacher of writing, regardless of the subject you teach.

Chapter 7: Best Practice Overview—What the Research Says

This chapter provides an overview of writing pedagogy, particularly in school settings, and offers of a map of the various approaches one might find in classrooms, usually in combination. It draws on a number of reviews of the research into the teaching of writing and draws some conclusions in respect of what works, both to improve the writing of students and to increase their motivation and self-efficacy as writers.

Chapter 8: Building a Community of Writing Practice

The starting point for this chapter is that writing is a socialized practice. I explore the implications of this assumption in respect of such things as the identification of roles in the writing classroom, notions of authenticity in relation to the meaningfulness of the writing task, and the primacy of audience. I also examine the kind of fluidity in identity that occurs when the writing classroom is thought of as a community of writers where expertise is distributed among members. In particular, I discuss ways in which response to text can be taught and fostered, and the place of talk and metacognition.

Chapter 9: Writing as Process

This chapter revisits writing as a process, both as involving a range of cognitive operations and as a sequence of tasks determined by the sociocultural context and rhetorical situation. It spells out the implications of what we know about the writing process for the development of learning strategies and shows how an instructional sequence can be constructed using the example of travel writing.

Chapter 10: Addressing (and Answering) the "Grammar" Question

The chapter begins with a brief summation of the issues that lay behind the so-called grammar wars. It then draws on current research and theorizations of practice, to suggest a range of ways that the explicit use of grammatical knowledge can contribute to the writing process. Underpinning this chapter is a recognition that acts of reading are intimately bound up with acts of writing and an assumption that the use of meta-language is rendered most meaningful and productive in the context of a rhetorical approach to writing and writing instruction.

Chapter 11: Writing as Technology, or Writing as ICRT

This chapter begins by arguing that the term "ICT" should be replaced by the term "ICRT" (Information, Communication *and* Representational Technologies).

It reviews some of the research, which has investigated the productive and not-so-productive ways in which the teaching of writing has changed through the integration of various ICRTs in classrooms. In particular, it focuses on word processing, multimodal storytelling and blogging.

Chapter 12: Writing Assessment as Negotiating Power and Discourse

This chapter begins by noting the disjunction that occurs between the evaluation of writing in educational settings and in the world beyond school. In providing an overview of assessment practice in the educational setting, it suggests that there are a number of discourses of assessment, including the widespread discourse of assessment for learning. Using the metaphor of a servant to two masters, it suggests that most teachers find themselves negotiating two broad discourses of writing assessment practice. The first, extrinsically oriented discourse, is "framed" or "constructed" by high-stakes testing or standards regimes that have been government mandated. The second, intrinsically oriented discourse, relates to the professional content knowledge of the teacher who understands the nature of writing and how it is best evaluated for the good of individual students.

ACKNOWLEDGMENTS

I would like to thank colleagues and teachers who worked with me over two years on the "Teachers as writers" project: David Whitehead, Stephanie Dix, Gail Cawkwell, Ruie Pritchard, Sally Barrett, Fiona Murphy, Hazel Redpath, Phillipa Grace, Helen Kato, Robyn Mills, Dawn Irvin, Tim Bullock, Bev Boyes, Therese Cargo, Gail Weston and Jenny Dalton. Special thanks go to those teachers who gave me permission to share their writing with the audience of this book.

I would like to thank the following scholars who have been prepared to act as readers for parts of this text, sometimes to check that I have not misrepresented their views and to check that I've said what I've thought I said: David Galbraith (University of Southhampton), and David Whitehead (University of Waikato).

I would like to thank: Jacinta Boon for permission to use the poem she wrote as a 10 year old; Teresa Cremin for permission to use her graphic to represent the teacher-writer, writer-teacher continuum; Sally Barrett for permission to use her feedback guide; Carolyn Frank for permission to use her neighborhood map; NCTE as the original publisher of the figure representing Flower and Hayes' (1981) Cognitive writing model ("A cognitive process theory of writing." *College Composition and Communication, 32,* 365–387); the Auckland Council for permission to reproduce the nature-trail pamphlet featuring the Shakespear Regional Park.

I would like to pay special homage to Naomi Silverman, my Routledge editor, for her exquisite tact and prodigious knowledge of the field. I would like to thank the University of Waikato for approving the study leave which afforded me the headspace to write this book.

Finally, I could not have completed this project without the support of my wife, Linda. She has always been my most encouraging critic and has supported me unstintingly throughout the writing of the book.

1

INTRODUCTION: ASSUMING THE IDENTITY OF WRITER

I would not be writing this book if I did not think of myself as a writer. As the reader of this book, here at the start of the journey, you might ask yourself what your answer would be to the question: "Do you think of yourself as a writer?" As you mull over this question, you'll be aware that this question is different from "Are you a writer?" It's easier to say yes to the latter, because of the extreme likelihood that you have already written something this very day—a shopping list, perhaps, or an email, or a text, or a comment on a student's work.

But thinking of ourselves as writers goes beyond recognizing that we engage in activities that require writing. It touches on identity—who we are—a quality of our being.

When I was studying English in high school, I was encouraged by my teacher to write poems and submit them for a school competition. I did so, without success. I still have these writings and am happy to confess that they are awful. I also wrote assignments—long, tortuous essays on Gerald Manley Hopkins and T. S. Eliot. But I did not think of myself as a writer. I was a student who submitted an unreadable poem for a competition and handed in literary essays.

The turning point in my journey occurred when I was studying American fiction in a postgraduate Arts program. My lecturer set us the task of writing a short story in the Hemingway style. The model was the kind of prose that you find in a story like "The Killers":

> The door of Henry's lunch-room opened and two men came in. They sat down at the counter.
> "What's yours?" George asked them.
> "I don't know," one of the men said. "What do you want to eat, Al?"
> "I don't know," said Al. "I don't know what I want to eat."

> Outside it was getting dark. The street-light came on outside the window.
>
> (Hemingway, 1962, p. 224)

I wrote a story about a gang-fight at a youth club I helped run at my local church and produced what I considered to be a fair imitation of Hemingway's "hard-boiled" style. What the activity forced me to do was think very carefully about *how* I was writing. I became *self*-conscious and, at the end of the experience, felt that I had stepped into a new pair of shoes—the shoes of a writer. Thinking of myself as a writer was not related to how good my writing was. But it had a *lot* to do with engaging in the activity and at the same time bringing a degree of reflection to what I was doing. I learned to think of myself as a writer by thinking about my writing as I wrote.

Teachers as Writers

The main focus of this introduction is the "Teachers as Writers" movement that has established a presence in the United States, England and New Zealand in the last four decades. The foundational belief of this movement is that when teachers embrace the identity of writer, their practices as teachers of writing undergo a transformation that enhances the experience of writing and writing performance of their students.

The National Writing Project (NWP) had its genesis in the United States in the Bay Area Writing Project (1973) and is currently a national professional development initiative with many sites. While it has received federal funding, it is a non-profit-making enterprise reliant on funding at local, regional and national level from a range of sources, including sponsors and local educational authorities. Its original and continuing spur was a gap in student achievement between writing and reading, where, according to Richard Andrews, "part of the problem is that teachers of all subjects, and at primary and secondary level, are less confident at writing and at the teaching of writing than they are at reading" (2008a, p. 5).

In a useful overview, Andrews summarizes the basic tenets of NWP thinking:

1. To teach writing, you need to be able to write;
2. Students should respond to each other's writing;
3. The teacher should act as writer alongside the students, and be prepared to undertake the same assignments as the students;
4. There is research about the teaching of writing that needs to be considered and applied, where appropriate, in the classroom;
5. Teachers can be their own researchers in the classroom;
6. The best teacher of writing teachers is another writing teacher; and
7. Various stages of the writing process need to be mapped and practiced: these include pre-writing, drafting, revising, editing, conferencing (see no 2 above) and publishing (2008a, p. 8).

In the U.S. context, the NWP has had good deal of research attention and commentary, which has confirmed the transformational potential of NWP-type professional development, while indicating that "much further investigation is clearly needed into the specific outcomes of NWP participation for classroom practices and for student outcomes" (Whitney, 2008, p. 151).

Influenced by the American project, a national writing project was established in New Zealand in 1987 with distinct projects based in four urban centres. A report on the project by Scanlan and Carruthers's (1990) found that:

- "as the teachers became writers themselves their attitude to the teaching of writing changed;
- "how the teachers *taught* writing changed;
- "student writing improved as a result of these changes; and
- "teachers demonstrated their new skills and knowledge to other teachers" (p. 14).

The report emphasized the way in which teachers trained in the project were "*seeded* back into the system to disseminate what they have learned" (Scanlan & Carruthers, 1990, p. 16), a cascading model also characterising the NWP in the United States.

From 1985 to 1988, a National Writing Project also took place in England, with a year's dissemination from 1988–89. Like its New Zealand counterpart, the project effectively came to a halt in the early 1990s. Both projects were overtaken by a raft of curriculum reforms that changed drastically the nature of teachers' work and which, with their focus on outcomes and levels, appeared out of step with the thinking behind the Teachers as Writers movement. In both countries, while the United States was soldiering on with its National Writing Project, it was another 20 years before steps were taken to reignite the movement.

Helen's Story

The decision to establish anew a writing project in the New Zealand context was realized in a two-year project, carried out in 2010 and 2011 with the title: "Teachers as Writers: Transforming Professional Identity and Classroom Practice." Some university colleagues and I approached 13 teachers in four high schools and four primary schools to engage with us in the project as teacher-researchers. Collectively we wanted to find out:

1. What practices around writing/composing pedagogy (and their attendant discourses) have the potential to contribute to the development of an effective, sustained Writing Workshop environment for teachers?
2. What Writing Workshop features are viewed positively by teacher-participants as contributing to increased confidence and competence in themselves as writers/text-makers?

3. To what extent are the self-efficacy profiles of teachers in relationship to themselves as writers/text-makers modified as a result of their engagement in the Writing Workshop experience?
4. What impact does involvement in the Writing Workshop experience have on the writing/composing pedagogical practices of participant teachers and how do they rate these changes in practice?
5. What pedagogical strategies have the potential to enhance the motivation and writing/composing performance of students of participating teachers and which of these can be attributable to changes in classroom practice prompted by engagement in the Writing Workshop experience?

Findings in relation to these questions are part of the repository of research data that underpins this book. Helen's story arises in this New Zealand context. I make no claim for her as either typical or exemplary, but I hope that you find some points of connection with her.

When I first met Helen Kato in 2010, she had been teaching for eight years in New Zealand secondary schools. She was now Head of English at a rural co-educational school with a role of around 470 students, of whom 32% were indigenous Māori and a significant number Pasifika (i.e., originating from a Pacific Island nation). The school drew students from a range of communities, some relatively affluent and others characterized by low incomes and welfare dependency.

Like other teacher-researchers, Helen attended two six-day Writing Workshops in January 2010 and 2011 and a supplementary one-day workshop in April, 2010. As a participant, she engaged in writing tasks in response to a range of stimuli, giving and receiving feedback in small groups, modeling teaching strategies of her own, and taking turns to share her writing with the whole group while occupying the "author's chair." In broad terms, she was engaged in a process approach to writing. Among the text-types (or genres) she produced were a child-hood memory, a biopoem, a personal narrative, a character poem, a group memory poem and a position statement. (For a detailed account of what happened and teachers' responses to the workshop, see Locke, Whitehead, Dix, & Cawkwell, 2011).

You'll notice I've been using the term "teacher-researcher." Teachers like Helen accepted the deal that they would be research partners in an action research project made up of a number of case-study sites. Lytle and Cochran-Smith (1992) usefully defined teacher research as "systematic, intentional inquiry by teachers about their own school and classroom work" (1992, p. 450). As a research partner, Helen was invited to engage in collaborative decision-making around: *what* she would try with her selected class by way of an intervention; *what* learning objectives she would plan for her unit of work; the data she would need to collect in order to ascertain what tasks/activities/approaches worked in terms of her objectives; and how these data should be analyzed.

In the reflective profile she wrote as part of the project baseline data, Helen described herself as a writer of emails, reports, letters of various kinds and job applications. She saw herself as confident about composing basic narratives and formal letters, but lacked confidence in "creative" writing. She had never considered identifying as "teacher as writer" and confessed that "writing as pleasurable" was not part of her previous study program. In her classroom writing program, writing was not included for anything other than gaining NCEA credits. (The National Certificate of Educational Achievement is New Zealand's qualification system and operates in the final three years of secondary schooling from Year 11 to Year 13.) "Writing as personal pleasure is not at the top of the list," she said.

In 2010, Helen had two Year 12 English classes. The class she chose for her "intervention" was the "least able" of these classes, containing students with a record of truanting, poor motivation and a lack of achievement in terms of NCEA credits at Year 11. The idea of trialling a unit of work based around the writing of poetry had its genesis in the January workshop. She wrote in her reflective journal:

> My approach, indeed even my contemplation of teaching a creative writing unit creatively, is most definitely colored and influenced by the Writing Workshop I participated in at the beginning of the year. With some sense of shame I am forced to admit that before attending the workshop, I had little confidence in my ability to teach creative writing. I feel brave, challenged and excited!! The workshop provided a model for teaching writing in a supportive and academically unthreatening environment, and then gave me the opportunity to actually write creatively. It was an indulgence and a hugely rewarding experience. Personally, and as a teacher, I felt enriched.

In what she described as a series of "brief experimentations," Helen had these students engage in writing freely on such theme as origins, and people and places. Encouraged by the quality of their writing and their enthusiasm, and emboldened by her own growing confidence as a creative writer, Helen decided to implement a poetry unit in the last two terms of the school year. (For a comprehensive account, see Locke and Kato, 2012.)

Helen's aim was to have her students write poetry on "place" or "character" for enjoyment, sharing and to gain NCEA credits at Level 2. Specifically, she was preparing a unit focused on Achievement Standard 2.1: "Produce crafted and developed creative writing," an internally assessed standard with an allocation of three credits. Rather than using a standardized national task (there isn't one for poetry), she herself designed a unit incorporating listening to selected poetry about place or character, reading (silently and aloud for an audience) and creating individual pieces of writing. As she wrote in her journal: "This is an ethnically diverse class so 'place' and 'character' will be widely defined—internal concepts of 'place' are also possible."

The specific learning objectives (SLOs) Helen developed for her students were:

1. Students come to understand that there are different views and descriptions of place/character depending on writers' backgrounds and/or experiences;
2. Students develop confidence in their ability to explore and express their own poetic voice;
3. Students appreciate the value of sharing the experience of writing with responsive peers;
4. Students can express ideas with effect in writing with a purpose;
5. Students can discuss their own and others' writing;
6. Students understand and can use a range of linguistic strategies that make poems powerful and effective.

Helen's intervention occupied a five-week period and was *not* easy sailing, with two students leaving and others absent for a range of reasons. When we analyzed her journal together, we identified five themes: (1) the teacher as writer; (2) reading aloud and discussion as an activity; (3) the use of Writing Project tasks; (4) motivation; and (5) frustrations.

In her Week 1 reflection, Helen wrote: "I feel slightly out of my depth—have never ventured to teach poetry which is more than analysis-centred." During the writing workshop, Helen had written a poem about her daughter, Anna, and decided to share this with her students. (Helen has allowed me to share this with you.) "They were silent for seconds after I had finished . . . then began asking questions: 'Why did you use *that* word . . . what does *that* mean?' Good start."

FOR ANNA MADISON PIPPI VICTORIA APRICOT KATO

A baldly beautiful E.T.
legs as substantial as
Daddy's
thumb,
ponga frond-shaped body nestled neatly along his forearm, wails
constantly imminent
as your headache throbs in your eyes

sorry for the rude entry my daughter.

Unfurling, delicate sensitive tomboy,
a fantail,
gumboots and water, magnolia tree and Granddad's homemade,

pixie-sized chair,
plum juice-stained t-shirts, sticky and smeared
only one limp tattered be-ribboned pigtail intact.

Tautly reaching tensile green koru body
tears
of
determination
streaking cheeks pinched with cold,
mixing with sweat in the foggy morning air,
petite rocket terrier child.

Tensile harp strings harmonising
unsourced DNA, gutsy, stubborn,
Asianly emotionally aware,
loving, with an ever-maturing sense of humour
building a bridge of steel and perfumed ether between us.

Vulnerable in recently born femininity
glossy, sun-kissed hair, straightened to attention,
txt happy, cuddle needy,
treasured daughter
sipping at life's cup, which is tantalisingly full
of yet unsavored flavours.

Blossom safely and fly high, falcon girl!

In Week 2, after setting her class an activity about an orange, she wrote a poem on the whiteboard with her students watching:

Fragrant,
teasing me

With waxy dimpled skin
Like armor
tangy
Squishy,
Slurp.

"Not a brilliant effort but it seemed to start discussion." The class proceeded to discuss Helen's choice of language: "Miss, you have a simile there." "You should use a different word . . . not 'skin'." "Why is it 'armor'?" She continued: "I was on shaky ground . . . really had to structure the class so that they felt confident to write their own. The interesting part was listening to them answering each other's questions, and responding to observations made. All agreed that they could smell/see the orange." Following this discussion, students wrote their own poems "very willingly." Helen used a number of photo prompts in her teaching. The following week she showed them a photograph of Pasifika women harvesting fruit. Again, she shared a poem that she wrote in response to the photograph, indicating in her Week 3 reflection that it promoted discussion.

A second theme was the place of reading aloud. Helen read aloud her own poems as well as anthology poems, carefully chosen to reflect the interests of her students and the writing focus she had selected. After reading some Glenn Colquhoun (1999) poems in the first week, she noted that her students had "amazing insights but little confidence in expressing their thoughts". She viewed them as needing a "poetic device vocabulary." However, the oral reading appeared motivating. After asking them to write impressions of a character or place they had in their minds or hearts, she wrote: "Absolute silence, all heads down. Have to remind myself that this is my lower ability class!! Scratching of pens, pages turning." In Week 2, she chose poems from *Whetu Moana* (Wendt et al., 2003), this time experimenting with reading in different voices and rhythms and following up by giving them their own copy so that they could read aloud to each other. In Week 5, Helen had the class listen to an Apirana Taylor CD (2004). Taylor had visited the school earlier in the year, and the students had listened to him read with "intense enjoyment." On this occasion, she wanted them to "hear his 'music" and his rhythm and resonant, Māori voice." She followed up by playing instrumental music "to see if it inspired them to settle and continue writing. It did." Helen's belief that these activities were motivating was reinforced the following period when her class smugly remarked that her other Year 12 class ("the highly academic class who are always in a hurry to cut to the chase for credits" and who had looked down their noses at the Taylor CD) wanted to know why they "did all the 'fun' stuff."

A third theme was the deliberate use of Writing Project tasks or activities. In the first week of the intervention, Helen invited students to write a biopoem, as writing workshop participants had done: "They tried hard, and I become aware that they need to become accustomed to not worrying about 'getting it wrong.' Writing for their own pleasure, and not assessment, is a foreign concept still" (Reflective journal). In the second week, students wrote a childhood memory. In introducing this task, Helen focused on concrete diction, extremes of emotion, assuming a retrospective viewpoint and building vocabulary. A vocabulary exercise "fed their appetite for using descriptive words. . . . Some of them immediately began ransacking (literally) the cupboard for a thesaurus" (Reflective journal). However, Helen adapted the activity by introducing the use of photos as prompts, using graphic organizers to help students structure their writing, and having them discuss poems which drew on memory in some way.

Another theme to emerge was student motivation and improved self-efficacy, instances of which we have met already. Reflecting in her journal on her lesson with her students on the Friday of the first week, Helen wrote:

> When the bell rang on Friday they were still writing. "Can I take my book home? I'm not finished." "I'm going to show Mum what I wrote." Rebecca [all student names are pseudonyms], my least able, asked me to read her work. . . .thinks she is "dumb" but is clearly proud of her first efforts. I asked them for some feedback as they left, most with their 1B5's in their bags. "This is great." "Cool, Miss!" . . . asked them to bring photos or drawings of their "people" or "places" for next week. . . . I am enjoying this so much.

In another lesson, Helen gave the class a newspaper article about a child who had briefly gone missing in Auckland and asked them to take the perspective of one of the family or the child himself. Helen noted that some of them wrote from their own experience. "Sandy, my Otara student with the baseball bat story, stayed behind to share her poem. Precious moments" (Reflective journal). In the third week, Helen wrote the following comment:

> Their inferential reading skills have improved . . . understanding of concepts, feelings, themes not directly stated was wonderful . . . discussion and some disagreements led to teaching opportunity . . . giving reasons/evidence for deductions and statements. Valuable. Students becoming more confident about thinking and almost no, "Why don't they say that if that is what they mean?" responses. (Reflective journal)

Engagement with writing was clearly motivating close reading; reading now had a point. Consequently, self-efficacy in respect of reading as well as writing increased.

A fifth and recurrent theme to emerge was Helen's continuing frustrations, not so much with her students, as with school climate and organization. In week three, we find this entry:

> Next class—students missing for sickness, trips, production, defensive driving. Beginning to worry as exams are soon, and we are not progressing as a class . . . completion of this creative writing is looking uncertain. However, the comments about this class from students are very positive . . . they really enjoy writing . . . considering this is supposed to be a reluctant group of students, this approach of being able to do their "own" writing has amazing results. Most of them take their journals home . . . and I know some of them share their work with family members . . . the tragedy is that this is not NCEA-measurable. (Reflective journal)

Two sub-themes emerge here: (1) the predations of extra-curricular activities on a teacher's classroom program with a class which has a record of non-attendance; and (2) the one-size-fits-all nature of NCEA creative writing assessment and the way it measures writing outputs. At the end of Week 4, Helen is beset with frustration and self-doubt:

> Beginning to feel the pressure! Have not done enough in terms of language terms etc.
>
> Will they be able to complete NCEA Creative Writing. . . . Feel that this is largely my fault . . . am trying to teach an integrated program in a school where they are proceeding as if we still have School Certificate—and all assessment is either at the end of the year (so catch-up is possible) or in bite-sized chunks ("teach" something quickly and then assess, then on to the next thing). I have let my students down . . .

But Helen survived this crisis and soldiered on into Week 5, knowing that in Week 6 she would lose most of her students to a physical education camp worth 6 NCEA credits and the focus would shift to exam revision. "These students (most of them) do not live in circumstances which are conducive to doing 'homework' . . . the fact that they even write in their journals in their own time is amazing. This makes the time they have in class so very important . . . and continuity is all" (Reflective journal).

There are two postscripts to this story. The first involves the thorny question of assessment, which I will be exploring in detail in Chapter 12. In the second six-day workshop, secondary participants agreed to mark independently and then cross-mark Helen's students' poetry portfolios according to an agreed rubric which was referenced to the achievement criteria related to the Achievement Standard Helen had entered her students for: "Produce crafted and developed creative writing." All students achieved the standard.

The second postscript relates to a letter to the project team Helen wrote at the end of 2011. Here is a section of it:

> How did a disparate, multicultural and mixed gender class of students who had little confidence in their abilities in English develop into a group who clearly enjoyed writing creatively, and sharing their work? Looking back over my personal journal, I realized that my own teaching practice had altered, fostered an environment in which this could happen. Initially, there were many challenges for me as a teacher. I had not been confident about teaching the genre of poetry. This had made my practice wooden, firmly structured and probably very boring. I had taught interpretation of meaning, but never writing. My lack of passion for writing had, I concluded, probably communicated itself to my students.

What had I done differently this time? The following is a list of practices which I learned from this class. They are now part of my practice for teaching all creative writing genres to all levels of students.

- Always write when students are writing. Model the practice.
- Begin by reading lots of writing and discussing with the class what they enjoy and why.
- Validate sincere personal responses from students.
- Model the creative process on the whiteboard: the alteration of vocabulary, the scribbles, crossing-outs, the reading aloud to "hear" rhythm, the alteration of structure.
- Respect the fact that no-one can write to order. If students can't write during class time and want to write later/at home/tomorrow, then try to accommodate their wishes. Sometimes this is difficult!!
- Share our own journal work if it is hoped that they have confidence to share theirs.
- Respect and be aware of the fact that some students will not want to share their thoughts about personal writing with others.
- Give them control over which work they wish to submit, if there is an assessment goal.
- Be acutely aware of the privileged position of teacher when asking students to write personally.

Helen, and other teachers, will join us in other conversations throughout this book. But now it is time to consider the voices of "teachers as writers" in other settings.

REFLECTIVE JOURNAL TASK 1.1

Is there anything in Helen's story that resonates with you? Use some aspect of Helen's story to reflect about some aspect of your own experience, *either* as a writer *or* as a teacher of writing.

Writing Projects in the United States and England

The United States

In July 2011, I was privileged to be invited to spend a day with teachers participating in a New York City Writing Project (NYCWP) summer "intensive" session based at Lehman University in the Bronx. The NYCWP was founded in 1978 as the New York City site of the National Writing Project in the United States and since that time had provided professional learning for over 15,000 New York City teachers. However, sitting in a classroom, watching teachers share a writing approach with other teachers, engaging in a writing task involving a brief story about "my name," and sharing their work with others, I felt myself occupying a familiar space. Hearing teachers discussing their frustrations with standards-based assessment models recalled all-too-familiar conversations in my own country.

The best overview of the National Writing Project is probably Ann Lieberman and Diane Wood's book, *Inside the National Writing Project* (2003), based on a two-year project undertaken in 1998–1999 to study two Writing Project sites, one based at UCLA and the other at Oklahoma State University. The book offers a comprehensive overview of the Writing Project model and how it operates as a network, and provides portraits of six teachers, three from each site.

Linda Thomas was one such teacher. Her first brush with Writing Project philosophy was through a "teacher consultant" in the early 1980s, at the start of her teaching career and at a time when her own children were beginning school. "Teacher consultant" (TC) is the U.S. term for a "graduate" of a NWP summer institute, who is prepared to take on the role of facilitating the professional learning of other teachers. The TC organized workshops in Linda's own school, modeling processes that Linda later came to recognize as typical of Writing Workshop programming. However, it wasn't until 1994 that Linda undertook her first summer institute at the Oklahoma State University site. By this time, she was heavily engaged in professional development in her own area, engaged in designing and implementing writing standards, rubrics and practices related to writing pedagogy.

Her aim in attending the summer institute was two-fold: to become a better writer/writing teacher and to become a better professional developer. Her "epiphany," as she described it, "came when she realized that learning to write, learning to teach others to write, and learning to teach teachers all required the same processes" (Lieberman & Wood 2003, p. 75). As she saw it, the needs of learners at all three levels were the same, namely:

- The need to have individual differences recognized and valued;
- The need to reflect critically as a vital component of learning;
- The need to take ownership of one's learning. (Lieberman and Wood recall visiting Linda's classroom and seeing her students "deliver minilessons on grammar and punctuation errors that many of them were making" [p. 76].)
- The need for a connection between learning in the classroom and a student's out-of-school life.

Lieberman and Wood, saw all six focus teachers as having something in common:

Although each of these teachers had an individual style and a unique set of challenges, they shared some common convictions. First, they were deeply committed to students' literacy and believed in the power of writing-to-learn. Second, each created classroom communities, capable of both critique and support, as an essential context for learning.

(2003, p. 78).

England

As mentioned previously, a National Writing Project flowered briefly in England between 1985 and 1989, before shriveling in the cold gusts of curriculum reform in the 1990s. However, there are signs of a spring awakening in that country. In the last few years, the situation in England has been characterized by a range of small projects based on "teachers as writers" principles, all committed to the fostering of professional autonomy and authority in teachers.

A major focus has been the facilitation of teachers' writing groups, based around five core principles:

1. Teachers as agents of reform supported by face-to-face meeting and closed VLEs [virtual learning environments];
2. Professional development through collaborative creativity and authenticity;
3. Sustained partnership in research, analysis and experience;
4. Free and structured approaches to teaching writing;
5. Leading teachers collecting and disseminating evidence of effective practice.
(Wrigley & Smith, 2010, p. 15)

In 2009, based in Buckinghamshire, a two-year Teachers as Writers project was set up with 12 primary and 4 secondary teachers, who began meeting twice a term, sharing writing both face-to-face and on a secure online forum and supported by various advisors, including Richard Andrews. Initial teacher reactions included "guilty pleasure at being asked to write," misgivings about sharing their writing with others, and doubts about the quality of their own writing (p. 15). Wrigley and Smith report that:

Project teachers are enthused by the agency which the project has given them and their children; writing journals have flourished and previously resistant writers have developed confidence in themselves and their work. . . . Teachers are capturing children's attention by sharing the process of their own writing more openly, and raising standards by NOT grading every piece of children's work.

(p. 16)

Such a finding resonates with an earlier project—"Writing is Primary"—run in clusters of schools in Bury, Kent/Medway and Worcester in the 2007–2008 school year, which demonstrated, among other things that (1) "teachers need a first-hand understanding of the writing process in order to be more confident teachers of writing; by developing their skills in writing, they can improve their leadership in writing; and (2) the writing workshops and other forms of CPD [Continuing Professional Development] provided through this programme had a positive impact on classroom practice" (Ings, 2009, p. 11).

REFLECTIVE JOURNAL TASK 1.2

You have now been given some sense of how "Teachers as writers" philosophy operates in three countries. Think about your *own* teaching context. What factors in your work situation do you think foster writing as a practice? What factors are hindrances?

Self-Efficacy and Writing

In her wonderful account of how a group of linguistically diverse teachers came to identify as writers, Carolyn Frank (2003) refers to writing apprehension and how common it is for teachers to have poor perceptions of themselves as writers and as having nothing to say. Self-efficacy pioneer, Albert Bandura defined "Perceived self-efficacy [as] concerned with judgments of how well one can execute courses of action required to deal with prospective situations" (1982, p. 122). If someone knocked on your door and asked you to help them write a press release and you felt your heart sink, then you could say that your self-efficacy in relation to this task was somewhat low.

QUESTIONNAIRE TASK 1.3

Complete the following self-efficacy writing scale. It was developed for use with the project described earlier in this chapter. For each item, give yourself a number between 0 and 10 (0 = no confidence at all; 10 = high degree of confidence).

OVERALL CONFIDENCE:
1. Overall, how confident are you as a writer?
2. Overall, how confident are you as a writer of fiction?
3. Overall, how confident are you as a writer of non-fiction?
4. How confident are you as a writer of poetry?

CONFIDENCE IN WRITING A COMPOSITION: How confident are you to perform each of the writing tasks below?

5. Write a clear, focused composition that stays on topic.
6. Use details to support your ideas.
7. Write a well-structured composition with a clear introduction, logically designed body and arresting conclusion.
8. Write well-structured, cohesive paragraphs.
9. Write with an engaging voice or tone.
10. Use effective words in the composition.
11. Use well-constructed and varied sentences in the essay.
12. Correctly spell all words in the composition.
13. Correctly use punctuation in the composition.

Further Reading

Stories About Transformation in Teacher Practice as a Result of Writing Project Involvement

- Whitney, A. (2008). Teacher transformation in the National Writing Project. *Research in the Teaching of English, 43*(2), 144–187.
- Seglem, R. (2009). Creating a circle of learning: Teachers taking ownership through professional communities. *Voices from the Middle, 16*(4), 32–37.
- Frank, C. (2003). Mapping our stories: Teachers' reflections on themselves as writers. *Language Arts, 80*(3), 185–195.

Accounts of Writing Projects in Different Countries

- Lieberman, A., & Wood, D. (2003). *Inside the National Writing Project: Connecting network learning and classroom learning.* New York, NY: Teachers College Press.
- Blau, S. (1988). Teacher development and the revolution in teaching. *English Journal, 77*(4), 30–35.
- Ings, R. (2009). *Writing is primary.* London, UK: Esmée Fairbairn Foundation.

Self-Efficacy in Writing

- Bruning, R., Dempsey, M., Kauffman, D., McKim, C., & Zumbrunn, S. (2013). Examining dimensions of self-efficacy for writing. *Journal of Educational Psychology, 105* (1), 25–38.

PART I

The Teacher as Writer

2

WRITING IN THE 21ST CENTURY

This chapter examines what it means to call ourselves writers. I discuss the nature of writing itself, viewing it as a historically and culturally situated and constrained activity that has changed over time. I look at different ways of answering the question, "What does it mean to be a writer?" I then set the scene for what happens in the remainder of this book by discussing writing (like literacy) as technologized, as a product as well as a practice, as a mode of expression and representation, and as a socially and culturally framed rhetorical act.

What It Means to Write

My four-year-old grandson Silas came to stay overnight and gave me an envelope with a sheet of white A4 paper folded inside. On the outside of the envelope (Figure 2.1), he had written in red felt-tip "Gradad nanny and." He had used a piece of hardware more accurately described as a fiber-tipped pen, and first produced in 1962, though its precursor, which used real "felt" was first patented in 1910. The words were formed from characters that were certainly recognizable and showed Silas to be what we might call, following the ground-breaking work of Teale and Sulzby (1986), an *emerging* writer. The words were accompanied by two graphic items in yellow and red on the right of the envelope.

Most of the white sheet was taken up by a continuous line drawing in yellow of circles and loops and one zig-zag. In the lower left corner, there was a two-story, yellow house, almost blotted out by solid strokes of red and next to it a yellow house, line-drawn, with one upper window, two lower ones, a peaked roof and what is presumably a chimney. I engaged Silas in conversation about his drawing, and he explained to me that the larger image represented lightning and thunder and the house that had been overdrawn by red felt-tip was on fire. The unscathed house was Nanny and Grandad's house.

FIGURE 2.1 Envelope of Silas's letter

I am sharing this example because it illustrates a number of features of what it means to write. Here are some of them.

- Silas learned to say "Grandad" before he learned to write it. Being able to write it, even in a crude form, meant that he had a way of representing speech, specifically five phonemes that occur in the version of English language he had been exposed to.
- This work of representation was accomplished through a set of sign characters, which within a particular culture had an agreed relationship to the voiced sounds (phonemes) this culture used in oral communication.
- There was a clear communicative intent, which subsumed other functions and purposes (e.g., self-expression, providing information, story-telling, scene-setting, instruction and persuasion).
- At any point in the process of production and dissemination, this piece of writing was available for interpretation by a reader (including the writer as reader).
- Writing was a means of getting something done with a degree of efficiency (i.e., a technology) utilizing means or "hardware" (e.g., felt-tip pens) and a medium or "software" (e.g., paper) (Gabrial, 2008, p. 23).
- A range of cognitive operations was at work in Silas's production of his written text. On the basis of my later conversation with Silas, the work of representation he was engaging in was also related to his self-expressive desire to

communicate his sense of the world in meaning, drawing on his own short- and long-term memory resources.

- Silas's act of "letter" production was socially situated. He happened to live in a culture characterized by letter-writing as one of its practices (though less so than formerly), had a parent prepared to guide him in this practice by printing for him the words he wanted to copy, and a grandparent who knew what a letter was and how to respond to it.

- Finally, the *meaning* of Silas's letter could be separated from what I will call *utterances* that preceded and followed it: a conversation with his dad that prompted it; conversations with his granddad and nanny where he explained it; and the discussion of it in writing that is occurring right now as I write this book.

To quote Haas (1996), "writing is at once individual, an act of mind; cultural, an historically based practice; and material, inherently dependent on physical, space-and-time artefacts" (p. 26).

The study of sign systems is called *semiotics*. According to Eco (1979), "there is a signification system (and therefore a code) when there is the socially conventionalized possibility of generating sign-functions" (p. 4). The English alphabet that Silas used is a direct descendent of the Latin alphabet, which in turn was a descendent of Greek script—the first alphabet to represent vowels, which came into being around 800BC.

In his first attempts at letter formation, Silas had been introduced to a writing system, defined in Wikipedia as "a symbolic system used to represent elements or statements expressible in language." Silas already knew that the letter "n" had a relationship to the spoken language he had been acquiring since birth, and that it signified the phoneme that occurs at the start of words like "nanny" and "no." Let's be clear that the writing system that Silas was learning with some effort does not "represent or depict the world directly but indirectly," that is, it represents spoken utterances used to make meaning (Olson, 2009, p. 7). The work being done by the letter "n" is what Eco means by the term "sign-function."

Silas had also been acculturated into an understanding of signs that do *not* rely on a knowledge of spoken language. During the same visit where he gave me his letter, we constructed a Lego model of the Sydney Opera House together, using a set of step-by-step diagrams using visual representations of the constituent Lego parts. He had no difficulty in matching the parts to their representations in the diagrams.

According to Hodge and Kress (1988), there are three types of signs. With *icons*, the sign resembles its object in some way, as in a road sign and the graphic representation of a Lego part. The graphic items in Figure 2.1 can be considered icons in this sense. An *index* is a sign whose meaning is based on association or causality (e.g., graffiti signifying anti-social behavior). In the case of a *symbol*, the meaning of the sign is conventional, for example, a rose as signifying love. That is why we describe written language as a *symbolic* system.

Drawing on Wikipedia, we discover that the writing system that Silas was being apprenticed into has four requirements:

- a set of "defined base elements or symbols" (*characters*) "collectively called a script;
- "at least one set of rules and conventions (*orthography*) understood and shared by a community, which arbitrarily assigns meaning to the base elements (*graphemes*), their ordering and relations to one another;
- "at least one language (generally spoken) whose constructions are represented and able to be recalled by the interpretation of these elements and rules;
- "some physical means of distinctly representing the symbols by application to a permanent or semi-permanent medium, so they may be interpreted (usually visually, but tactile systems [for example, Braille] have also been devised)" (Anon, 1212a, "General properties," para 3).

The second bullet point supports the point made by Eco (1989) that, for a signification system to be workable, there needs to be conventionalization, that is, tacit agreement in a community in respect of its governing rules (e.g., that the character "n" signifies the initial sound in "nanny"). It is this feature of the system that enables children to make up secret "codes" by coming up with their *own* conventions (e.g., using the letter "s" consistently as a substitute for the letter "n"). A "grapheme," as graphic element, is a somewhat wider term than "character." An inverted comma is a grapheme, but not a character.

The fourth bullet point is a reminder that as a technology, writing requires a material medium. Silas applied a felt-tip to paper. Paper is a relatively permanent medium. A classroom whiteboard is less permanent—writing applied by a felt-tip to such a surface is likely to be short-lived. As will be explored elsewhere in this book, the digitizing of type in a range of software applications means that text characters have become fluid, that is, they can be easily transformed in terms of such qualities as font size, type, style and color.

Eco (1989) follows his definition of a signification system by noting that what is required for a "communication process" is for "the possibilities provided by a signification system [to be] exploited in order to physically produce expressions for many practical purposes" (p. 4). At a very basic level, this is what Silas did in producing what is in effect a personal letter to his granddad and nanny, regardless of the comparative absence of written script. The mention of *purpose* here anticipates a major focus in Chapter 4, where I focus on *genre*.

REFLECTIVE JOURNAL TASK 2.1

Think about some of the signs that you encounter in your own culture. Identify an example of an icon and an index and write an explanation of them for someone from a different culture.

Writing and Literacy

In 1996, the Australian Association for the Teaching of English (AATE) published a resource on critical literacy, which included an address by Wendy Morgan (Morgan, Gilbert, Lankshear, Werner, & Williams, 1996). It is a useful resource, which I still use with my pre-service secondary English teachers. At what I now take to be a key moment in her address, Morgan told her audience that "These days, we hear less about literary criticism and more about critical literacy" (p. 35). Morgan was drawing her audience's attention to a shift in discourse from a focus on the "literary" (related to the prominence of literary study in English teaching in her country) to a focus on "literacy"—just one letter, but a world of difference. Her observation is an important reminder that *how* we think about anything is affected by the language available to us.

How we think about ourselves as teachers (including teachers of writing) depends on the language available to us throughout our professional lives (through our training, the resources we use, the texts we read, in-service professional learning, curriculum and assessment documents and so on). How we think about ourselves as writers in our out-of-school lives (if we do) also depends on the language available to us through our out-of-school lives (through text-based leisure pursuits, engagement in secondary associations, and so on).

In my own case, the concept of "literacy" was very much a Johnny-come-lately. In the 1980s, I worked as an English teacher with a New Zealand curriculum document that was quite radical for its time, in that it had shifted the central focus of English Language Arts away from literature and towards "language." "Language" was the key concept, illustrated in such sentences as: "Students need to acquire competence in language through participation in a variety of activities appropriate to their needs, interests, and stages of development" (Department of Education, 1983, p. 11). Interestingly, there was not a single reference to the word "grammar" in the entirety of the document. (I will be exploring the significance of this in Chapter 10.) This displacement of "literature" in favor of "language" was a feature of subsequent curriculum documents also.

A Crisis in Literacy?

The term "literacy" began filtering into my vocabulary in the 1990s in two significant ways. The first was through a concern of a number of governments that their international, economic competitiveness was likely to be affected by a quality in its population signified by the term "literacy levels." In 1994, the first International Adult Literacy Survey (IALS) involved seven countries, including the United States and Canada. Five other countries, including New Zealand, Australia and the United Kingdom were added in 1996. The survey defined literacy as:

> The ability to understand and employ printed information in daily activities, at home, at work and in the community, to achieve one's goals and to develop one's knowledge and potential.
>
> (NALD, n.d.)

The survey was adamant that literacy could not be reduced to a single skill, given the range of written texts people in industrialized countries encounter on a daily basis. The IALS, therefore, assessed literacy under three categories:

- **"Prose literacy**: the ability to understand and use information from texts such as editorials, news stories, poems and fiction.
- **"Document literacy**: the ability to locate and use information from documents such as job applications, payroll forms, transportation schedules, maps, tables and graphs.
- **"Quantitative literacy**: the ability to perform arithmetic functions such as balancing a chequebook, calculating a tip, or completing an order form" (NALD, n.d.).

I want to make three observations. First, the emphasis is clearly on reading rather than writing. Second, the assessment has a strong "skills" focus. Third, the focus is clearly on the individual.

By the late 1990s and into the first years of the 21st century, governments in a number of English-speaking countries were acting as if there was a literacy crisis, especially when these countries eyed the "performance" of economic competitors in terms of cross-national literacy surveys such as those conducted by the International Association for the Evaluation of Educational Achievement (IEA) (i.e., PIRLS or Progress in International Reading-Literacy Study), and by the Organization for Economic Co-operation and Development (OECD) (i.e., PISA or Program for International Student Assessment). The reports generated by these organizations are available online. These surveys are heavily oriented to reading rather than writing. (To read a critical view of how such reports can "produce" crises, read Elley, 2004.)

For U.S. citizens, the talk of crisis reached a peak with the release of a report entitled *A Nation at Risk* (National Commission on Excellence in Education, 1983), which viewed the country's students as falling behind counterparts in other countries and whose poor performance was rendering the country less competitive globally. In the United States, this crisis talk precipitated a "universal movement towards government-regulated standardization and high-stakes assessment, resulting in the No Child Left Behind Act (NCLB) of 2001" (Rubin, 2011, p. 407). As Rubin further suggested, if you were a teacher in the United States, your school would be required to prove via frequent standardized assessment that students were achieving, "with all students required to be 100% proficient in reading and mathematics by 2014" (p. 407). The merits of NCLB have been fiercely debated. However, one thing that is clear is the privileging of reading over writing (see McCarthey, 2008). The publication in the United States in 2003 by the National Commission on Writing in America's Schools and Colleges of *The Neglected "R"* report certainly suggests that institutions of learning were focusing on reading at the expense of writing.

Similar crisis talk occurred in England, fueled by an Ofsted report, *The Teaching of Reading in 45 Inner London Primary Schools* (Ofsted, 1996) which, according to Stannard and Huxford (2007) "found pervasive weaknesses in the teaching of reading in three inner London education authorities" (p. 7), and a widespread perception that teachers had scant knowledge about language and disagreed on how best to teach basic literacy skills and knowledge. The National Literacy Strategy (NLS), implemented in schools in England in a number of phases commencing in 1997, was a coherent and comprehensive measure aimed at a radical transformation of the educational landscape. Like NCLB, the NLS engaged in target-setting and standardized testing. However, its most radical feature was its focus on professional development for the entire teaching force in England, with the State determining not just the curriculum question of "what to teach" but also the pedagogical question of "how to teach." (For a critical review of the NLS in England, see Goodwyn & Fuller, 2011.)

In my own country, New Zealand, the crisis talk was fuelled by successive international literacy surveys from 1990 onwards indicating a wide gap between the highest and lowest levels of reading achievement and worrying levels of performance in particular groups of children, in particular Maori and Pasifika children, boys, and children from low socio-economic schools. A government-commissioned *Report of the Literacy Taskforce* was subtitled "Advice to the Government on achieving its goal that: 'By 2005, every child turning nine will be able to read, write, and do maths for success'" (Ministry of Education, 1999, p. 2). For New Zealand teachers, the National Literacy Strategy meant a set of evolving strategies that were rolled out to teachers in primary and intermediate schools as a series of distinct measures that were certainly aimed at changing teaching practices and, of course, outcomes for New Zealand students (see Dix, Cawkwell, & Locke, 2011). Like so-called reforms elsewhere, the focus was on reading rather than writing, as if reading success would somehow translate into writing success. There has also been a pronounced shift towards National Standards and standardized measures for assessing literacy in children.

I draw attention to these big-picture changes because those of us who aspire to develop as writing teachers cannot avoid being implicated in them. These policy initiatives pervade our lives in all sorts of ways. Now, in the 21st century, they will be affecting us discursively, in that we will find ourselves being encouraged to use different language to think about our profession. I have always used the word "standard" in a casual way, in phrases such as "up to standard." But it wasn't until the mid-1990s that it began to replace the word "objective" in the language I was expected to use in the assessment of student work. Implicit in this shift was the potential to change my thinking about assessment from student-centered goal-directedness to an emphasis on attaining a level of performance (what the student knew or could do) fixed in the one-size-fits all language of standards. I return to this topic and these pressures in Chapter 12.

Literacy as a Social Practice

The second way the term "literacy" began filtering into my vocabulary in the 1990s had a markedly different origin than government policy, the construction of "literacy" crises, target-setting, teacher bashing and the widespread uptake of standardized measures of "literacy" achievement. A typical starting point for this alternative way of thinking about literacy is James Paul Gee's book, *Social linguistics and literacies: Ideology in discourse* (1996, first published in 1990). What may strike you about this title is that "literacy" has been rendered plural—"literacies." In a section of his book entitled "Literacy and Social Practices," Gee begins by alluding to the traditional and commonsense view of literacy as the ability to read and write texts—to decode writing (as a reader) and to code language in graphic form (as a writer). He then compares and contrasts this traditional view of literacy, which is very much focused on the individual and his or her cognitive process, with a view of literacy as a social practice, a view of literacy which began to emerge in the 1970s and 1980s (see below).

Gee occupies a position on literacy, which he opposes to a view where literacy becomes caught up in what he calls "the commodity myth." In this myth, such things as time, work and money become separated from their association with human experience and relationships and become seen in abstract terms as commodities. In terms of this myth (way of thinking),

> literacy = functional literacy = skills necessary to function in "today's job market" = market economy = the market = the economy. . . . Literacy is measured out and quantified, like time, work, and money. We get "reading levels," "graded texts," "levels of literacy skills," "levels of literacy," "amounts of literacy and illiteracy," and "rates of literacy." We match jobs with "literacy skills" and skills with "economic needs'" Literacy, thus, becomes itself intertranslatable with time, work, and money, part of "the economy" . . . a commodity that can be measured, and thence bought and sold.
>
> (pp. 122–123)

I draw attention to Gee's critique of "literacy as a commodity," because you will see that the language in which it is couched resonates with the language used about literacy in the last section on literacy crises.

Gee's description of this alternative view of "literacy" grew out of the work of scholars associated with the "New Literacy Studies." Drawing on the work of scholars such as Brian Street, David Barton, Allan Luke, Gunther Kress and Gee himself, and drawing on such disciplines as linguistics and social anthropology, the New Literacy Studies challenged the view that

> literacy is concerned with the acquisition of a particular set of cognitive skills, which once acquired can be put to use unproblematically in any new context. . . . It takes as its starting point the position that literacy is not a unitary concept; reading and writing—literacies—are cultural and social practices, and vary depending upon the particular context in which they occur.
>
> (Lea, 2004, p. 740)

Central to Gee's argument that literacy is multiple is the concept of discourse or "Discourse," a term I use throughout this book. This is how he defines a discourse:

> A *Discourse* is a socially accepted association among ways of using language, other symbolic expressions, and "artefacts," of thinking, feeling, believing, valuing, and acting that can be used to identify oneself as a member of a socially meaningful group or "social network" or to signal (that one is playing) a socially meaningful "role."
>
> (1996, p. 131)

Thinking back to Silas and his letter, we can think of him as engaging in a set of "Discourse" practices that clearly identify him as a particular kind of grandson and member of a particular family group. Writing the letter the way he did made him a particular kind of person. Gee uses a capital "D" to distinguish his use of the word "discourse" from its more ordinary usage as a formal speech or essay on a particular subject, or an abstract noun denoting language in use as a social practice with particular emphasis on larger units such as paragraphs, utterances, whole texts or genres. (I will not be using the capitalized form generally, since the context will suggest the meaning that applies.)

Having defined "Discourse," Gee makes a distinction between "primary" and "secondary" discourses.

> Primary Discourses are those to which people are apprenticed early in life during their primary socialisation as members of particular families within their sociocultural settings. Primary Discourses constitute our first social identity, and something of a base within which we acquire or resist later Discourses. They form our initial taken-for-granted understandings of *who* we are and *who* people "like us" are, as well as what sorts of things we ("people like us") do, value, and believe when we are not "in public."

"Secondary Discourses are those to which people are apprenticed as part of their socialisation within various local, state, and national groups and institutions outside early home and peer-group socialisation—for example, churches, gangs, schools, offices. They constitute the recognisability and meaningfulness of our "public" (more formal) acts.

(1996, p. 137)

The verb "apprentice" denotes the way we "acquire" rather than "learn" a discourse because of the subconscious nature of the process, the process of trial and error and the absence of formal instruction. (This is how Silas learned to speak English.) For Gee, a discourse can't be taught. Thinking about Silas, and using Gee's terms, we can say that he was apprenticed into a primary discourse that *values* letter-writing as a practice. However, he had to be *taught* letter-sound relationships and how to form the characters of the alphabet used by his social group. (You may find yourself wondering somewhat about Gee's primary/ secondary distinction. While I know for certain that letter writing is a valued practice in Silas's wider family, it may also have been a valued practice in the Montessori kindergarten that he attended.)

Gee needs to sustain his distinction between primary and secondary discourses, since he asserts that "any socially useful definition of literacy must be couched in terms of these notions of primary and secondary Discourse" (1996, p. 143). For him, literacy consists of *mastery of a secondary Discourse*. It follows then, that literacy has to be a plural—*literacies*— since there are multiple secondary Discourses into which we can be apprenticed: church groups, clubs, and of course schools. In Gee's terms, "acquisition must (at least, partially) precede learning; apprenticeship must precede overt teaching" (1996. p. 139). There is a political implication in what Gee is arguing here. It is easy enough to see that the discourse Silas has acquired through such activities as letter-writing will equip him well for school. For other children, who have been apprenticed into different kinds of literate practice, the transition will not be so easy. And, in many instances, the school may not be sympathetic to their difficulties.

This "pluralization" of *literacies* has become widespread. For example, academic literacies can be thought of as the repertoire of textual practices (involving the production, reception and dissemination of texts) that enable successful participation in a formal academic or scholarly environment, setting or community. A university department or faculty is an example of one such setting. A high school is another. There is nothing universal about this repertoire of practices, which demand the mastery of a range of genres, for a variety of audiences and purposes. As we shall see, one of the characteristics of a genre is its dynamic, historical and socially situated nature. It's not surprising that students moving from one tertiary institution to another may find themselves having to adjust to a different set of conventions and expectations in writing an essay for an assignment.

REFLECTIVE JOURNAL TASK 2.2

Write an account of your primary discourse, thinking particularly of your life before you turned 5. What kind of person were you encouraged to be? What sorts of activities did you typically engage in? What were you encouraged to believe and to value? In particular, were there practices related to reading, writing, and the visual and performing arts that you were encouraged to engage in? To what extent would you say that your primary discourse has shaped the kind of person you are today?

Writing as Cognition

You may be wondering whether I've gone too far with this emphasis on literacy (and therefore writing) as a social practice. What about the brain? What was going on in Silas's brain as he struggled to place letters on a page in the right order? (You'll have noticed that he didn't get the *order* of the words quite right.) What's happening in my brain right now as I use a keyboard linked to a laptop (hardware) to sequence graphemes on a Microsoft Word file (software)? Well, the simple answer is: Quite a lot and it is all of interest to contemporary researchers into the role cognition plays in writing and to teachers who realize the relevance of these understandings to writing pedagogy. I will have more to say about this in Chapter 9. However, a few general comments are in order as we consider writing in the 21st century.

In a historical overview of writing research, Martin Nystrand (2006) reminds us that writing research took off in the 1980s as the result of a new way of thinking about writing which "posited the individual writer's mind as the seminal organizing principle of writing." These researchers "sought to explicate the cognitive structure of writing processes that transformed thought and agency into text" (p. 12). The groundwork for this new approach had been laid as early as 1966 at the Anglo-American Conference on the Teaching of English, which was held at Dartmouth College. As one American participant, Herbert Muller noted, "Characteristically the seminar was most interested in the value of composition for the development of children. By writing they learn how to order and shape their experience, thereby learning more about life and themselves" (1967, p. 98). The focus here is on writing as a cognitive, expressive, meaning-making process. Another Dartmouth participant, Englishman John Dixon, referred to "the swing to process" (1975, p. 12). Dixon was at the forefront of a group of educators (including James Britton and Nancy Martin) who defined English in terms of process, by which they meant such language-based activities as selecting, shaping, choosing, which, in Dixon's opinion led to the construction of "a representational world . . . to fit reality as [the child] knows it" (1975, p. 6).

Another precursor discussed by Nystrand (2006) was the Cambridge cognitive revolution at Harvard and MIT in the 1960s and 1970s, which, drawing on Chomsky's model of linguistic competence, linked the study of language to the structure of the human mind and therefore the disciplinary province of cognitive psychology. Researchers such as Janet Emig (in the 1970s) and John Hayes and Linda Flower (in the 1980s) all conceptualized writing as a cognitive process. One of the best known cognitive models of the processes involved in writing was developed by Flower and Hayes (1981), who identified the elements, organization and interrelationship of long-term memory, task environment, planning, reviewing and what they called the "translating" of thought into text (see Figure 2.2).

One of the challenges to a model of linguistic knowledge anchored in cognitive psychology came from ethnography, with Dell Hymes' development in the mid-70s of the concept of "communicative competence" and a "speech community" (1974). The concept of a *speech community* highlights how the linguistic resources a writer has available are a property of the community itself. Nystrand (2006, p. 19) cites Faigley (1985, p. 238) as arguing that "within a language community, people acquire specialized kinds of discourse competence that enable them to participate in specialized groups." This is not Gee's (1996) discourse with a capital "D." However, in the use of the term "acquire" we can see a connection with the view of literacy as a social practice discussed in the last section.

Does such critique mean that researchers such as Flower and Hayes were wrong? Well, no. What we can say is that writing is and always has been a complex

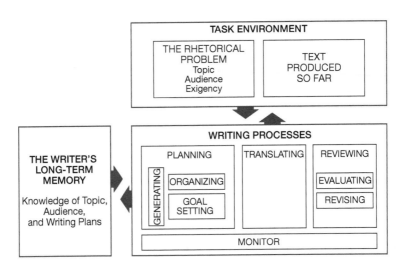

FIGURE 2.2 Flower and Hayes: cognitive writing model

human activity, and that it is multifaceted. Adopting the lens (or discourse in Gee's sense) of a cognitive psychologist allows us to focus on one facet of this multifaceted activity. In this respect, then, researchers such as Flowers and Hayes have *added* to our knowledge of writing; but their account is necessarily partial. Hayes himself, in 2006, called his model a "framework"—a representation "designed to help us think about complex processes or situations" and provide a "common language for discussing cognitive processes in writing" (pp. 35–36). Later, Hayes (1996) himself made substantial changes to the 1991 model (Figure 2.2), adding a focus on working memory and motivation/affect, removing the term "translation" for the realization of ideas in written language form, and referring to the "social environment" rather than to a "rhetorical problem" as a context for thinking about audience.

In the last decade of the 20th century, cognitive neuroscience revolutionized brain research through the development of brain-imaging technologies and by providing new insights into brain function in relation to writing and other processes. Berninger and Winn (2006) succinctly define the brain as "an organ that allows an organism to:

1. "receive information from the external environment through the sensory input modalities and code that information internally;
2. "compute new mental structures from the incoming sensory information, existing mental structures, and operations performed internally and externally; and
3. "act upon the environment through the motor output system" (p. 98).

Brain imaging is allowing us to discover: (1) what brain regions are activated exclusively in relation to a particular process (e.g., writing an individual character in the external environment) and (2) which regions are functionally connected. When Silas produced the letter "g," his brain integrated both orthographic and motor codes. Brain imagining tells us that, since his writing was not automatic, different distributed neural processes occurred than had he been a practiced writer (Berninger & Winn, 2006, p. 100).

Berninger and Winn (2006) highlight a number of studies, which highlight the importance of automaticization in relation to the function of working memory in the writing process, especially over time, noting how it "reduces the temporal constraints on working memory" (p. 102). Working memory is a concept used in cognitive psychology to describe "a limited capacity system allowing the temporary storage and manipulation of information necessary for such complex tasks as comprehension, learning and reasoning" (Baddeley, 2000, p. 418). Once Silas's "low-level" handwriting becomes automatized, it might be expected that working memory will become freed up for the purpose of "high-level composing goals by reducing the temporal constraints on it (the number of component processes that need to be orchestrated in real time)" (pp. 102–103).

Writing as Artifact

An artifact is a useful or decorative object made with human hands. Regardless of function, a technology is required to produce an artifact. A range of technologies would have played a role in producing the hardware (felt-tip pen) and paper and envelope (medium) Silas used for his letter to me. When, around 2600 BCE, a Sumerian scribe used a chisel to inscribe personal names on a lapis lazuli object (artifact) to be buried in a tomb, he was using characters that needed to take *material* form in the first instance before the process of widespread subscription and conventionalization could take place as prerequisite to establishing a writing system. As early as 1916, John Dewey was arguing that it is this world of artifacts that "allows children to attain rapidly what humanity took ages to develop" (Prior, 2006, p. 56).

Young Children's Understandings About Writing

Liliana Tolchinsky, who has spent a good deal of her life studying emerging writers like Silas, reminds us that "writing" (as noun) has three distinct meanings:

1.   Notational system;
2.   Mode of production;
3.   A collection of genres or discourse styles (2006, p. 83).

In regard to a notational system, an artifact imprinted with writing in most languages features a linear string of distinctive characters, clearly defined units or groupings, regular spaces and directionality. According to Tolchinsky (2006), children like Silas already understand that writing is a "particular activity that produces a specific formal output distinct from drawing, in that it is linear and discrete" (p. 88). He will also be aware that writing is related to language in some way. In Silas's case, his father would have spoken the word "grandad" as he wrote it down, thus creating an artifact that operated as template for the 4-year-old boy to follow.

In regard to mode of production, the special quality of writing as a linguistic mode is that it leaves a visible trace and as artifact (e.g., legal document, court record, poem, letter) offers the possibility of relative permanence. Tolchinsky (2006) refers to research that shows that when toddlers produce graphic marks, they don't do it because of the activity, but rather because of the traces themselves. She cites the work of other scholars who have shown that children much younger than Silas *know* that drawing and writing are quite different activities.

Tolchinsky's third category of meaning is perhaps the most fascinating in respect of what has been discovered about emerging writers. She reminds us that in literate communities, children grow up surrounded by textual artifacts, not just from their own era but often from times past. Silas would be *most* surprised if I opened a storybook and read him a recipe (p. 86), since, according to the research, he has already developed some sensitivity to the conventions and constraints of a number of genres. Tolchinsky (2006) cites research that shows that even with children who are yet to master phonographic conventions, "the graphic layout of [their] text imitates the features of different genres" (p. 86). It is quite possible that the rectangular graphic on the right hand side of Figure 2.1 is meant to represent a stamp.

Two aspects of children's mental development in relation to their early exposure to features of a writing system should give us pause. The first is Tolchinsky's (2006) suggestion that "writing . . . develops at many levels simultaneously" (p. 87), and not in a sequence that moves from smaller to larger textual units. This has implications for the way teachers need to think about the sequencing of formal learning in respect of writing (see Chapter 7). The second is the degree and internal logic of young children's understandings about what writing is and the nature of its production. These findings appear to challenge Gee's (1996) contention, mentioned in the first section of this chapter, that literacy is mastery of a secondary discourse.

Writing as a Material Practice Shaping Thought

There is mounting evidence that literacies as repertoires of social practices taking material form in texts (including written texts) have the capacity to change the way we think. According to Christina Haas (1996), a Vygotskian perspective suggests that "culture and cognition mutually construct one another" (p. 13) since, for Vygotsky, "semiotic signs or psychological tools are the mediational means by which high psychological functions develop—and therefore the means by which the unique human quality of consciousness is brought into being" (p. 14).

In 1982, Walter Ong asserted strongly that those of us who are "functionally literate" are:

> beings whose thought processes do not grow out of simply natural powers but out of these powers as structured, directly or indirectly, by the technology of writing. Without writing, the literate mind would not and could not think as it does, not only when engaged in writing but normally even when it is composing its thoughts in oral form. More than any other single invention, writing has transformed human consciousness.
>
> (p. 78)

Ong was looking back to the print revolution, ushered in by Gutenberg's invention of the letter press in the 1450s, which made mass-produced printed artifacts available to all. Ong argued for a range of print effects on mind, for example, "distancing" which ". . . develops a new kind of precision in verbal-ization by removing it from the rich but chaotic context of much oral utterance" (1982, pp. 103–104). He also argued that print honed human beings' analytical skills because, without the extralinguistic support on offer in oral situations, words had to do more. Moreover, backward scanning allowed revision to be undertaken effectively. Ong even claimed that writing made possible "increasingly articulate introspectivity," thus giving birth to the "great introspective religious traditions" (p. 105).

In respect of computer-based hardware and software, Gavriel Salomon (1988) has argued for a kind of artificial intelligence in reverse, that is, that we need to think not only of human beings creating artificial intelligence in the form of computers, but that interfacing with computer technology has a cognitive effect in human users who internalize their symbol systems and functionalities. In her own studies, Hass (1996) found that "writers' spatial understanding of text was eroded when they read that text on a standard personal computer. . . . Retrieving information was slower on a standard personal computer than it was on either paper or a more sophisticated computing system with an advanced display", and that "critically reading to reorganize a text was better when writers used hard copy or screens that displayed more text than when they read from small screens" (p. 69).

Such studies by Haas and others draw our attention to the material medium on which writing appears and the variable effect on our mental processes of different media. A key point made by many theorists is that writing and other forms of graphic representation are a way of *externalizing* our thinking (process) and thoughts (product), thereby making them available in a form that is more effective for such processes as reflection, revision and critique, than maintaining these representations in our internal memory. As I write this, I recall observing a beginning teacher conducting a lesson on persuasive speeches at an élite, private girls' school. The girls were sitting in groups, each with an identical laptop. There was virtually no paper evident. The teacher modeled a brainstorm-to-mindmap process for a topic she had chosen, inviting contributions from the class. Her technology was whiteboard and felt-tip marker pen. When students were asked to do their own brainstorming, no particular technology was suggested nor insisted upon. However, the girls engaged in this task on screen. After a while, I asked how many felt they would be more efficient at the brainstorming task had they been using a pencil and paper. All said yes. The moral here is that different media are not equally effective in aiding the externalization of inner thought. As suggested by Haas (1996), a pencil and paper may be more effective (because less distracting) than mind-mapping software in externalizing thinking oriented to whole-text considerations such as structure.

In his seminal work on *The Working Brain* (1973), Alexander Luria, a younger colleague of Vygotsky, developed the concept of *functional brain systems,* defined as "sets of component processes that are orchestrated to achieve specific goals" (Berninger & Winn, 2006, p. 103). In a series of experiments conducted as part of the Literacy Trek Project based at the University of Washington, Berninger and colleagues (2006) found evidence that functional brain systems for beginning writers develop differently if a keyboard is used rather than a pencil, a finding which has implications for the way we think about working memory and the way we integrate various technologies into formal writing instruction. Hayes (2008), for example, raised the interesting speculation that training students to type to the degree that demands on working memory resources are reduced should facilitate the learning of other writing skills (pp. 32–3). Berninger and Winn (2006) raised the further possibility that the "new technologies may alter the developmental timetables in which writing skills emerge, are scaffolded, and are practiced" (p. 104). For the 21st century then, the pen may still be more powerful than the sword, but it is certainly not more powerful than the keyboard or touch-pad.

In concluding this section, I would like to draw further on Berninger and Winn (2008) and highlight two recent ideas about the "role of action and interaction with environments during learning. . . . The first idea is that cognition is not just a mental activity, but involves the mind interacting with the environment" (p. 108), which, of course, includes the semiotic, text-saturated environment we all inhabit in the 21st century. The second idea is that "if the bounds of cognition expand to include the body in an environment, then it is no longer possible to say with certainty whether an idea came from the environment, the student, or their interaction" (p. 108). Berninger and Winn's response to these ideas has been to propose a unitary view of the writing process that does away with brain/mind and mind/environment dualisms. They propose that

> The writing process is supported by a single system—the writer's internal brain-mind interacting with the external environment (including technology tools).

(p. 108)

This interactional model of writing offers much for us to think about as 21st-century writers. In particular, it discourages our thinking of one part of the system (for example, the mind's inner workings) in isolation. It also encourages us to think about the contribution the external environment makes to internal processing. As will be discussed in Chapter 8, thinking about writing in terms of a community of practice, is one way of drawing productively on this interactional view.

REFLECTIVE JOURNAL TASK 2.3

This task invites you to compare and contrast how you go about using different technologies to perform a similar writing/composition task. Think carefully about the distinct operations you need to perform the task, how you go about performing them, and how they are sequenced. Write an account for *each* technology that sets out how you went about the writing task. What differences and similarities emerge when you compare the two accounts? Are there implications from these findings for you as a writer or teacher? [If you find yourself stuck thinking about a writing task, try writing a short poem, first using a pencil and writing long-hand on paper and then using a word-processing program.]

Further Reading

History of Writing

- Olson, D. (2009). The history of writing. In R. Beard, D. Myhill, J. Riley, & M. Nystrand (Eds.), *The Sage handbook of writing development* (pp. 6–16). Los Angeles, CA: Sage.
- Schmandt-Besserat, D., & Erard, M. (2008). Origins and forms of writing. In C. Bazerman (Ed.), *Handbook of research on writing: History, society, school, individual, text* (pp. 7–22). New York, NY: Erlbaum.
- Gabriel, B. (2008). History of writing technologies. In C. Bazerman (Ed.), *Handbook of research on writing: History, society, school, individual, text* (pp. 23–34). New York, NY: Erlbaum.
- Ong, W. (1982). *Orality and literacy: The technologizing of the word*. London, UK: Methuen

Writing as a Social Practice

- Gee, J. P. (1996). *Social linguistics and literacies: Ideology in discourse* (2nd ed.). London, UK: Taylor & Francis.
- Prior, P. (2006). A sociocultural theory of writing. In C. MacArthur, S. Graham & J. Fitzgerald (Eds.), *Handbook of writing research* (pp. 54–66). New York, NY: Guilford.

Writing as Cognition

- Berninger, V., & Winn, W. (2006). Implications of advancements in brain research and technology for writing development, writing instruction and educational evolution. In C. MacArthur, S. Graham, & J. Fitzgerald (Eds.), *Handbook of writing research* (pp. 96–114). New York, NY: Guilford.

Developmental Aspects of Writing

- Tolchinsky, L. (2003). *The cradle of culture and what children know about writing and numbers before being taught.* Mahwah, NJ: Erlbaum (especially Chapter 3: "What children know about writing before being formally taught to write").
- Berninger, V., Abbott, R., Jones, J., Wolf, B., Gould, L., Anderson-Youngstrom, M., Shimada, S., & Apel, K. (2006). Early development of language by hand: Composing, reading, listening, and speaking connections; three letter-writing modes; and fast mapping in spelling. *Developmental Neuropsychology, 29*(1), 61–92.
- The Literacy Trek Project: see http://education.washington.edu/research/projects/literacytrek.html

3

WRITING THE SELF THROUGH STORYING

Out of the dimness opposite equals advance—always substance and increase, always sex;
Always a knit of identity—always distinction—always a breed of life.

Walt Whitman: *Song of Myself*

The focus in this chapter is on personal or expressive writing. To begin with, though, I want to invite you into some sustained writing, using some writing prompts that have been used over time in a range of situations, including Writing Workshops. I will also be sharing with you some examples of teacher writing, *not* as models of excellence, but rather to highlight the uniqueness of personal experience and the quality of voice that articulates this experience in writing.

This chapter assumes a close relationship between voice and identity. However, as I will explain, there is no single way of understanding these two concepts. In between the concreteness of working with specific writing activities, I will be engaging in some theorizing. That is, I will be sharing my understanding of such concepts as "voice," "identity," "writing to know and be" and "self-expression."

Biopoetics

Ever since I wrote my first biopoem in 1988, I have used them with students and teachers. As you'll see, a biopoem does two things to lower the threshold into writing, (1) it solves the problem of form and (2) it cues content. Without further ado, I'd ask you to read the prompt in Writing Task 3.1 to generate some content. Then write your own biopoem.

WRITING TASK 3.1

[This can be written in a hard-copy or digital reflective journal; the choice is yours.]

Prewrite for Biopoem

Name an adjective that describes your current life.
Name something that you watch or have watched or seen over time.
Name an object that you once possessed or name something that you once did or had to do
Name something you once had, but no longer possess.
Name your age or reference to era (over 30, middle age, under 25, Generation X, Baby boomer)
Name something you have seen in the past
Name something you have heard, smelled, or touched in the past.
Name an important belief or fact
Name another important belief or fact, one that you now doubt or have changed your mind about
Name two or three things that you hate and something that you detest
Name something/someone that you love
Name something/someone that you used to love
Name objects, beliefs, feelings, person that you have lost (2 or 3)
Name something/someone that you miss
Name objects or dreams that you are seeking or hoping for (2 or 3)
Create two metaphors for how you see yourself.

An elementary teacher, Therese Cargo, generated the following pre-writing ideas:

Happy
My children grow up
Be the anchor in my home.
A dog named—Sioux
Half century
The Great Wall of China
Shanghai
That we are all equal
That we are not all equal
Dishonesty, lying and cheating
Jason

5 O'Neill Street
My Mother
The one above
Good health, a life of happiness.
One's life ripens with experience.
An idea is a vehicle for change.

She then produced a full draft which, with her permission, I share with you below.

I am leading a happy life.
I am watching my children grow up.
I had to be the anchor in my home.
I had a dog named Sioux—but she died.
I thought of her as a special friend.
And now at a half century,
I have seen the Great Wall of China.
I have heard and smelled the metropolis of Shanghai.
I know that we are all equal—I often see inequality.
I don't know why people feel the need to discriminate.
I detest dishonesty, lying and cheating.
I hate it when people lack integrity.
I love Jason.
I used to love my home at 5 O'Neill Street,
Now I am going to sell it.
I have lost my mother.
I miss her greatly.
I'm looking for good health and a life of continued happiness.
And my heart tells me:
      An idea is a vehicle for change and
      My life ripens with experience.

There is no correct way of writing a biopoem, of course, and if you search "biopoem" on the Internet, you will find other formulas. Even with the above formula (which Ruie Pritchard introduced me to), there is nothing to stop one writing in the third person, nor taking on the persona of a character in a novel. (A biopoem written by Captain Ahab might contain the line: "I hate Moby Dick.")

Self (Expression)

In an epilogue to *Growth through English Set in the Perspective of the Seventies,* educator and participant at the 1966 Anglo-American Conference on the Teaching of English, John Dixon (1975) shared a view of language in use as having two poles. The first was based on the language-user's *communicative* goals and the need to

---

REFLECTIVE JOURNAL TASK 3.2

Write a reflection in response to one or more of the following prompts:

- Did you find some biopoem pre-writing prompts more difficult to jot notes for than others? If so, why might this have been?
- Did you actually resist the idea of doing a prewrite and simply write your biopoem straight off? If so, why did you do this?
- How did you feel at the moment you started writing your biopoem?
- How did you feel once you had written it?
- If you were to share your biopoem with someone, who would that someone be?
- If you have shared it with someone, how did you feel before and after you shared it?

---

organize language with others in mind. The second, which he called "(self-) expression," was self-oriented in terms of its organization. "Instead of considering the effect of our feelings and attitudes on others, we just let them loose. Instead of having to take care that everything's clearly ordered, we can switch back and forward on impulse, to suit ourselves" (p. 133). He used the word "pole" to suggest that in practice, writers move to and fro between these two orientations. About the same time, in the United States, Peter Elbow was arguing a case for something similar, which he termed "freewriting." "It is like writing something and putting it in a bottle in the sea," and the "habit of compulsive, premature editing" is resisted (1973, pp. 3, 6).

From Dixon's point of view, the advantage of a self-expressive orientation is that it frees the writer from audience *demands* while at the same time allowing for audience *support*. The distinction between audience support and demand is an interesting one, I think, because as Dixon explains it, having a "sense of an audience can encourage us to take verbalizing further than we anticipated, to realize new possibilities. . ." without the need to justify our ideas nor frame them rhetorically with a particular audience in mind (1975, p. 134). Pedagogically, Dixon saw expressive writing as "the natural precursor to more careful, deliberate learning, when we are ready to meet the demands of an audience" (p. 135) and sadly lacking in school settings.

A year earlier than Dixon was writing, the National Writing Project (NWP) was getting under way across the Atlantic at the University of California in Berkeley. A blueprint was being laid down for the professional learning of teachers, which included an expectation of daily writing of around 20–30 minutes for later sharing with members of a response group. As Anne Whitney pointed out (2008, 2009), there has been a longstanding debate in NWP circles about the relative merits of inviting teachers to engage in "personal" or "professional" writing, with just a suspicion in this age of accountability, that having teachers explore personal topics in an "expressivist" manner was an indulgence. However, the case is often made that personal writing can operate as a "precursor" to professional or transactional writing, citing James Moffett's (1989) idea of "bridging." "Writing in the 'comfort' of the personal domain might increase confidence for writing in the more intimidating professional domain" (Whitney, 2009, p. 239). Interestingly, Sheridan Blau (1988), in an article reviewing the early years of the NWP, suggested that participants went through two stages as they developed as writers, an initial stage focused on simply developing fluency and conquering fears (similar to Dixon's expressive pole) and a second stage where the focus shifted to audience and publication (Dixon's communicative pole).

On the basis of her study of one NWP teacher participant, Laura, Whitney (2009) suggested that the dichotomy between the personal and the professional is a false one. Certainly, when Dixon used the term "expressive," he was not intending to restrict writers to "personal" subjects. Rather, the focus was on giving oneself permission to explore any topic at all. When Laura first became involved in a Writing Workshop, she engaged in writing that focused on her life as a mother rather than her professional life as a teacher. But she felt that somehow she was not fulfilling her responsibilities as a course participant. However, as she put it, "Through her work on family and mothering, Laura entered a space where she could explore issues of authority and role—issues that cut across the domains of family and workplace." However, through response group participation, Laura was able to reframe "her sense of self as a writer, a teacher, and a mother to reveal how these selves are not parallel or divergent trajectories, not discrete identities, but rather comprise her whole meaning" (pp. 254–255).

The argument for the value of expressive writing can also be found in the EFL (English as a Foreign Language) literature. Bilton and Sivasubramaniam (2009) hypothesized that engaging their EFL students at the University of Bahrain in "expressive, self-actualizing writing . . . without any fear of intimidation, grammar correction, teacher-dictated topics, critical comments or grades" (p. 303) would enhance student motivation and performance. They found that students engaged with a series of literary texts in rich and increasingly fluent ways, which allowed them to explore in a meaningful way their responses to these texts.

The "Self" that Writes

Who is the self that writes? There is no simple answer to this question and, if I look back on my own journey, I have found myself answering the question in quite different ways, sometimes using words like "identity" and "voice." If, as you read this, you ask *yourself* this question, you'll find that any answer you come up with is going to need language and you will be realizing that language is a slippery commodity at the best of times. Any language I use to answer this question is going to *frame* my answer to it in a particular way.

Let me share with you an 1869 poem from *Leaves of Grass* by Walt Whitman that offers a particular sense of the self.

A noiseless patient spider,
I mark'd where on a little promontory it stood isolated,
Mark'd how to explore the vacant vast surrounding,
It launch'd forth filament, filament, filament, out of itself,
Ever unreeling them, ever tirelessly speeding them.

And you O my soul where you stand,
Surrounded, detached, in measureless oceans of space,
Ceaselessly musing, venturing, throwing, seeking the spheres to
    connect them,
Till the bridge you will need be form'd, till the ductile anchor
    hold,
Till the gossamer thread you fling catch somewhere, O my soul.

Does this poem speak to you? Is the word "soul" part of your own vocabulary? There was a time in my life when this grand and heroic picture of the self appealed to me. But, like any single picture, there are certain things that don't appear in the frame. For example, this picture seems to present a view of the self as isolated or autonomous, overlooking the extent to which we are inextricably woven (to continue the metaphor) into a range of family, cultural and discourse communities. Some people would say that the self is *not* unitary, but is constituted of a complex of sometimes conflicting Discourses (see Chapter 2). Nature here is viewed as somehow empty and requiring thought to make sense of it. Many cultural traditions would see this view as rather blasphemous. Moreover, some people would say that meanings are mostly made *for* us (for example, by the various Discourses we acquire)—not *by* us. Regardless of such caveats, of course, we can still enjoy the poem in its own terms.

If you have a look at the way Whitney described Laura's reframing a few paragraphs back, you will see that she uses a language about the self that constructs it as both one ("sense of self," "whole meaning") and multiple ("selves," "identities"). Is there a single or essential self that endures over time? Can I look back at myself as an adolescent and say: "Yes, that was still me, even though in many ways I am not the same person as I was then." Cognitive neuroscientist, Antonio Damasio, has come up with the term "autobiographical self" to describe this "single" self that endures.

The autobiographical self is based on autobiographical memory which is constituted by implicit memories of multiple instances of individual

> experience of the past and of the anticipated future. The invariant aspects of an individual's biography form the basis for autobiographical memory. Autobiographical memory grows continuously with life experience but can be partly remodelled to reflect new experiences. Sets of memories which describe identity and person can be reactivated as a neural pattern and made explicit as images whenever needed. Each reactivated memory operates as "something-to-be-known" and generates its own pulse of core consciousness. The result is the autobiographical self of which we are conscious.
>
> (1999, p. 174)

Memory as a theme recurs later in this chapter.

What about self-as-multiple? If we take up the argument made by Gee and others in Chapter 2, we can assert that all of us, as socialized beings, are apprenticed as we grow and develop in a range of Discourses (coherent stories about this or that aspect of the world). I use the word "subscription" (Figure 3.1) to indicate the way we can be thought of as "signing up" to a particular way of viewing the world, while acknowledging that we may not be fully aware of this process of subscription. I use the word "inscription" to denote the way we can be thought of as being "inscribed" by discourses—how we are acted *upon* in the process of apprenticeship. Our attitude to any discourse, once we become aware of our subscription, can vary from compliance to resistance. I use the term "self as negotiator" to suggest that as individuals we have agency over the subscription process and can contest the way the world is storied in discourse. Figure 3.1 has Discourse 1 and Discourse 2 to suggest that we can subscribe to more than one discourse, and that often these discourses can appear to be contradictory. For example, I would argue that a person can be both evolutionist and Christian. Finally, one way of managing this paradox of the one and the many is to think of ourselves as having a single sense of *self* that is constituted by multiple *subjectivities*. I think of myself, for instance, as constituted by a number of subjectivities, for example, a subjectivity that is sympathetic to certain Christian ways of making meaning and a subjectivity that endorses Darwinian explanations for a range of human capabilities.

How does this relate to the concept of voice in writing? As Peter Elbow comments, "voice is a lightning rod that attracts ideological dispute" (2000, p. 218). In his essay, "What Is Voice in Writing?" Elbow takes issue with views that argue that either (1) "self" is no more than a series of roles that are created through text for rhetorical purposes, or (2) is inaccessible through textual engagement. Elbow's rhetorical strategy is to begin with a discussion of the literal, physical voice, which you and I would be using were we in the same room having a conversation. He then distinguishes five distinct senses of the concept of voice as applied metaphorically to something we *hear* in/through (the prepositions matter!) a written text. These are:

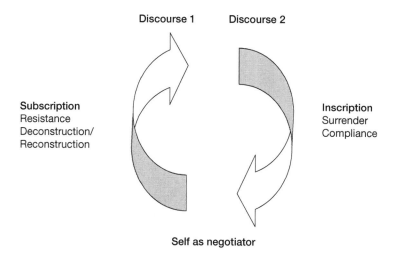

Discourse 1   Discourse 2

Subscription
Resistance
Deconstruction/
Reconstruction

Inscription
Surrender
Compliance

Self as negotiator

FIGURE 3.1 Self and discourse

1. "audible voice or intonation (the sounds in a text);
2. "dramatic voice (the character or implied author in a text);
3. "recognizable or distinctive voice;
4. "voice with authority;
5. "resonant voice or presence" (p. 193).

The first of these refers to ways in which certain features, such as intonation and other qualities of the physical voice find their way into writing. The second refers to our habit of associating a text with a speaker who exhibits certain *characteristics*. The third refers to the recognizable qualities in a voice, which enable it to be distinguished from other voices. The fourth relates to the degree of confidence we perceive in the way writers position themselves authoritatively, allowing us to distinguish between those who have *found* their voice and those who have yet to find it. According to Elbow, none of these senses demands a theory of the self as single or unitary.

In explaining the fifth sense of the word, Elbow suggests that the idea of *resonance* suggests a perceptible relationship between written text and the unconscious, where voice in a way that is hard to explain, captures something of the "rich complexity" of the person (2000, p. 206). "Resonant voice in writing is not a picture of the self, but it has the self's resources behind or underneath it" (p. 208). This does not necessitate a belief in the self as coherent and having an identity that persists over time. What Elbow *does* argue for is that we can "make inferences about the relation between the voice in a text and the actual unknown historical writer behind the text" (p. 211) and that we have been trained to do so, for example, as a way of making decisions about a "speaker's" trustworthiness or genuineness.

Interestingly, Elbow's claim here is backed up by evolutionary theory and *theory of mind*, which Brian Boyd describes as a unique human capability "to read one another, and therefore social events, in a far finer-grained way than any other species" (p. 141). Despite the strictures of literary theories that caution teachers and students away from seeking authorial intention in/through texts (the *intentional fallacy*), teachers and students in practice tend to ignore such advice and act as if some kind of voice is accessible (Locke, 2011).

REFLECTIVE JOURNAL TASK 3.3

Think back to Anne Whitney's description of Laura as having multiple selves. List your selves. Try to identify some of the values and beliefs associated with each of these selves. Which self do you feel most private about? What social context do you associate with each self?

Memory as a Resource

Carolyn Frank (2003) recalls how she managed to help a group of linguistically diverse teachers think of themselves as writers by having them draw neighborhood maps and engage in personal narratives about childhood memories. Her first experience of a neighborhood map as prompt was in 1996 during a summer institute of the South Coast Writing Project at the University of California. The purpose of the exercise was to illustrate the importance of memory for writing. For Frank, the memory map was a personal turning point (see Figure 3.2.).

> I remembered my neighborhood in the San Fernando Valley in Southern California when it was still mostly fields of turnips, tomatoes, and corn. . . . As I drew the map, my mind was flooded with memories of past experiences. I remembered digging the swimming pool in the dirt with my sister, my brother falling out of the car, and my biting the head of my sister's chocolate Easter egg.
>
> (p. 186)

The map was crucial in helping her overcome her fear of not having something to write about. In the research she describes later in her article, the memory map is a key prompt in helping a group of culturally and linguistically diverse elementary teachers explore their cultural identities, and develop confidence as writers and culturally responsive teachers.

It is not altogether surprising that a visual prompt such as a map can trigger language. In 1971, Allan Paivio published a theory of dual coding, a theory of

FIGURE 3.2 Carolyn Frank's annotated map of the neighborhood

cognition arguing that the human brain has both verbal and visuo-spatial (pictorial) codes for representing information in discrete memory systems. According to this theory, concrete words (such as "tree" and "bicycle") are easily encoded twice, once in the verbal system and once in the non-verbal system, hence "dual-coded." Abstract words (such as "love" and "ambition") are preferentially encoded in the verbal system, but concrete analogies (as in the famous line from Robert Burns, "My love is like a red, red rose") would allow them to be encoded in

WRITING TASK 3.4

Childhood Memory

Choose from your childhood a moment you remember and write it down. Now, with your eyes closed, imagine this moment caught in a photograph or a movie that is playing in your mind. Notice as clearly as you can details of people and places and happenings. Quickly make a set of jottings based on these rememberings.

Now, using the first person "I", present this experience in a personal narrative, recording what is happening. Your purpose is to evoke the immediacy of the experience so that you "put the reader there", so you may want to use the present tense. Try to emphasise concrete, sensuous impressions. You might think of a reader as eavesdropping on an interior conversation. Feel free to use the features of stream-of-consciousness: for example, fragments, lists, abrupt transitions, and snippets of dialogue.

the non-verbal system. Pictures are preferentially encoded in the non-verbal system, but through referential connections to words. Thus the picture of a cat will link to the word "cat" in the verbal system. Again, we can say that the picture and the word are "dual-coded." Frank's neighborhood map, as a concrete representation of early lived experience, appears to have referentially stimulated the recall of words encoded in the verbal memory system, even though it is currently unclear how the two memory systems interact. Dual coding theory in general explains why graphic representations can be helpful in written tasks, for example, having a structural outline before writing.

A Scottish-born English teacher, Hazel Redpath, produced the following piece of writing in response to this task.

TITIAN

On Saturday my mum and I take a trip to Edinburgh to visit the National Gallery on the same day that my friend Mandy and her mum are going to Marks and Spencer's—a shop which, in my imagination, is an Aladdin's cave full of coloured tights and pretty printed scarves and knitted berets. I feel thwarted.

We wait patiently for the bus, exposed to the full blast of the wind from the sea, but we do not board the first one that arrives. My mum has a bad feeling about this one and so we let the bus pass for some unspoken reason that I trust and do not question. It is intuition; she knows things that I do not always understand.

We sit downstairs. The top deck of the bus is the preserve of the people who smoke and we do not want to go there. Instead, we position ourselves, if possible, on the side seat—from where we can view most of the other passengers and still watch the shops and houses rumble by outside the windows.

I look out, anxiously, for old women who might need a seat. If I see one, I must jump to my feet immediately and offer my place. This shows manners and is the right thing to do. Failure to complete this movement in the allotted time will result in a disapproving look from my mother and I prefer to avoid that, whereas successful completion of the task will result in a nod and a smile of satisfaction, which I enjoy.

Today the bus is quiet and I have time to look around.

In the corner, a young woman has fallen asleep. Her head rests against the window, which has steamed up to form a barrier against the cold, and as the bus shudders from stop to stop, her ringlets bounce and sway in time to some unrecognisable rhythm. I am drawn to the patent leather shine of her high heeled shoes and the neat seam on the back of her stockings. I think she is stylish and that she probably shops in Marks and Spencer's on Saturdays—which is where I imagine she will be going today.

Opposite her, sits a much older woman, her small frame cosseted inside a coat of rough tweed. A woollen headscarf, neatly tied, obscures her hair, and her legs are encased in heavy knit tights that wrinkle just above her sturdy ankle boots. She clutches a handbag with both hands and sits very still. Her back is straight and firm and she does not lean on the seat for support. I do not imagine that she could ever fall asleep on a bus.

The air in the bus begins to grow stuffy and the cigarette smoke from the upper deck is snaking down the stairs towards me. I squirm and fidget as the rough woollen cloth of the seat starts to scratch the back of my legs. I take this as a signal that we are nearly there.

Although I covet the trip to the Princes Street shops that I believe everyone else will be enjoying this afternoon, I love the National Gallery. It is a place that I have come to regard as my own—and I am sometimes a little bit surprised to find other people there.

My mum and I each have our favourite paintings that we like to visit and we head off in different directions; we will meet from time to time, but the feeling of freedom is immense. I wander around on my own. The size of the building always impresses me and I love to look up at the domed ceiling that curves towards a pinpoint of light high above my head. The sense of space is palpable, overwhelming.

The rubber soles of my new winter shoes squeak as I walk across the varnished wooden floor and I glance cautiously over my shoulder—embarrassed at first by the sound until I realize that no one seems to have heard. Perhaps it was not as loud as I had imagined. Nevertheless, I adjust my footing and twist my ankles outwards slightly in an attempt to shift my weight to the edge of my feet and silence my steps.

I shuffle, awkward in my newly adopted gait, and smile at the motionless attendants who stand in each of the rooms watching over the paintings. I feel unsettled today; none of the paintings are demanding my attention.

It's warm inside the gallery and, after a while, I decide to sit down to relieve my tired ankles and loosen the toggles on my duffle coat. I wish that I had not worn my scarf because I can feel the fibres of the wool tickling my neck. I should have taken it off and left it in the cloak room after all.

I sit more comfortably after I have struggled loose from my outdoor clothing and start to admire the paintings. I am in my favourite room of the gallery and these works are as familiar to me as the faces of my own family—perhaps more so. I study the paintings more closely and look at them for a long time; I think that sometimes I barely glance at the people I know well.

Today, though, there is something new. I sit up straight. For a moment, I am puzzled. Then I see it clearly—although I am not yet able to put it into words.

There is something secret and female and powerful here. I know it. I realize that I saw it earlier in the different faces of the women on the bus and I see it now in the paintings. Venus, as she rises from the waves wringing her hair, casually glances to the side and reveals to me the message that she has been carrying with her for centuries. Diana, too, has something important to share.

I stand up, in awe. These paintings have endured: the women are strong here, against men, but against other women too, and their strength has nothing to do with printed scarves or coloured tights or anything else that can be sold and bought at Marks and Spencer's.

I rush off to find my mum.

Writing to Know and Be

As I reread Hazel's piece, I have a strong sense that she has discovered something in the act of writing, something to do with gender and her developing sense of herself as a woman. As a reader, I detect a shift, for example, from the child who trusts her mother's decision-making and desires her approval to the girl, whose sense of herself has become enlarged as she finds herself responding deeply to certain paintings and rushes off to her mother to share *her* new knowledge.

In 1927, English novelist E.M. Forster gave a series of lectures, which were later published with the title *Aspects of the Novel*. At one point, Forster notes approvingly an assertion of an old lady accused by her niece of not understanding and appreciating logic: "'Logic! Good gracious! What rubbish!' she exclaimed, 'How can I tell what I think till I see what I say'" (1976, p. 99). Is writing a means of discovering what we already know? Is it a means of bringing new knowledge into being?

In his classic text, *Writing Without Teachers*, Elbow (1973) is in no doubt of the answer to this question, and we find him attacking the "commonsense, conventional" view of writing as a "two-step process," where one makes an outline or plan *before* starting writing (p. 14).

This idea of writing is backwards. That's why it causes so much trouble. Instead of a two-step transaction of meaning-into-language, think of writing as an organic, developmental process in which you start writing at the very beginning—before you know your meaning at all—and encourage your words gradually to change and evolve. Only at the end will you know what you want to say or the words you want to say it with.

(p. 15)

In part, Elbow's advocacy for freewriting is related to this strategy, which John Hayes (2006) terms *interactive* as opposed to "outline first" (p. 32).

Earlier cognitive accounts of the writing process, as discussed in the last chapter, very much saw the generation of ideas as related to the retrieval of content from long-term memory. Much early research was focused on ways of reducing the impact of processes that hinder this process of retrieval, for example, the pressure to spell correctly and write neatly, hence the push to *automatize* these processes. In the 1990s, Kellogg (1994) conducted a number of studies suggesting that when writers construct a clearly organized outline as a pre-writing strategy, thus reducing cognitive overload *during* writing, the final product will be better.

Another important factor related to the way knowledge is generated and transformed in the writing process, as British researcher David Galbraith (2009b) argues, is a difference in goal orientation. "While novice writers appear to define writing as primarily a matter of expressing what they know about a topic, expert writers define it as a matter of achieving communicative goals" (p. 53). In 1979, Linda Flower had described the prose of novice writers as "writer-based" and that of experts as "reader-based." The following year, Flower and Hayes (1980) reported on a study that used think-aloud protocols to compare the writing practices of expert and novice writers, finding that the latter generated 70% of their ideas in relation to the topic alone, whereas the former generated 60% of their ideas in relation to their rhetorical or communicative goals.

Later in the decade, and also operating out of a cognitive paradigm, Bereiter and Scardamalia (1987) developed their knowledge transforming model of writing which had a dual focus, with ideas reflecting both what the writer knows and how these ideas function rhetorically in a process of communication. As Galbraith (2009b) sums it up:

> The contrast between the knowledge telling model and the knowledge transforming model is a contrast between writers who ask themselves questions like, "What do I know about this?", "Does this sentence correspond to the idea I want to express?", "What else do I know about this?", and writers who, having thought about the goals they want to achieve, say things like, "If I want to achieve this, then the first step I need to take is . . .", "I can do this by saying . . .", "Having said that, what do I need to do next. . .".
>
> (p. 55)

Bereiter and Scardamalia's (1987) model further viewed the development of content as a continuing process that coincided with the production of the text itself. Looking back on this work, however, Galbraith (2009b) pointed out that although there is an implication that writing might be a source of discovery, these models don't adequately explain how *new* content can emerge in the writing process.

Since the early 1990s, Galbraith himself has engaged in research in an attempt to investigate how the act of writing serves to develop understanding. In selecting his research subjects, Galbraith distinguished between two types of writers: *low self-monitors*, who are assumed to focus on directly expressing their beliefs about a topic (and hence would be expected by Bereiter and Scardamalia to be knowledge-tellers); and *high self-monitors*, who are assumed to tailor their content to their communicative or rhetorical goals (and hence would be expected by Bereiter and Scardamalia to be knowledge-transformers). (See Galbraith, 2009b, for a detailed account of his findings over a number of years.) By 2006 his research had generated findings that appeared to be at odds with the Bereiter and Scardamalia model:

1.   While high self-monitors *did* generate new ideas during writing, these ideas were neither associated with increased understanding nor with coherence;
2.   Low self-monitors *also* generated new ideas when they wrote, but contrary to expectation, deepened their understanding and organized these ideas coherently.

As Galbraith bluntly put it, "precisely the wrong kinds of people, according to the knowledge-transforming model, appear to develop their understanding through writing" (2009b, p. 58).

Galbraith's explanation for this finding was to suggest that writing is more than a "knowledge-telling" or "knowledge-transforming" process. In his terms, writing is a *knowledge-constituting* process, that is, writing is not just about retrieving content; it is also about *synthesizing* content. For him, viewing writing this way provided a glimpse into a mechanism whereby new content can be created in the context of producing a written response to the demands of a rhetorical situation. Galbraith described his model as a "dual process," because he saw it as a combination of "rhetorical planning" and "dispositional text production." Rhetorical planning, concerned with the selection and arrangement of content, draws on memories connected with previously held ideas and how these have been organized in the past for communicative purposes, and is subject to working-memory constraints. A person's disposition relates to an implicit point of view— values, beliefs and his or her sense of self in the world. Dispositional text production involves the synthesis of propositions during the construction of a text guided by the implicit organization of the writer's belief system. If you've ever prepared a report for presentation to a meeting where you have been careful *not* to reveal your real feelings about some issue or other, you have experienced a conflict between your *dispositional* and *rhetorical* goals. In short, writing, viewed this way, allows for a discovery of what we think and feel about something. In Galbraith's words, "Text production . . . rather than being something that gets in the way of thinking, is in fact where thinking takes place" (2009b, p. 63).

Writing is not just about *coming-to-know* (epistemology). As Carolyn Frank found when working with culturally diverse teachers, writing can also play an important role in one's *coming-to-be*—in the development of identity (ontology). Ros Ivanič has written much about the way writers assume an identity as they write. As we write, we *construct* ourselves as a particular kind of person. (When we write, we are affirming our subscription to one or more discourses; see Figure 3.1.) Ivanič (1994) puts it this way:

> Every word a writer writes contributes to the impression she is creating of herself to a reader. Writers are positioned, a multiple identity is constructed for them, not only through what they have said but also through the discourses they have participated in to say it.

(p. 5)

In a later work (*Writing and Identity*, 1998), Ivanič argued that four dimensions of identity are involved in the act of writing: (1) an autobiographical self (similar to Damasio's concept quoted above); (2) a discoursal self which relates to how we position ourselves in relation to an anticipated audience by the discourses we subscribe to and project outwards; (3) an authorial self, very much related to Elbow's fourth sense of "voice"; and (4) possibilities for selfhood. The last of these has implications for all of us who seek to develop our sense of ourselves as writers, because it suggests that there are certain social conditions that favor our willingness to take risks in trying out or asserting or discovering identities (or "selves") in the act of writing itself (finding our "voice"). (See Ball & Ellis, 2008, for the implications of this for teachers in culturally diverse settings.)

REFLECTIVE JOURNAL TASK 3.5

Reflecting on Your Childhood Memory

As a result of writing your childhood memory, did you find yourself developing some kind of awareness of yourself that you did not have *prior* to the act of writing? If so, what did you "discover"? Can you identify some aspect of what you did in the process of completing the task that helped you in this act of "discovery"?

The personal narrative below was written during a Writing Workshop by Robin Mills, a teacher who works in a small, rural school. She gave permission for me to share this with you. Please be aware that the narrative you are reading is *not* a first draft and went through a number of drafts and was subject to response group sharing as it wended its way towards this version.

WRITING TASK 3.6

Personal Narrative

All of us have stories to tell. The word narrative comes from the Latin verb *narrare*, "to tell" and can be thought of as synonymous with "story." However, I use the word *narrative* to suggest that the story-maker has given some thought to *how* the sequence of events that make up the narrative has been shaped. In this task, I invite you to tell a story based on your own experiences or the experiences of people you know, that suggests an overarching theme, issue or idea. You can focus on a single episode, or draw on a number of episodes separated in time but which are linked to your theme. You don't have to *tell* your reader what the theme is, but trust that if you shape your narrative in a particular way, your reader will infer it.

A theme, of course, can mean a number of things. It might mean a particular insight about the nature of relationships, for example, how easy it is to hurt somebody. It might mean an insight into yourself, for example, that you really enjoy entering the imaginative worlds of children. It might mean a reflection on some aspect of society, for example, injustice, so that the events you weave together focus on the treatment of members of a minority group.

Having said all this, of course, you may choose to take up Peter Elbow's advice, and simply *freewrite* without forethought, trusting that a thematic center will emerge as knowledge in the narrative you write. Concrete detail is important, because that will give your writing vividness. However, you can be selective in your use of detail, providing just enough for the theme to emerge.

STAGE STRUCK

The applause faded and a wave of proud parents swooped towards their excited children. Actors, dancers, musicians all, the kids tossed their props into waiting baskets, seized bits of discarded costumes and burst into the chair strewn auditorium. Exhilarated with the success of the thirty-minute show I gathered together the abandoned instruments and left the children to enjoy their moment. This is what children's musical theatre should be about: limitless innovation, experimentation and creativity unfettered by adult expectations. The children themselves were the keystone. There had been no adult written script or formally composed music but simply a favourite legend retold through the children's own language, drama, music and dance from their own stories, designs, sound-scapes and motifs.

The satisfaction of realising our dreams was enormous. The time-frame involved, little more than a week of creating, learning, practicing and performing to the school and finally the parents. A week to realize a dream that had been nearly a lifetime growing.

I barely remember the piano. Hidden away in a dim back corner of Mr Oslaar's second-hand shop in deepest, darkest Dannevirke, it was probably unloved and out of tune. My nose remembers the smell of borer-chewed dust and cracked, sticky varnish. My fingers recall the pock-marked, gritty feel of old ivory keys. I wriggled onto the high stool, its brocade-covered seat greasy and threadbare. I started to investigate: touch and listen, touch and listen. The sounds bore little resemblance to the brilliantly executed piano music I had heard on records at home. My mother bustled in followed by an agitated Mr Oslaar. "Robin, you must always ask before you touch anything," she scolded. I scarcely heard her. "Mummy, how does it work?" I wanted to know. My mother, apologising and fussing as mothers do when their offspring break the rules, was interrupted by Mr Oslaar as he reached over and opened the front casing of the instrument. I don't remember what he told me but I have never forgotten the sight of the tightly stretched, brass-skinned and slender steel strings, and then the sound as I was encouraged to drag my fingers across them. A humming, jarring array of dissonant noise calling images into my mind of the wind, of storms and the roaring rapids of a river. The images in my mother's mind were somewhat different. She was visualising her daughter as a musical prodigy, a future concert pianist and was already planning my impending musical education.

The phases and fads that followed must have held endless frustrations for her quietly nurtured ambitions. My mother is a woman of very strong mind and she was determined that I would have the opportunities to learn music that she had secretly wished for as a child and been denied. However her initial attempts to reincarnate Mozart met with gentle but firm rebuttals from a succession of teachers. I was too young to learn piano, my hands were too small, I had no sense of rhythm, I should learn dancing first, preferably tap. This last suggestion I approved enthusiastically but was instead enrolled in a beginners' ballet class. Looking at my first recital photos showing a chunky child with elbows forming right angles matched by another perfect right angle created by an ankle that was never intended for extension to point a toe, I don't wonder that the ballet lessons didn't last long.

Next I begged to learn the bagpipes and spent hours dressed up in a tiny kilt that had been sent from Scotland, doing the Highland Fling and inventing noise pollution with a set of toy bagpipes. Later, after we moved into town I fell in love with the entire pipe band and would trail round after them at practice while my friends pestered their parents for ponies.

Formal piano lessons began at the age of eight with Miss Willison, an ex-primary-school teacher with a tight-lipped mouth and a steel-edged ruler. We had practically to mortgage the house in order to afford lessons, so I didn't dare say that I hated them. Practice was instant drudgery, exams were torture and recitals a fate worse than Easter without chocolate. I hated being on show and suffered from nerves of earthquake proportions. Unfortunately, I also played very well, so no one noticed my agony. The only part I really enjoyed was the theory. Learning how to build chords and write simple compositions was fun. Miss Willison, however, had other ideas. I was too young (again) to master the intricacies of music theory so I didn't "qualify" to sit the exams. I believe to this day that it was she who struggled.

The terrors of the weekly lesson with Miss Willison didn't last forever, because I found the perfect excuse to drop out. School homework demands left little time for practice, especially when I had to bike to secondary school every day, and home again via the local teenage gathering place, Sherson's Milkbar, for an obligatory Coke. What did interest me, however, was the school orchestra, so I lined up for a flute or an oboe which would have meant more practice but time out of class for lessons. Unfortunately, I was late for the muster and all the flutes and oboes had been claimed. Would I be interested in learning violin?

How proudly I biked home that first day with my violin and my dreams of playing solo with the National Orchestra. But, oh horror, the sounds that came from that instrument. The dreadful wailing was far worse than bagpipes. Our Siamese cat competed and the shrieks and squeals brought ridicule and complaint from the neighborhood. I did become proficient enough to play third violin in the school orchestra and that led to romance with the percussion. Graeme played the timpani and Graeme was gorgeous. Gorgeous enough to make me practice in earnest to improve my bowing technique and to spend hours mastering drums and cymbals in his dad's garage.

The romance blossomed until school prizegiving. The orchestra's second item was Greensleeves, a real dirge but a solo showcase for Vonnie, a budding clarinettist. She was dreadful: off key, out of time, nervously breathless and squawking like a parrot. That instrument fairly yodelled. My watering eyes met Graeme across the spinney of cello scrolls and we started to laugh. Soon everyone was in silent stitches, except Vonnie, who continued to blow her way into musical oblivion.

After that incident both Graeme and I were retired from our orchestral yearnings and took to the stage where we encountered mixed success, me in musicals and Graeme in Shakespearean productions. My poor mother must have wondered whatever became of her piano prodigy. There I was in the back row of the chorus having the time of my life and there I remained for years, never with the ambition or the voice for more than minor roles, but absorbing more than I realized of the workings of the theatre.

Meanwhile, after we moved to Hamilton, I had trained as a teacher and was loving the work, looking forward to every day and somehow managing to balance planning and rehearsals for shows with Musikmakers, an amateur theatrical company. The various schools I worked in were lucky to have enviably energetic and talented teachers, always keen to showcase children's abilities in a production of some sort, but refusing help from anyone but their closest cronies. I watched. They worked themselves ragged, revelled in grumbling and moaning about the hours they put into it, and threw glorious tantrums in the principal's office, an opportunity I would have relished.

The kids also loved the attention they got, the pageantry and the glamor. I could relate to that. The trouble was it all seemed a bit pointless. They rehearsed, performed and that was it. A fairly hollow experience enjoyed by a select few and from which no one really learnt a great deal. I remembered the flat feeling after my own school productions when we had to settle back into routine and nothing was any different from before, despite the efforts we had put into entertaining people and the fun we had had. The embryo of an idea was beginning to uncurl in my mind, although it was to be some years before I would recognize it. Could the children and I write and stage a musical production based on the learning that happened in our classroom?

The school I work in now is the ideal place for experimentation such as this. Teachers' visions are like plants in a prolific garden. They are allowed to grow organically, never sprayed and only pruned if they get out of control. Here children and their relationship to the arts are nurtured, not only by the staff but by support people from outside the school whose freely shared experience enriches everyone's growth. Angela, whose drama devices and soft Scottish accent captured the attention of the most disrespectful teenagers, and Cath, who would arrive armed with parrot-coloured boom-whackers and other outlandish instruments that made her my friend for life. It was Cath who gave me that vital encouragement to look beyond the conventional, opening the doors and windows for children to interpret and create with their own voices. Choice, encouragement, empowerment and success are the hallmarks. Every child takes part in his or her chosen aspect of class productions. Children write, design, choreograph and perform, learning as much about themselves as they do about theatre. Their skills are learnt over weeks, their productions are developed over days but their memories and interest will last a lifetime.

REFLECTIVE JOURNAL TASK 3.7

Reflecting on Your Personal Narrative

1. You'll be aware that Robin's narrative covered a range of events happening over a long period of time. What theme or themes do you see emerging in this story? If you were to give this piece a title, what would it be?

2. We have not talked about sharing writing or having others respond to our writing yet, have we? It may be that you are using this book as a member of a group of teachers who are meeting from time to time to discuss it and engage in writing together. Or, you may be working your way through the book individually. However, if you do have an opportunity to share your personal narrative with another person, ask them to share with you positive comments about your narrative and any suggestions they might have for changes or improvements.

Further Reading

Expressive Writing

- Elbow, P. (1973). *Writing without teachers* (2nd ed.). New York, NY: Oxford University Press.
- Bilton, L., & Sivasubramaniam, S. (2009). An inquiry into expressive writing: A classroom-based study. *Language Teaching Research, 13*(3), 301–320.

Memory as Writing Prompt

- Frank, C. (2003). Mapping our stories: Teachers' reflections on themselves as writers. *Language Arts, 80*(3), 185–195.

Writing to Learn

- Galbraith, D. (2009b) Writing as discovery. In V. Connelly, A. Barnett, J. Dockrell, & A. Tolmie (Eds.), *Teaching and learning writing* (pp. 5–26). Leicester, UK: British Psychological Society (*British Journal of Educational Psychology* Monograph Series II, 6).
- Hayes, J. (2006). New directions in writing theory. In C. MacArthur, S. Graham, & J. Fitzgerald (Eds.), *Handbook of writing research* (pp. 28–40). New York, NY: Guilford; see especially pp. 32–35.

Voice in Writing

- Elbow, P. (2000). What is voice in writing? In *Everyone can write: Essays toward a hopeful theory of writing and teaching writing* (pp. 184–221). New York, NY: Oxford University Press.
- Ivanič, R. (1998). *Writing and identity: The discoursal construction of identity in academic writing.* Amsterdam, The Netherlands: Benjamins.
- Ball, A., & Ellis, P. (2008). Identity and the writing of culturally and linguistically diverse students. In C. Bazerman (Ed.), *Handbook of research on writing: History, society, school, individual, text* (pp. 499–514). New York, NY: Erlbaum.

4

"ONE'S-SELF I SING"

The Democratic Self in Writing

This chapter begins by revisiting the ancient concept of *rhetoric* and the *rhetor*—the person with designs on an audience and who fashions his or her text accordingly using the semiotic resources at his or her disposal. I argue that all texts have a rhetorical purpose and are produced in order to get something done, whether we're talking about a literary text such as a poem or the carefully structured closing address of a prosecuting attorney. It locates writing at the heart of the democratic forum, as enabling speakers to develop, sustain, defend, negotiate and modify a position in dialogue with others. While texts generally engage in one of three "super" functions—describe, narrate and persuade—the fact is that for many texts these functions overlap; texts are usually multifunctional. Even literary genres such as the lyric poem and memoir can be thought of as having a persuasive force. Like earlier chapters, this one will provide you with ways into various types of writing and examples of such writing from practicing teachers.

Rhetoric: Writing with an Audience in Mind

My own understanding of rhetoric has had a long gestation. I first became aware of it in the term "rhetorical question"—a kind of non-question that is used to invite agreement ("Should we continue to put up with this!")—and in phrases such as "empty rhetoric." Such phrases have tended to give rhetoric a bad name, suggesting that rhetoricians (people who practice rhetoric) are manipulative people whose primary aim is to somehow deceive others into agreeing with them. However, as Richard Andrews (1992) and others associated with the "new Rhetoric" have argued, rhetoric has a proud history dating back to the ancient Greeks' preoccupation with the "arts of discourse" and, with some dusting off and refurbishment, deserves to be reinstated as a fundamental concept in our understanding of how language (including written language) works. The definition I offer my students is that "Rhetoric is the art of making language work for you." I generally follow up this definition by explaining that language function is the *work* that a text is doing at any point. Function is always *social*. We produce texts in order to get something done, that is, to achieve a goal with a reader or audience.

Cognitive accounts of the writing process have not omitted to recognize the place of audience. For example, in a 1996 version of the cognitive model of writing first propounded with Flowers, Hayes included two components, the "task environment" and "the individual." "Audience" was an aspect of the "task environment" (as was the "physical environment). However, the rhetorical approach to writing I am presenting here is more consonant with a sociocultural view of writing (see Chapter 2).

Figure 4.1 is a way of representing this approach. Let's start with the *rhetor,* the word I am using here in preference to either *writer* or *composer.* You can think of the rhetor as a purposeful text-maker or designer who is aware of the semiotic resources available to him or her as a means for achieving the best possible outcome in a communicative situation. As Kress (2010) puts it, "in each instance of interaction it is essential to assess the social environment and the social relations which obtain; to adjust forms of communication accordingly. . . . The competence of clear and detailed analysis of social environments of communication is now becoming a required commonplace" (p. 243). In Figure 4.1 I draw on the linguists Halliday and Hasan (1985) and identify two dimensions to the communicative situation: *context of culture* and *context of situation.*

Let me illustrate this by imagining that you and I are writing a cookbook. The context of situation refers to the immediate environment within which this writing project occurs. It could include our purpose in writing the book (to develop tasty, gluten-free recipes), our intended audience (people who find gluten-free food somewhat drab), and a commissioning agent (a publisher who is convinced of our credentials to produce this kind of recipe book). The context of culture is the broader institutional and cultural environment within which we will be working. As Ivanič points out, meaning is "dependent on the way in which language has been used in the past: only certain meanings are possible because of socio-historical constraints. The language system itself has been socio-culturally constructed" (1998, pp. 39–40). For us as writers, our language use will be profoundly influenced by current discourses around nutrition, healthy eating, environmental responsibility and so on.

As you're reading this, you'll be realizing that all these aspects of the rhetorical situation will be impacting on the *kind* of content that we will be including in our book. For instance, because we are imagining an audience that is environmentally aware, we will be designing recipes that make use where possible of local, seasonal produce. Our completed text, then, will be an outcome of our

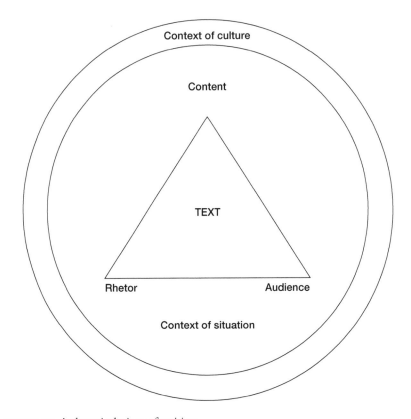

FIGURE 4.1 A rhetorical view of writing

analysis of the rhetorical situation. The exact shape our text assumes will be very much the result of how we engage with the genre of "recipe book." However, *genre* is a big topic, which I mention here but will treat more thoroughly later in the chapter.

This rhetorical approach can be summed up in the following statements:

1.   People construct texts with a view to achieving a desired result with a particular audience.
2.   Text is a product of function (form follows function).
3.   Texts are generated by contexts. Social/cultural contexts call forth texts.
4.   All texts assume a kind of social complicity between maker and reader.
5.   The expectations of people participating in such acts of complicity become formalized in the conventions of genre.
6.   These conventions can apply to such language features as: layout, structure, punctuation, syntax and diction in the case of print texts, with other configurations of features operating for other modes and modal combinations.
7.   In a rhetorical approach, literature is not devalued but revalued.

In relation to text as a product of function, think of a business letter and the various structural components that comprise it and the way they are sequenced. In the first of these components, the sender is identified via letterhead and/or address. It occurs first because it is useful to have a component at the top of the page that clearly identifies the sender (function). Form is being dictated by function. And so on for the other components of such a letter. In relation to texts assuming a kind of social complicity between maker and reader, think of a text that I imagine that you have produced at some stage in your life and probably keep in digital form—your curriculum vitae (CV). When you apply for a job and send off your CV (usually accompanied by a letter of application), you are doing something quite remarkable. You are assuming that a person you have probably never met will recognize your CV *as* a CV. The complicity arises because you and the

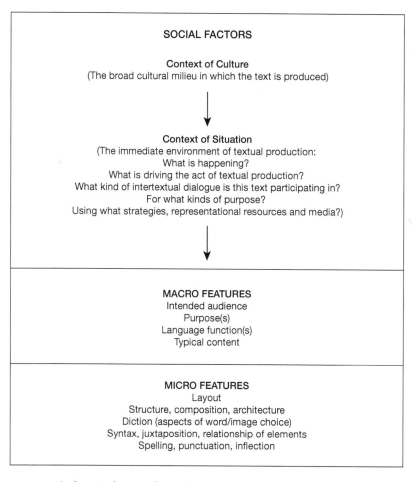

FIGURE 4.2 A rhetorical view of textual production

addressee are both members of a society in which the CV is an agreed-upon (or *conventional*) way of conducting a particular kind of transaction. Figure 4.2 is another way of representing this rhetorical approach to writing. This is a "top-down" view of writing, where the function of language features at the micro level are explained by the relationship of the text to its context.

REFLECTIVE JOURNAL TASK 4.1

Draw up a three-column table. Make a list of some of the types of text that you produce as a regular part of your personal and professional life. Put these in column one. Aligned with each of these texts in column two, name the audience for each of them. Then, in column three, write some of the features associated with each text that you would regard as determined by the audience. For example, in column one you might write "personal letter," and in column two you might right "family members." In column three you might realize that, when you write personal letters, you use "colloquial language" and "run-on sentences." (You might explain to yourself that you use run-on sentences because you tend to write personal letters as if you're talking.)

Lyric Poetry

The following poem was written by 10-year-old Jacinta Day from Wigan in England and published in an anthology of poetry by children, edited by Chris Searle and published in 1972. It is a poem I have shared with my students over many years.

MY TEACHER

Her hair is like smog clinging to a building.
Her eyes are like death's army marching
towards me.
And her teeth are like jagged rocks,
devouring ships.
Her nose is like a blunt pencil.

When I was writing this book, I managed to locate Jacinta and she told me that she submitted this poem to a competition organized by the *Times Educational Supplement* and that, although she did not win, she was contacted by Chris Searle for her permission to have the poem published. She told me that the teacher described here was her teacher at the time and that this was how she imagined her. My students have always responded to the very direct way in which Jacinta communicated her attitude to the teacher.

In this part of the chapter, I invite you to write a poem about a person you know and have feelings for. While poetry is actually a *form* of writing (as prose is a form), once we start rhetorically framing a poem, by describing it as a lyric poem, or a didactic poem, or a satirical poem, or a narrative poem (ballad), we are really talking about genres (of which more later). "My teacher" is a lyrical poem, where the speaker is exploring feelings or attitudes in relation to a person, event, or situation.

The rhetorical is not the enemy of the literary! As Terry Eagleton (2007) pointed out: "A poem . . . is a rhetorical performance, but (unlike most rhetorical exercises) not typically an instrumental one. It does things to us, though not usually so that we can get something done" (p. 89). In Jacinta's case, her little poem, with its sequence of similes, convinces us to see her teacher in a particular way. There is quite some argumentative force in her description.

Earlier, I described a rhetor as a purposeful text-maker or designer who is aware of the semiotic or representational resources available to him or her as means for achieving the best possible outcome in a communicative situation. To allay student anxiety around poetry, I often suggest that writing a poem can be reduced to two basic operations: selecting words and arranging them on the page.[1] Let me try to set out some of the representational resources available to a poet/rhetor under each of these headings:

SELECTION

Diction is a grammar category related to word choice. A person with a large vocabulary has a large "lexis" to choose from. Simply having a large vocabulary will not make you a good writer, of course. Rather, it's your ability to choose words appropriate to subject matter, audience and purpose. It's also knowing which *types* of words best suit your purpose.

A key distinction here is between *concrete* and *abstract* diction. Concrete words enable a reader to respond sensuously to an experience. Sensuous language can be visual (images of sight), aural (hearing), tactile (touch), gustatory (taste) or olfactory (smell). For example, "The old man lay huddled on the pitted surface of the dusty and rutted road. His skinny arms clasped a ragged and dirty child. Its head lolled back and its eyes had a marble stillness. Near its open mouth, buzzed a large, blue fly."

Abstract diction is the language of ideas or concepts. It is useful for reasoning through generalization and argument. For example: "There is no such thing as a just war. There may be just causes. But there can be no justification for the notion that arguments can be solved by force." Words like "thing," "just," "war," "justification," "notion," "argument," "solve," and "force" are abstract. You cannot see, touch, smell, taste or hear a "justification."

A second key distinction is between *literal* and *figurative* diction. Literal language denotes objects actually present in a situation being written about, whereas figurative language draws on images from outside the literal situation as a way of saying something about or expressing an attitude to the literal situation itself. The most common *figures of speech* are: *metaphor* (where the comparison is a blunt identification: *He's a lion of a man*); *simile* (where the comparison is softened by the use of "like" or "as": *She was like a wildcat when put upon*); and *personification* (where a non-human object is described in terms of human characteristics: *The cold hand of death was upon her*). In the example of concrete language above, the word "marble" is figurative. The child's eyes are not literally made of marble, but have a quality in death that reminds the writer of the lifeless but beautiful qualities of marble.

Another way of thinking about words relates to the formal/informal continuum. In this regard, the writer's view of his or her relationship with the audience and the demands of the genre are crucial. Words for death and dying are obvious examples here. You will be aware of the phrase "passed away" as a euphemism for "die," and that using a slang expression such as "carked it" (more familiar to U.K. and Australasian readers) risks causing offence.

Finally, but not exhaustively, there are the sound qualities of words. English has a large range of vowels (pronounced differently according to one's accent). Some are long (as in "moon"), while others are short (as in "hit"). *Figures of sound* is the collective term for devices which exploit the sound qualities of language, such as *alliteration* (the repetition of identical consonants in proximity), *assonance* (the repetition of identical vowels in proximity), *onomatopoeia* (words whose sounds echo the sound made by the objects referred to, as in "hiss" and "drone") and *phonesthesia* (words whose sound seems to suggest certain meanings or feelings, such as "slimy" and "slattern").

In terms of word selection, Jacinta's poem is both concrete and figurative. There is a sequence of four similes. However, within the similes themselves, we find metaphor (smog "clings," rocks "devour") and personification (death is a military leader).

ARRANGEMENT

Words can be arranged at different levels.

1. **Syntax (Level 1).** A rhetor, who is syntactically fluent, confidently combines words into groups such as phrases, clauses and sentences. As Chomsky discovered, and as cognitive neuroscientists such as Stephen Pinker (1995) have written about at length, the brains of human beings appear to be "wired" for syntax. That means that, without being taught, we can recognize sentences that are nonsense syntactically and generate correct

sentences we have never encountered before. Poetry is a form that allows writers to combine words in ways that defy conventional syntax (see the first stanza of Helen's poem in Chapter 1). However, Jacinta chose to use conventionally correct syntax in her poem. Having said that, there are certain *notational* devices that can be used in the *lineation* of a poem (setting it out in lines).

a. Notated pauses (increasing the gap between words beyond a single space);
b. Dropped lines (dropping to the next line without returning to the left-hand margin);
c. Controlling for line length;
d. Line-breaks.

In Jacinta's poem, the line-breaks are mostly dictated by the presence of a period or comma. However, she also introduces a "non-syntactical" line break after "marching."

2. **Text section (Level 2).** Some texts have identifiable sections that have a structure of their own. Here are three examples:

a. *Paragraph:* Sometimes, but not always, a paragraph will have an explicit *topic sentence* which needs to relate clearly to other sentences within the paragraph. *Cohesion* is the grammatical term used to describe the way in which sentences clearly relate to each other in the context of a paragraph and other kinds of text section.
b. *Stanza:* This is a verse paragraph, which can be described in terms of, for example, a regular number of lines, a rhyme scheme and meter. In English poetry, a meter is an artificial pattern of stressed and unstressed syllables made up of units called *feet,* which have the same pattern. The most common pattern is *iambic:* an unstressed followed by a stressed syllable. Jacinta's poem has a single paragraph and might be described as *non-metrical,* since it relies for its rhythmic effects on the natural rhythm of English speech. (English is a stress-timed language, meaning that its words *already* have a pattern of stressed and unstressed syllables.)
c. *Directions:* Look at a recipe, and you'll find a section, often numbered, with a set of directions. Directions are characterized by a logical succession of sentences using imperatives verbs (e.g., "Mix carefully).

3. **Text (Level 3).**

a. *Structure:* In this book, I mostly use the word *structure* to refer to the relationship of components to one another within a whole text. The structure of a text organizes the content in a meaningful way and contributes to textual meaning. For example, each sentence in Jacinta's poem is a clear reference to the teacher she is describing. You could also say that there is an overall attitude towards the teacher (tone) that each sentence (as structural component) reinforces.

b. *Composition:* This is a useful term for thinking about the way design elements in a text (especially pictorial elements) are arranged in relation to one another and some kind of frame. In arranging content, a designer will consider audience impact. *Layout* is another term referring to the arrangement and formatting (see below) of elements on a page.

c. *Format:* I'm writing this chapter using Microsoft Word. If I lift my gaze from the page to the top menu bar, I see a drag-down menu entitled "Format." Format refers to a number of visual textual features which relate to the "look" of a text but are not particularly determined by content: size of margin, font, number of columns, width of guttering, style of bullet, size of indentation, and so on. As often happens, each line of Jacinta's poem is indented and the title is in bold and left justified.

Let me emphasize that the above overview of selection and arrangement is not meant to be exhaustive. How could it be! However, I hope it will indicate to you the immense possibilities a rhetor has at his or her disposal when he/she is considering shaping content for an audience. A distinguishing characteristic of poetry, of course, is that of all forms of writing, it is the one that offers the *most* resources to a writer. That makes poetry both fun and challenging to write and read.

WRITING TASK 4.2

Poem About a Person

Imagine a person you know and that you feel something towards. Describe that person concretely, using a mix of literal and figurative language to communicate your attitude. Write your text in such a way that none of your lines arrives at the right-hand margin.

When you have some kind of draft, you might like to use the following as revision prompts (or have a friendly reader discuss these prompts with you):

1. *Content:* Are there telling details about the chosen person that you have overlooked? Try imagining them engaged in a typical activity? What do they typically wear? Are there certain objects you associate with them? Or colors?

2. *Rhetorical strategy:* Do you have a particular reader in mind as you write? What difference would it make to your poem if you did?

3.   *Structure:* Is there a logic in the way your poem is sequenced? (Think of Helen's poem in Chapter 1.) Do you want to rethink the sequence?

4.   *Layout:* Are your lines too long? Would certain details stand out more if you had shorter lines or line-breaks at particular points.

5.   *Syntax and punctuation:* Are you being too fussy about correct syntax? Could you omit words that are not really adding to your poem (like "very")?

6.   *Diction:* Are your words as particular as they could be? For instance, "amble," "strut," "stride" are more particular than "walk." Could you replace an abstract expression with words that help your reader see, hear, smell, touch and taste? Are you over-focusing on the visual at the expense of other senses?

Bakhtin, The Utterance and Genre

I want you to imagine that a good friend of yours is having relationship problems. Because you want to be a supportive friend, you arrange to meet him for coffee. (I'm making the friend a "him" in this instance as a way of resisting the gendered expectation that it is only women who engage in this kind of relationship discussion.) As it turns out—in our imagined scenario—the conversation goes well, your friend has an opportunity to unburden, you are a good listener asking probing questions without being too intrusive and offer insightful feedback without being pushy.

Let's bring in Bakhtin here, a Russian scholar with broad interests in literature, philosophy and language, and see how he might encourage us to think about our imagined scenario. I'll start with a comment about Bakhtin made by Freedman and Medway in *Learning and teaching genre* (1994). "Bakhtin's primary interest in language is not in abstract systems of formal rules (for grammar, for example). Rather it is the instances of language in actual use that interest him" (p. 9). Despite his literary training, Bakhtin would have been just as interested in your conversation with your friend as in a novel by Dostoyevsky. He would be unwilling to privilege one kind of language situation over another. Novels and informal chat would have equal claims to attention. He would see your conversation over coffee as a typical area of human activity (this is one way friends support one another) and would have been interested in the key role played by language as used by you and your friend as participants in this encounter. He would have seen the language used as influenced by the conditions prevailing in the situation (the level of trust operating between you and your friend, could your conversation be overheard, and so on) and the goals you both brought to the conversation.

In a famous essay written around 1952–53, "The Problem with Speech Genres," Bakhtin made the claim that "Language is realized in the form of individual concrete utterances (oral and written)" made by participants in some area of activity (1986, p. 60). For Bakhtin, the boundaries of each concrete utterance are determined by a *change of speaking subjects,* that is, a change of speakers. In our scenario, I imagine that there would have been a large number of utterances. (The same would be the case had you decided to have your conversation via Skype.) Remember that an utterance, in Bakhtin's terms, can be written. A personal letter written to a friend is a single utterance, as would be a letter sent in reply. There are two other features of an utterance besides its being marked by a change of subject:

1   *Finalization:* Bakhtin includes three aspects of an utterance under this term.
    • The way in which there is a kind of completeness in a single utterance in the way it treats a topic or theme, even in a single response such as "I see what you mean."
    • *Goal-directedness:* Bakhtin uses words such as "plan" and "speech will" to refer to the way in which participants bring certain purposes or intentions to the production of an utterance.
    • *Generic form:* This refers to the way in which utterances are composed in typical ways, with typical structures and stylistic usages. If you decided to engage in a follow-up conversation with your friend, you would find on reflection that it would be typified by many language features present in your first conversation because of the *similarity in the conditions* that prevail.

2   *Relation to participants:* In his essay, Bakhtin refers to "The relation of the utterance to the *speaker himself* (the author of the utterance) and to the *other* participants in speech communication" (1986, p. 84). In this instance, Bakhtin distinguishes two aspects which determine a person's choice of language and genre:
    • "The referentially semantic assignments (plan) of the speech subject (or author)" (p. 84). Think of this as the meaningful content of an utterance—the theme or topic a speaker or writer is addressing.
    • "The *expressive* aspect, that is, the speaker's subjective emotional evaluation of the referentially semantic content of his utterance" (p. 84). What Bakhtin is talking here about is what we might simply call *tone,* that is, how a speaker or writer feels about (attitude towards) something or someone.

The implication of all of this is that language is only *truly* meaningful in the context of an utterance. Think of the possible shades of meaning to the sentence, "I love you," and you will appreciate what Bakhtin means when he writes: "Neutral dictionary meanings of the words of a language ensure their common features and guarantee that all speakers of a given language will understand one another, but the use of words in live speech communication is always individual and contextual in nature" (1986, p. 88).

But Bakhtin goes further, making an additional claim that utterances themselves can only be fully understood in the context of their relationship to other utterances. The term I will be using for this relationship is "intertexuality." (You may have spotted it in Figure 4.2 earlier in this chapter.) I'm guessing that this makes perfectly good sense to you in the case of your imagined conversation with your friend. At some point you may have produced the utterance, "I see what you mean." But for me to understand this fully, I would need to see a transcript of the section of the conversation where this utterance occurs.

But what about an utterance like this book I am writing and which you are reading in its published form? In a memorable passage, Bakhtin introduces the idea of an "organized chain of utterances" as a metaphor for intertexuality:

> Moreover, any speaker is himself a respondent to a greater or lesser degree. He is not, after all, the first speaker, the one who disturbs the eternal silence of the universe. And he presupposes not only the existence of the language system he is using, but also the existence of preceding utterances—his own and others'—with which his given utterance enters into one kind of relation or another (builds on them, polemicizes with them, or simply presumes that they are already known to the listener). Any utterance is a link in a very complexly organized chain of other utterances.
>
> (1986, p. 69)

To extend the picture, a speaker or writer is not just a respondent to preceding utterances. He or she is also a respondent to the anticipated utterances of others in the immediate and more distant future. Bakhtin's term for this aspect of intertexuality is "addressivity." When he asserts that "the utterance is constructed while taking into account possible responsive reactions, for whose sake, in essence, it is actually created" (p. 95), he is taking us back to the rhetorical view of language with which I commenced this chapter.

The linguist, Norman Fairclough, one of the founders of critical discourse analysis, is a good example of a contemporary theorist who has drawn on and extended Bakhtin's ideas about intertexuality. In fact, in his own definition he quotes Bakhtin:

> Intertextuality is basically the property texts have of being full of snatches of other texts, which may be explicitly demarcated or merged in, and which the text may assimilate, contradict, ironically echo, and so forth. In terms of production, an intertextual perspective stresses the historicity of texts: how they always constitute additions to existing "chains of speech communication" consisting of prior texts to which they respond.
>
> (1992a, p. 85)

In his own writing, Fairclough distinguishes between:

1. *Manifest intertextuality:* Where specific other texts are overtly drawn upon within a text. Among the many examples of this in this book is the above quotation from Fairclough.
2. *Interdiscursivity* or *constitutive intertextuality:* In this case, I am not directly quoting or referring to other texts. However, I am writing out of a discourse that is shared by others in *their* production of texts, even if I have not read these texts. As a reader, you will have picked up that while I appreciate the contribution of scholars who operate in terms of a cognitive discourse, I am mostly drawing on a sociocultural discourse of textual production. My emphasis on rhetoric is part of this. This book has an interdiscursive relationship with other books that are framed in terms of a sociocultural discourse.

There is another Bakhtinian concept I want to introduce before addressing genre—the concept of *dialogism* or *dialogue*. Bakhtin writes:

> The utterance is filled with *dialogic overtones,* and they must be taken into account, in order to understand fully the style of the utterance. After all, our thought itself—philosophical, scientific, and artistic—is born and shaped in the process of interaction and struggle with others' thought, and this cannot but be reflected in the forms that verbally express our thought as well.
>
> (1986, p. 92)

When we write, we engage with the thoughts of others. This is a powerfully simple idea and in part explains why I have referred to the "democratic self" in the title of this chapter. As I understand Bakhtin, dialogue involves an attitude of respect for the other. Dialogic engagement is not about getting the other to subscribe to your views because you know best. (This is what fascism is all about.) As a democratic principle, it is not about a tyranny of the majority suppressing individual freedom and impeding social justice. Rather it celebrates diversity, viewing truth not so much as the possession of a particular individual or group, but as something dynamic and fluid emerging in the dialogic process itself—not something *in* persons but *between* persons. For Bakhtin, the carnival was a metaphor for the co-existence of multiple voices (which he termed "polyphony"), jostling against each other in the social forum (or in a great novel), each representing what we might call a "partial" truth.

I conclude this chapter section by addressing the thorny question of genre. I begin by assuming that you already *have* a sense of genre. Let's imagine visiting our local DVD rental store (fast becoming a thing of the past). My local store is divided into sections with headings such as "drama" or "thriller" or "sci-fi." I imagine yours is too. When you go into a section, you have an expectation that a DVD is going to be characterized by a particular treatment of a theme, that is, it will be using the representational resources of motion pictures to tell a story in a particular way. In simple terms, a genre is a particular way of doing something in a text using semiotic resources.

Let's return for a minute to Bakhtin's essay which, although it has the words "speech genres" in the title, is not just about spoken language. He makes the strong claim that "We speak only in definite speech genres, that is, all of our utterances have definite and relatively typical *forms of construction of the whole*. Our repertoire of oral (and written) speech genres is rich" (1986, p. 78). (What I asked you to do in Reflective Journal Task 4.1 was to explore your own "repertoire" of written genres.) The definition of genre implicit here focuses on the typical forms of construction of an utterance. So, while a genre is social in origin, there is a clear emphasis on individual agency and creativity. A description of a genre may refer to such formal features as vocabulary, syntax and structure, but it is the social context that makes these features meaningful and, we might say, calls them forth. A genre is a relatively stable type of utterance or utterance cluster. Writing from a new rhetoric perspective, Freedman and Medway defined genres as "typical ways of engaging rhetorically with recurring situations" (1994, p. 2). Around the same time, Australian genre theorists Cope and Kalantzis were defining genres in this way: "Genres are social processes. Texts are patterned in reasonably predictable ways according to patterns of social interaction in a particular culture. Social patterning and textual patterning meet as genres" (1993, p. 7).

How stable is stable? Because genres are social products, they come into existence at certain times in response to particular social conditions. The lyric poem is a much older genre than the novel. However, both these genres have changed enormously over the centuries. There are many ways to write a lyric

---

REFLECTIVE JOURNAL TASK 4.3

Imagine you have found yourself sitting next to Bakhtin on a long train journey (maybe on the Trans-Siberian Railway). Think of some comments you might like to make to him about his views. Think of some questions you might ask him. Write your conversation with him as a piece of dialogue, for example:

Me: I'm sorry to trouble you, but am I right in guessing that you are Mikhail Bakhtin?

Bakhtin: Yes, how did you recognize me?

Me: I saw your photograph on Wikipedia.

poem or a novel. Genres also hybridize. For example, you can think of the epistolary novel as a hybrid of the novel and the personal letter. Bakhtin makes the telling point that while style is individual, "... not all genres are equally conducive to reflecting the individuality of the speaker in the language of the utterance, that is, to an individual style" (1986, p. 63). Think of genres as operating along a continuum from open to closed. A "closed" genre allows the producer very little room to deviate from conventions of content, structure, style, layout and so on. A piece of legislation is closed, in these terms. A CV is relatively closed. A lyric poem is open. A newspaper column is somewhere in between.

From Personal Narrative to Memoir

In Chapter 3, I invited you to write a personal narrative. You'll recall that I linked the writing of personal narrative to expressive writing. In contrast to a personal narrative, a memoir is a recognized genre that people write and publish for particular audiences. The memoir, as a sub-class of autobiography, is characterized by certain conventions. Here I describe a memoir, using headings that could apply to many genres.

1. **Context of culture**: The memoir is a relatively recent genre, emerging in the 19th century as the public appetite grew for the reminiscences of people who were prominent in public life.
2. **Context of situation**: People write memoirs at a point in their lives when the past is sufficiently distant for them to have developed a particular perspective on events that they deem worthy of sharing with an audience.
3. **Function/purpose**: According to Kirby and Kirby (2010), the memoir writer "is using the genre to do more than just remember or describe people and events. Readers have the sense that memoirists use the form to experiment, solve puzzles and riddles present in their lives, pose sometimes unanswerable questions, and advance hypotheses and what ifs about their lived experiences" (p. 23).
4. **Typical content**: A memoir focuses on a significant event or series of events in the memoirist's life and interprets these events. Thoreau's *Walden* is a prominent 19th-century example.
5. **Features**:

    - *Layout*: As per prose fiction and non-fiction.
    - *Diction*: As for prose fiction and poetry, the range of possibilities is large in terms of diction.
    - *Punctuation*: Conventionally correct punctuation is expected.
    - *Syntax*: There is scope for a range of sentence types, but conventional correctness is expected (unlike poetry).

- *Structure*: Like any narrative, a memoir gains power from the way in which the writer manipulates the arrangement of plot elements, including:

  o *Predicament*: A difficult choice, often early in a narrative, where a character is presented with a choice between unpalatable alternatives.
  o *Conflict*: A situation where the interests of characters or groups of characters are opposed.
  o *Complication*: An unexpected problem or misfortune that disrupts the smooth flow of action of a story.
  o *Resolution*: A choice or event, which sorts out a complication one way or another.
  o *Rising Action*: The suspenseful part of a story leading up to its climax.
  o *Turning Point*: A crucial choice or event, which changes the course of a story in a radical way.
  o *Climax*: The decisive moment in a story towards which events appear to be heading.
  o *Denouement*: The process of unravelling or winding down that occurs in the aftermath of a story's climax.

WRITING TASK 4.4

Memoir

There are two steps you can take as a way of orienting yourself to this task.

1. **Mine your own past.** Are there events or episodes in your own life that you find yourself returning to in memory in an ongoing attempt to make sense of them, or because you learnt a valuable lesson from them, or because they were significant somehow? Choose one and make notes about what happened, using as much concrete detail as you can (including snatches of conversation). Tell yourself that none of us has photographic memories, and that while your memoir will be based on events in your own life, your text will be a *reshaping* of these events. (Our word *fiction* derives from the Latin verb *fingere:* to shape.)
2. **Read examples of memoirs.** A useful site that I have used in Writing Workshops is "Write it" (see Further Reading). This site publishes a range of student work in various genre categories, including memoir. A nice example is "Of Red Clay and Sugar Cane" by Addison M., a 16-year-old New York student.

Clearly, there is no prescribed length for a memoir. Here is a relatively short piece of memoir writing by Phillipa Grace, a history teacher:

Near-Miss

The news flashed on. "Bombs in London. Devastation on the tube and buses." Red buses, and redder streets. Leafy trees, cobbled roads, bodies, sirens and moans. Carnage in the morning sun. Shots of a congested underground entry with pillared smoke, erupting black, replicating Twin Towers.

"Oh, my God," "Oh, my God," "Oh my God," taps out in my head as I push each digit in my brother's number. The line was overloaded. "No, no, no, no," repeats itself in my brain as I try my sister's also. Same response—none. I waited with impatience for the computer to access my email, and I rattled off an urgent 'Contact Me!' to them both. I followed with cell-phone texts—desperately abrupt.

My sister responds. She is sitting in a café having coffee with my niece. Patiently whiling away the time waiting for the "mayhem" on the tube to settle so she could get herself home. It's "only another suicide train-jumper," she had reasoned—an unfortunately familiar occurrence in the mindset of Londoners bred with an indifference towards such an act of desperation. An indifference endemic to their historical class structure and an apathy towards mayhem massaged into the mundane by the murderous acts of militants spurned during the Irish "Troubles." Then shock and disbelief as I tell her that *our* news channel, aired in the antipodes, has related the police connection to coordinated terrorist attacks. She abruptly disconnects in an anguished attempt to contact her other children.

I try my brother's work number. The crisp, cultured English tone of a bored secretary informs me that he is in a meeting and isn't available. I impatiently tell her that I'm calling from New Zealand and she can "damn well put me through." His disbelief is palpable when I tell him of the scenes streaming through satellite to the other side of the globe. This is followed immediately by a sharp intake of breath as realisation dawns on him, and he recounts how it was his usual train on the tube that was bombed. He had overslept and mistimed his departure to work. He had been forced to alight one tube stop sooner than necessary and had looked on with vague annoyance at the 'congested underground tube entry' with its 'pillared smoke, erupting black' all over his usual morning cheer. He had assumed, as it is so sadly predictable and credible to do, that it was 'just another train-jumper' causing all the fuss.

How lucky had we been? How selfish in our sense of narrow escape? To be grateful that those mangled, twisted forms were not one of our own. Arbitrarily snatched from their loved-ones' care. The guilt of relief is hard to own, as the continued stories of horror visually unfold.

Newspaper headlines proclaim the multiple stories of shock and pain. Voyeuristic addiction ensures we watch the saga continue. Unpacked by feverish media, populist headlines and sensationalized personal accounts. "There but for the grace of God go I," had been my brother's parting words.

We can see why Phillipa chose this event to focus on, as we see her exploring the complex feelings of guilt and relief that occur when we or a loved one has a narrow escape while others are not so lucky.

Once you have a draft, I suggest you follow a similar revision routine as I suggested earlier in this chapter in relation to poetry. In particular, think about the way you have structured your piece. Consider sharing a draft with a critical friend, asking if the particular meaning you have attached to the events you have narrated has come through clearly.

Note

1. In using the word "selection", I'm aware of Ivanic's caution that this usage can be misleading, since it seems to imply that a writer is choosing freely among alternatives, that choice is a function of an individual will, and that it is conscious. I don't want to imply this, and agree with her point that "the very idea of selection and the possibilities for selection are social constructed" (1998, p. 54).

Further Reading

Rhetoric

*   Andrews, R. (Ed.) (1992). *Rebirth of rhetoric: Essays in language, culture and education*. London, UK: Routledge.

Poetry

*   Eagleton, T. (2007). *How to read a poem*. Malden, MA: Blackwell.
*   O'Connor, J. (2004). *Wordplaygrounds: Reading, writing, performing poetry in the English classroom*. Urbana, IL: National Council of Teachers of English (NCTE).
*   Collom, J., & Noethe, S. (2005). *Poetry everywhere: Teaching poetry writing in school and in the community*. New York, NY: Teachers & Writers Collaborative.

Bakhtin

- Bakhtin, M. (1986). The problem with speech genres (V. McGee, Trans.). In C. Emerson & M. Holquist (Eds.), *Speech genres and other late essays: M.M. Bakhtin* (pp. 60–102). Austin, TX: University of Texas Press.
- White, E. J., & Peters, M. A. (Eds.) (2011). *Bakhtinian pedagogy: Opportunities and challenges for research, policy and practice in education across the globe*. New York, NY: Peter Lang.

Genre

- Freedman, A., & Medway, P. (Eds.). (1994). *Learning and teaching genre*. Portsmouth, NH: Boynton/Cook Publishers.

Memoir

- Kirby, D. L., & Kirby, D. (2010). Contemporary memoir: A 21st-century genre ideal for teens. *English Journal, 99*(4), 22–29.
- Write it (n.d.) Retrieved from http://teacher.scholastic.com/writeit/readwork.asp?Genre=Memoir

5

WRITING AS ENACTING THE PROFESSIONAL SELF

The setting for this chapter is the professional life of the teacher. I argue here that writing has a key role to play in a teacher's professionality and explore the relationship of professionality to writing. I raise questions around the teacher's voice—to whom or to what does this voice address itself and how? In particular, how can the professional self be sustained through writing in a context where teachers' voices can be silenced and where "audit" cultures operate to disempower and deprofessionalize teachers.

Being a Professional

If you are a practicing or aspiring teacher, I have no doubt that you consider yourself to be a professional, and that this professionality is part of your identity. But what is a profession? There has been considerable debate over the years about this, and I will touch only lightly on it here. The first point to note is that the word "professional" is value-laden, that is, it posits an ideal for a sphere of human activity. When we compliment someone on doing a "professional job," we are suggesting that this person sets high standards for him/herself (rather than having standards imposed on him or her by someone else). Second, if we observe actual professionals going about their business and adopt a *criterion approach* (Hoyle & John, 1995), we can generate a set of defining characteristics (criteria) against which the conduct of a profession can be measured. Hoyle (1982) defined a profession in terms of its central social function—its length of training, a body of knowledge, high levels of skill, a code of ethical conduct, client-centeredness, autonomy, independent decision-making and adaptability, self-governance and the requirement that it play a central role in relevant public policy-making.

Interestingly, there is widespread agreement on three criteria: knowledge, autonomy and responsibility (Hoyle & John, 1995). Educators such as Hargreaves and Goodson (1996) and Sachs (1997) subscribe to a view of *classical democratic professionalism* as characterized by: *expertise* (the possession by an occupational group of exclusive knowledge and practice); *altruism* (an ethical concern by this group for its clients) and *autonomy* (the professional's entitlement to exercise control over entry into, and subsequent practice within, a particular occupation).

REFLECTIVE JOURNAL TASK 5.1

Does this make sense to you? Write a journal entry in response to the following:

1. What kinds of knowledge do you have that someone who is *not* trained as a teacher is unlikely to have?
2. Which aspects of your "professional" life are you able to make your own decisions about? What sorts of decisions are made for you by others?
3. There is much research that suggests that teachers enter the profession to "make a positive difference" to others. How important is altruism to you?

Each of these characteristics is problematic. Let's take knowledge. Shulman (1986) asked the question: "Where did the subject matter go?" (p. 5). He categorized teaching knowledge in terms of *content knowledge, pedagogical content knowledge* and *curricular knowledge.* If we combine curricular knowledge with content knowledge, then we end up with two broad categories, *what should be taught* and *what practices enable the teaching to occur effectively.* But how should a body of teacher professional knowledge and expertise be constituted? In whose interest? How stable does it need to be? If this body of knowledge is provisional and culturally specific, how relevant is it for a culturally and linguistically pluralistic society? Just how altruistic *are* teachers? Certainly, the media in many countries are fond of representing teachers as largely concerned with their *own* interests rather than with the interests of children. What version of "altruism" are we talking about? Where does altruism end and paternalism begin? Then there is the question of autonomy. What degree of autonomy do teachers *really* have, particularly at a time when governments seem determined to control many aspects of teachers' work? Isn't autonomy *always* constrained in some way? Can a teacher be collegial or collaborative and still be autonomous?

Despite such problematics, I believe that the classical view has much to offer in terms of our thinking about our identities as professionals. I'll start with altruism. Altruism is typically defined as the principle of living and acting for the interest of others. Such a definition connects with the public expectation that teachers

---

REFLECTIVE JOURNAL TASK 5.2

Write an entry in your journal responding to one or more of the above questions.

---

exercise a duty of care towards their students. All professions and individuals are going to be self-interested to some extent. However, an altruistic disposition can co-exist with self-interest. We can also expect that different cultures will construct altruistic practice differently. Our relationship to the other we teach raises hard yet inescapable ethical questions, such as: "Who is the other I teach?" and "What kind of covenant with the other does teaching imply?"

To address such questions, Noddings (1986) drew on concepts of *fidelity* and an "ethic of caring," viewing *fidelity,* not as

> faithfulness to duty or to principle but as a direct response to individuals with whom one is in relation. Natural caring—the sort of response made when we want to care for another—establishes the ideal for ethical caring, and ethical caring imitates this ideal in its efforts to institute, maintain, or re-establish natural caring. From this perspective fidelity may be interpreted as a precondition for subjectively satisfying relations and a continuing condition for their maintenance.
>
> (p. 497)

According to Noddings (1986), teachers guided by an ethic of caring ask questions such as "What effect will this have on the person I teach? What effect will it have on the caring community we are trying to build?" (p. 499). Such questions serve to condition a teacher's way of thinking about the place of relational goals within a wider context of institutional goals and responsibilities. Achieving this balance is not easy (as Chapter 12 will indicate).

It is clear that an ethic of caring constrains our autonomy as teachers. But then, autonomy around professional decision-making has *always* been constrained. Raising questions about autonomy inevitably raises questions about *agency*, the status of various stakeholders in educational decision-making and the nature of collaborative action. A teacher's decision-making has always been constrained by professional knowledge, ethical demands (however defined), the discourses one subscribes to and the network of obligations to colleagues, institutions and systems. For instance, Hargreaves and Goodson have talked about the professional need for "Commitment to working with colleagues in collaborative cultures of help and support as a way of using shared expertise to solve the on-going problems of professional practice, rather than engaging in joint work as a motivational device to implement the external mandates of others" (1996, p. 20).

There are constraints and constraints. *Intrinsic accountability* occurs when professionals submit to constraints that are consistent with their altruistic ideals and with their body of expert content and pedagogical knowledge. *Extrinsic accountability* involves a professional in negotiating constraints that are imposed by some other agency (usually the state), and which seek to determine his/her relationship with students, what should be taught and how. Extrinsic accountability technologies (assessment regimes, curriculum standards, performance measures, for example) pose problems for teachers when they encourage a relationship with students and teaching practices that are in conflict with a teacher's altruistic ideals and professional knowledge. Teachers in many countries currently struggle to reconcile what they know about teaching writing with the practices encouraged by the testing regimes accompanying the introduction of national or state standards. As discussed in Chapter 1, the National Writing Project in the United States is a good example of teachers developing the sort of collaborative culture that Hargreaves and Goodson write about; drawing strength from that culture can mitigate the effects of negative forms of extrinsic accountability.

We need to accept from the outset that professional knowledge is provisional, unfinalizable, culturally produced and historically situated. My approach in this book is that knowledge about writing and how to teach it is multiple, that is, there are various discourses (e.g., cognitive or socio-cultural accounts) that offer contrasting stories about writing and writing pedagogy. These discourses don't have to be thought of as enemies. Rather, adopting Bakhtin's notion of dialogue, we can view them as partial truths, all contributing to the bigger picture. (I explore these discourses in more detail in Chapter 7.)

Finally in this section, I would like to draw further on the work of Roz Ivanič. Although her book on *Writing and Identity* (1998) was concerned with academic literacy, I believe her work has relevance for those of us for whom "writer" is an element in the composition of our professional identities as teachers. Ivanič's overarching argument in her book is that:

> Writing is an act of identity in which people align themselves with socio-culturally shaped possibilities for self-hood, playing their part in reproducing or challenging dominant practices and discourses, and the values, beliefs and interests which they embody.
>
> (1998, p. 32)

As argued in Chapter 3, the discourses we subscribe to, knowingly or unknowingly, shape our identity (who we are). Ivanič argues that writing is a particularly powerful form of social action for the negotiation of identity since it is relatively permanent; it forms a statement of who we are and what we stand for. Ivanič terms the impression we project to others in our writing the *discoursal self*. She notes that "The relations of power, interests, values, beliefs and practices in institutional settings [such as school] enable and constrain people's possibilities for self-hood as they write. Some discourses are more powerful, and/or more highly valued than others, and people are under pressure to participate in them through adopting them in their writing" (p. 32). The position we adopt when we write either aligns us (as *compliant*) with these powerful discourses or puts us at odds with them (as *resistant*). Like the autobiographical self (see Chapter 3), the discoursal self is multiple and subject to change over time.

As professionals, it is incumbent on us to develop an awareness of the discourses we ourselves subscribe to and the powerful discourses that shape what it means to be a teacher (and teacher of writing) in our own educational settings. There is nothing neutral about the act of writing. Whatever type of writing we produce in our own professional setting—reports, lesson plans, observations of colleagues, analyses of problem situations, letters to parents, submissions to a board, a scheme of work or a policy statement—we are operating out of a particular discursive frame, that privileges certain values, beliefs and practices and neglects others.

REFLECTIVE JOURNAL TASK 5.3

There are three potential sources of knowledge about writing practice that we draw on as teachers:

1.   How it operates in society and across cultures.
2.   How it is constructed in the context of undergraduate and graduate degree programs in such "disciplines" as English, Professional Writing and so on.
3.   How it is constructed via curriculum documents, qualifications systems, high-stakes assessment practices, textbooks, and online or hard-copy resources.

Which of these sources would you rate as most central to the formation of your understanding of the practice of writing? Which is least central? Are you aware of conflicting messages about writing (how it is best practiced, taught and assessed) from these sources? If so, how do you manage this conflict in your own life?

The Power of Observation and Reflection

I argue that there is a close connection between what I call aesthetic knowing and the quality of *attention* (Locke, 2010a). A wonderful description of this quality can be found in poet and teacher Anne McCrary Sullivan's (2000) *Harvard Educational Review* article, "Notes from a Marine Biologist's Daughter: On the Art and Science of Attention." Sullivan argues that aesthetic vision is a kind of complex attention, a "high level of consciousness about what one sees. It suggests an alertness, a 'wide-awakeness' that Maxine Green . . . has urged educators and researchers to learn from artists," involving a "sensitivity to suggestions, to pattern . . . a fine attention to detail and form" and so on. (p. 220). "My mother, the scientist," she writes, "taught me to see" (p. 221). Sullivan is not just talking about the narrow sense of "seeing" (the sense of sight), but rather to an attentiveness involving all our senses.

Description is a major language function and has a part to play in many genres (including oral genres). Think of a witness in a trial offering testimony about what they saw and heard. Think of a piece of travel writing which is setting out to provide a reader with the sense of being in a place and attempting to communicate something of its sights, sounds, smells and tastes. Think of the role description plays in all kinds of narrative, both fictional and non-fictional. All narrative utilizes both recount and descriptive language functions. Indeed, scene-setting, where not a lot appears to be happening, is an important aspect of story-telling. (You might like to visit your memoir and review the balance between description and narration.)

I cringe when I hear teachers terming adjectives "describing words." Parts of speech (or word classes) fit into two categories: *content words* (nouns, verbs, adjectives and adverbs of manner) and *function words* (pronouns, prepositions, conjunctions and determiners, other adverbs). Content words have meaning even when separated from other words, whereas function words help content words relate to one another. (If you do a cloze test where the content words in a passage are replaced by nonsense words, it will still make a kind of sense, whereas the same passage where the function words are replaced by nonsense will make no sense at all. Lewis Carroll's famous "Jabberwocky" poem is an example of the former.) All content words can contribute to the descriptiveness of a piece of writing.

Attention (as a disposition), observation (as an activity) and description (as a language mode) are all important to teachers as professionals. As a teacher educator, it is part of my work to observe students on "practicum" and to write up my lesson observations in a report. You may have been asked to observe a colleague's lesson. Observation, of course, is an important "data collection" method in qualitative research. David Silverman (2006) reminds us that observation is "fundamental to understanding another culture" (p. 19). Recall that in a socio-cultural approach to writing, the context within which writing occurs is not separable from the individual who is engaged in producing a text of some kind. That is why, when observing a lesson, taking in the environment is as important as noting what individuals are doing and the interactions that occur between them.

Some years ago, I led a project on teaching literature in the multicultural classroom. In the course of that project, I was invited into classrooms of participating teachers to observe lessons. Rather than make notes on an observation schedule, I resolved to write a narrative account of what I saw without predetermining what I would look for. In doing so, I was adopting a writing practice or stance advocated by Elliot Eisner (2002), who theorized the idea of the "educational connoisseur," the knowledgeable observer who enters a classroom and writes up what he or she observes in much the same way as an art critic might visit an exhibition and write a review. According to Eisner, "Observation schedules are tools that can guide one's attention, but their mechanical use can blind one to what is significant" (p. 216). There is no such thing as an "objective" observer, since observation and describing are inevitably filtered through a particular discursive lens or set of lenses (ways of thinking and valuing). Eisner defined description as the "vivid rendering of the qualities perceived in the situation" (p. 234). However, interpretation and evaluation are inevitably implicated in the way we describe a situation. The three functions of description, interpretation and evaluation are not easily separated in practice (Locke with Riley, 2009).

Let me share with you the start of an observation report I did in the classroom of Janet Sturgess, a teacher-researcher in the above project, who at the time was engaging with some interesting work with her ninth grade class on fairy-tales and stereotyping (see Sturgess & Locke, 2009). The name of the school has been changed and some material has been removed.

Huia College is brand spanking new. Janet was appointed as HOD English and ESOL for the school's first year, when it was a Year 9-only school. Four years on, it is a Year 9–12 secondary school with a roll of around 1200 students. Next year, it will have a Year 13 class for the very first time.

Driving along Chapel Rd, I'm irresistibly recalling my childhood (now over 50 years ago) when I would go blackberrying with my parents. Right now, the huge expanse of the Huia community and shopping complex extends on my right. New subdivisions sprawl as far as the eye can see and to my left, coming up, is the school—a gleaming, two-storey structure that looks cast in aluminium. I think of the school as four, large, blocks that relate to one another rather like the arms of an "H" on its side. The buildings on each side of the "H" are linked by bridges. Each arm is a cluster of classrooms and facilities which open on to interior, covered, communal areas.

Janet's classroom—G1.1—is on the ground floor of a building which is colour coded like other blocks (in this case green). As I walk along the way between the parallel arms of the "H," I notice words in frosted glass in the exterior walls of the buildings—words such as "Discover," "Spirit," and in the case of G-block, "Koru." I'm not quite right in talking about "Janet's classroom." After she greets me in the common space, she points out to me that this is a classroom she shares with other teachers and expresses her frustration in not having a home room. However, by good fortune, the class that might be occupying the classroom at this point is elsewhere, with only their bags in evidence, so that we can both go about our respective preparations.

I'm always struck by the snappy way Janet dresses. Today she is wearing a white blouse, a dark grey skirt and ear-rings that are matched by the sparkling red of the heavy necklace around her neck. What stands out, though, are the bright, red ankle boots.

. . .

The unit the students are doing is based around a study of Maurice Gee's novel *The Fat Man*. Students have already done some preliminary work in the library, and Janet comments with some curiosity on the reluctance of some boys to share their findings. We also discuss the issue of teacher professional knowledge (especially related to content). As a HOD, this is very much of concern to Janet in respect of ways of ensuring that professional development opportunities are made available to staff. She draws my attention to some items of the room that she *is* responsible for—full-length, representations of characters from the novel *St Agnes' Stand* by Thomas Eidson, which she uses with her Year 12 class. . . . Janet extols its virtues as a teaching text, especially in relationship to its evocative style. I'm aware of the speed with which we're covering these topics, rather like two helicopters covering quite a large terrain without really having the time to land.

11.33. As the students begin to enter the classroom, Janet poses a problem. "What shall we do?" She means the bags of the other class. One young girl suggests: "Carefully put them on the floor?" Janet instructs them firmly. "Place them outside." "Pick them up, please, and put them outside." She wants to get on with the lesson. We both know how much she has planned. "Can we settle quickly!" It's a command, not a question.

Indeed, the students do settle quickly. It's time for SSR and Janet directs them to read *The Fat Man* and also indicates that there are newspapers that they could also read. She gives them another reminder to settle, commenting that they appear to have taken longer than usual. It certainly doesn't appear to have taken long to me. She tells them that she, herself, has a really good book that she wants to get through.

The room is quiet. Students are sitting at clusters of mottled, blue formica desks in black plastic chairs in five clusters of around six students each. The low-angled sun is pouring into the classroom, or would be if I had not lowered a series of blinds behind me, and it is warm despite our being in late autumn. Nevertheless, most of the students are wearing regulation maroon jerseys. The rest of the uniform is made up of white, pin-striped shirts, navy trousers or skirts, and long socks with a wide maroon band. The majority of students are Asian, but with mixed ethnicity (Chinese, Indian) with a minority of Europeans.

By the time the students have settled, there is not a lot of room for a teacher to move around between the clusters of desks. The space is well lit, with fluorescent light being diffused via opaque ceiling panels. It all comes across as new, white and extensively glazed. Indeed, there is glass on all four sides of the classroom. On one wall, you can see through to the open, common space of G-block. On another wall, to my left, at least half of it is glazed and provides visual access to the class next door. On my right, windows extend the length of the wall, and allow one to view the school fields and, behind them, the sprawling Huia subdivisions with their pastel walls and tiled roofs. The front wall of the classroom has least glass, with a stretch behind the teacher's desk, which is in the front right. Most of the central part of the wall is taken up by a white-board (W/B) which doubles as a projection space. With the help of one of the students, Janet has already set up a data projector (to which her laptop has a wireless connection) on a desk near the front of the room ready for use later in the period. Not that the room is short on connectivity. At regular intervals in the purply, carpeted floor there are recessed boxes with jackpoints of various kinds. There are also jackpoints in the ceiling. On two walls, there is blue pinboard. In addition to the *St Agnes' Stand* figures, there are student posters ("Education in the Elizabethan Era," "Health," "Punishment").

WRITING TASK 5.4

Descriptive Writing: "Wish You Were Here"

Think of a place you know well or reasonably well and where you have spent time on vacation or visiting. You are writing or emailing a family member about this place, extolling its virtues and describing some of the activities you have been engaging in since arriving. Keep your writing as concrete as you can, but aim for a tone of infectious enthusiasm. (You can take some fictional liberty with the facts.) This task has a relationship to Writing Task 6.3 in the next chapter.

The Stance of the Observer, Voice, and Point of View

There is a concept that has been lurking in the wings for some time now and pressing to be invited into the spotlight. It is the concept of *point of view*. We both use the concept to indicate a particular perspective on something, as in, "That's your point of view and you're quite entitled to it." In this instance, point of view is associated with a person and relates to his or her identity. However, in this book, I will be mostly using this concept to denote a technical aspect of writing, particularly narrative. Used in this sense, point of view answers the question, "Through whose eyes or from what vantage point am I viewing the action that is being presented in this account?" In prose narratives, we refer to the narrator (different from the author) as occupying a point of view. We can also talk about the narrator as being distinguished by a particular kind of voice.

I'm using the term "vantage point" metaphorically. I like it because it is spatial—a reminder that a point of view is always *located* somewhere in relation to the action and that it *privileges* a particular angle of vision on what is being recounted. In the example above, where I described Janet's classroom, you will be aware that my voice is privileged and that in describing her classroom in this way I am co-opting you to see things *my* way. The metaphor of the helicopter is *my* metaphor, not Janet's. You'll realize that there is an ethical issue demanding our attention here. Janet could have been offended by and rejected this choice of metaphor.[1]

Of course, we can't explore point of view as a technical feature of writing without mentioning those pesky little function words called pronouns. Table 5.1 shows subject pronouns, that is, pronouns that occupy subject positions in English sentences. My description of Janet's classroom is a first person narrative. You'll see that it offers opportunities for immediacy but also limits a reader's access to a single voice and vantage point. (William Faulkner, gets around this in his novel *As I Lay Dying*, 1963, by retaining first person but giving different chapters to different characters.) You get a sense of what I was doing before the lesson, but no sense of what Janet was doing. We might call this single voice *univocal*. Second person narrative is not common in narrative writing. Third person narrative is commonplace, and gives a writer a good deal of flexibility around the provision of access to readers. Third person narrative allows the use of a technique that is sometimes called the "roving narrator." This happens when the vantage point shifts from one character to another in the telling of a story.

TABLE 5.1 Subject pronouns

Person	Singular	Plural
1st person	I	we
2nd person	you	you
3rd person	he, she, it	they

To highlight the ethical issue mentioned previously, let me share with you an extract from a contributor to Eisner's book (2002), Mary Burchenal.

Class moves, accordingly, at a startlingly quick pace. **[Description]** This is clearly a teacher who knows the direction of class before it begins. **[Interpretation]**

Class isn't slowed down by tangential discussion. In fact, Bill habitually directs the students' comments more than I, as a teacher, would find desirable. **[Evaluation]** He has a habit of playing "Match Game." For the uninitiated, this game show of the 1970s was hosted by Gene Rayburn and highlighted a panel of dim Hollywood stars. Gene would read a sentence to the contestants with a "blank" in it. The contestants would try to fill in the blank and match as many of the stars' answers as possible. Perhaps this comparison is unfair, but I found the students in Bill's class doing much the same thing. Bill rarely asked open-ended questions, and instead asked questions such as the following:

"He's a very—what? Yes a, a shrewd man."

My insertions in bold indicate the way in which Burchenal evaluates and interprets as well as describes. Do you feel uneasy about what's happening here? Burchenal's writing is lively, but it is also passing judgment. (She herself may be having misgivings: "Perhaps this comparison is unfair.") My unease comes from the fact that Bill has no opportunity to assert his own voice. The observation is univocal. As the focus of the observation, Bill is actually having something done *to* him. Sadly, in the professional context of teaching, it is often teachers who are having things done *to* them. Too often "their" stories are told by others and they are at the mercy of how others represent them (Goodson, 1999). Dialogue, in the sense that Bakhtin talks about it, does not appear to have occurred.

In 2007, I had an opportunity to observe David Riley, another teacher-researcher in the Teaching Literature in the Multicultural Classroom project. At the time, David was Head of English at a predominantly Pasifika high school in South Auckland, and was teaching a critical literacy lesson with his tenth grade class on Hip Hop videos. Following Burchenal's example, I wrote an account of the observation using the approach of connoisseur that Eisner was advocating (2002). However, *after* writing the account, I shared it with David and asked him to tell me what was going on in his mind at various points in my first-personal narrative. He did so in detail and also shared with me written comments from the students. Unsurprisingly, there were discrepancies between what *David* was thinking and what I *imagined* he was thinking. As a result, I produced a different kind of observational report, this time using third-person narrative and attempting to introduce the "voices" of David and his students—a *multivocal* account. You'll see that I'm not slavishly following chronological time in this extract, giving myself freedom to move between past, immediate present and future.

The third Group 1 video is Wyclef Jean and Ying Yang Twins, "Dangerous."

I see the fire in her eyes
Fire in her eyes

The way she moves
She got the fire in her eyes
Fire on her waist
Fire in her thighs

At this point, as Terry sees it, the modeling and joint negotiation of textual response with a focus on action and dress have worked well. For his part, David is aware that he has been doing a lot of modeling already and that it is a teacher role he endorses. So he says, "Just write it down." Because he wants students to think of the classroom as "our class," he asks for a contribution from someone who hasn't contributed yet, a "different voice."

What everyone is seeing on the screen right now is a music video which is cutting between two men in a car and a lone woman in an alleyway who is gyrating in a sinuous manner and easing her short blouse from her

---

REFLECTIVE JOURNAL TASK 5.5

According to Cochran-Smith and colleagues (2009), "A key assumption [of practitioner research] is that those who work in particular contexts have significant knowledge about what the problems and questions are and how to solve those problems through systematic data collection and analysis" (p. 19).

Describe a problem that you have observed in your own teaching context. What knowledge do *you* have that would enable you to address this problem?

WRITING TASK 5.6

Moving from Univocal to Multivocal Writing

Use first-person point of view to write a relatively short teaching episode that you have observed in a classroom (yours or a colleague's). Be as detailed and concrete as you can. I suggest you use present tense. If you have observed a colleague, share your draft with him or her, asking for comments on what he or she was thinking at "key" points. You might also like to chat with students to ask them what they were thinking and feeling at particular points of the episode. On the basis of this additional information, rewrite your observation as a third-person, multivocal, account.

shoulder to her upper arm. In response to her teacher's invitation, Krissie introduces the word "seductive" into the discussion. Like other students, she sees herself as benefiting from having been introduced to the word "portrayed" and will use it in the reflection she will write the next day. As Krissie sees it, thinking about who's actually in charge in these videos has been a useful exercise. From her perspective, the woman in this video is doing just that, taking charge.

Narrative researchers sometimes refer to this as a "co-constructed" account. Technically, it is about the management of point of view in the description of a teacher's practice.

From Narrative to Argument

So far in this book, you may be thinking that I have focused too much on narrative and have neglected a major function of writing, namely *argumentation* (the process of mounting an argument). If so, I would want to respond that in most genres, language functions such as *narrate, describe* and *argue* frequently overlap. Take the fables of Aesop. A fable is a fictional tale with animals as characters that illustrates a moral lesson, usually ending with a maxim stating a general truth such as, "It is best to prepare for the days of necessity" ("The ant and the grasshopper"). A fable is a story that makes a case for a proposition. There are a number of genres that do this, for example, *parable* and *cautionary tale*. But then, you could argue a case that all narratives are making an implicit case for a particular way of viewing the world.

A *proposition* is a statement expressing an opinion about something, and is central to argumentation. The Latin prefix "pro" indicates supporting something. If we break up the word into its two parts—*pro-position*—a proposition might be termed a position that you adopt in support of something. It is something that others can disagree with also. Propositions use abstract diction. Perhaps the most famous proposition ever (first written by Thomas Jefferson) occurs in the second sentence of the United States Declaration of Independence, and states: "All men are created equal."

In *Teaching and Learning Argument*, Richard Andrews (1995) defined argument this way:

> Argument can be taken to be *a process of argumentation, a connected series of statements intended to establish a position and implying response to another (or more than one) position, sometimes* taking the form of an actual exchange in discussion and debate, and usually presenting itself in speech and/or writing as a sequence or chain of reasoning.
>
> (p. 3; his italics)

In this book, I use the term "proposition" and "statement" interchangeably when I discuss argument. I suggest you keep the following statements clear when you think about argumentation:

- Your **position** is where you stand on some issue.
- Your **case** is the sum total of points you use to justify your position.
- A **point** can support your own position or oppose someone else's.
- A point is made up of a **statement**, the use of **reasoning** and the provision of **evidence**.
- There is no one correct way of **sequencing** your points.
- There are **many kinds** of reasoning and evidence.

Other useful terms for thinking about argumentation come from a model first developed by Stephen Toulmin in 1958. Toulmin used the word "claim" in place of the word "position." He used the word "grounds" as a collective term for the reasons and evidence one draws on (the "what"), and the term "warrant" for "how" one marshals evidence and reasoning to support a claim.

A Diversion on the Transition from the Expressive to the Communicative

In Chapter 3, I put considerable emphasis on expressive writing, noting how expressive or "free-writing" (to use Peter Elbow's term) can enable us to discover what our position is. Teachers who engage in practitioner enquiry will often keep a reflective journal. In a recent article on using journaling to improve professional practice, Shepherd (2006) quotes a passage from Zehm and Kottler (1993, p. 101):

> A journal is a place you can talk to yourself. It helps you develop self-discipline, greater precision and sensitivity in your communication. In this process of systematic self-reflection, you become more insightful about your own inner world and thus better attuned to your desires and needs. You are able to work through internal conflicts, solve personal problems, remember significant events that take place, and be more like the person you want to be.
>
> (p. 335)

You will see how the description of journaling here resonates with the description of expressive writing in Chapter 3, where the focus is on talking with oneself rather than engaging with another.

Cognitive theorist Linda Flower (1979) explored the process required for a writer to move from self-focused prose to audience-focused prose, making the point that "effective writers do not simply *express* thought but *transform* it in certain complex but describable ways for the needs of a reader," using the term "Writer-Based prose" for writing that is "undertransformed" in respect of its recognition of the needs of a reader (p. 19). Flower argued that while the style of writer-based prose was not illogical, certain features potentially posed a barrier for reader understanding and created problems of cohesion:

1.   the "organization of sentences and paragraphs reflects the shifting focus of the writer's attention" but the "psychological subject" may not be "reflected in the grammatical subject of the sentence."
2.   "the writer may depend on code words to carry his or her own meaning" (p. 29).

For all that, Flower saw writer-based prose as a "major, functional stage in the composing process and a powerful strategy well fitted to a part of the job of writing" (1979, p. 34) since, as discussed previously, it can help writers access the reservoir of memory. Journaling, for example, in the professional context, whether used for reflective processes or as part of formal research, can be thought of as a key stage in the discovery process, producing a rich resource of data/evidence to be mined at a later date to contribute to findings transformed for public consumption. So far in this book, I have mentioned a number of theorists who have used particular terms for distinguishing between writing which is focused on the self and writing that is focused on the reader. Table 5.2 is a summary.

WRITING TASK 5.7

Journal Reflection

- Step 1: Write a reflection on an event of some significance to you that has occurred in your own or someone else's classroom. Treat the writing as a self-expressive exercise, that is, write for yourself and get your ideas down as quickly as you can.
- Step 2: Read your reflection carefully and ask yourself the question: "Is this piece of writing making a case for something?" or "Am I adopting a position on something in this piece of writing?"
- Step 3: If the answer is yes, try writing your position as a proposition or group of propositions. For each, begin with the words: "I believe that . . ."
- Step 4: If you have arrived at a group of propositions, imagine that you want to convince your principal of your position. How would you *sequence* your propositions to make your case?

TABLE 5.2 From writer focus to reader focus

Theorist	Focus on the writer	Focus on the reader
John Dixon (1975)	Self-expression	Communication
Peter Elbow (1973)	Free-writing	
Linda Flower (1979)	Writer-based prose	Reader-based prose
Sheridan Blau (1988)	Developing fluency and conquering fears	A focus on audience and publication
Bereiter and Scardamalia (1987)	Knowledge telling model	Knowledge transforming model
David Galbraith (2009)	Dispositional text production	Rhetorical planning

Shaping an Argument: Writing a Position Statement

Something that may have occurred to you when you were engaging in narrative writing is *time*. Narrative can be thought of as a reworking of a *temporal* sequence of events involving one or more characters in one or more settings. You may even have been struggling at times to manage questions of *tense*. Beginning writers of narrative tend to adhere to *chronological time,* that is, they sequence events in the order they occurred in "real time." As storytellers become more experienced, they experiment with what might be called *psychological time*—the order of events as they are recalled or reconstructed in the mind of a narrator. Such writing will make use of devices such as flashbacks and flash-forwards. (The passage about David Riley's classroom is an example of this.)

The primary function of a *position statement* is argumentative rather than narrative. A position statement might be thought of as a half-way house between a piece of expressive writing, where you explore your views about an issue, and a public genre such as a newspaper column, where you mount a carefully considered argument on a topical theme for a particular audience in a particular publication. When you develop a position statement, you certainly have a reader in mind, but have not fully decided on a particular audience or purpose. The position statement is a genre that I use often in Writing Workshops,

---

WRITING TASK 5.8

Writing a Position Statement

- Step 1: Think of a position about education that you hold dearly. As you begin to put this in words, try starting with the words "I believe that."

- Step 2: List as many positive points you can think of in support of your position.
- Step 3: Imagine you are seated with some people whom you imagine might object to your position. Imagine yourself sharing your position with them and recording what they say to you. Imagine each of these people beginning, "Yes, but . . ." Write down a negative point (a point of rebuttal) that addresses each of these "Yes, but's."
- Step 4: For both positive and negative points, draft reasons and evidence that support each of them. These pieces of writing will provide the raw material for your position statement.
- Step 5: Construct a box plan (Figure 5.1) to help sequence your points in a way that takes account of a possible audience.
- Step 6: Write a first draft of your position statement.
- Step 7: Engage in *substantive* revision. That is, either conferencing with yourself or with a critical reader, ask questions such as: "Am I as convincing as I could be?" "Is there a clear link between my evidence and reasoning and the point being made?" "Have I given due recognition to other positions?"
- Step 8: When you are satisfied that you are substantially there, engage in an editorial revision to address mechanical errors and syntactical awkwardness.

because it eases the transition from expressive reflections to the development of arguments in genres such as submissions, editorials, letters to the editor, columns and opinion pieces.

In contrast with narrative, I suggest you think of the planning of an argumentative piece in spatial terms—and distinguish it from the time-bound nature of narrative writing. For some years, I have encouraged writers to plan their writing of narrative by using a box plan (see Figure 5.1). In Figure 5.1, the position adopted is that the legal drinking age should be raised. Each point to be made in support of this position is placed in a box on a sheet of paper. This also applies to points that anticipate an objection that might be raised against the position taken. For example, in Figure 5.1, the point that "Teens can still learn responsible decision-making in other contexts and situations," anticipates an objector who argues that teens are being deprived of the opportunity to learn how to act responsibly.

The main use of the box plan, however, is to allow writers (or speakers) to think carefully about *how* they sequence their points. Let's suppose that you're mounting an argument for a position and have four positive points (reasons for) and two negative points (points of rebuttal, where you anticipate objections to your position). You have a good many options in terms of how you order your points. Do you enter the fray making your positive points first and follow up by anticipating objections? Or do you adopt a more subtle approach, and begin by recognizing that there may be listeners or readers who will *not* be sympathetic to your position and attempt to win them over by addressing their concerns immediately? As I said, the possibilities are endless. Once you *have* decided on your sequence, then arrows are added to the box plan to show this.

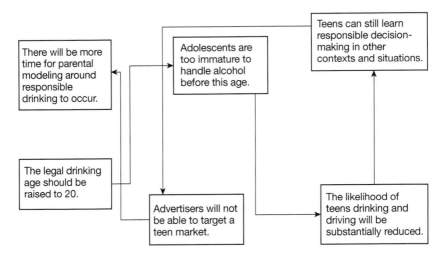

FIGURE 5.1 Using a box plan for shaping an argument

I would like to share with you a piece of writing of my own, written alongside other teachers writing in the context of a Writing Workshop. I offer it as an example of work in progress, at about Step 6 in the above sequence:

CHILDREN SHOULD NOT BE LIED TO

When I was fourteen, I was propositioned in the Civic movie theatre by a man who was probably homosexual and who drove me home and who suggested a picnic in the Waitakere Ranges, west of Auckland, for the following weekend. I was excited about discovering a new friend, but when I reported the events of the evening to my parents, they told me in no uncertain terms that I was to convey to my "friend" at the proposed meeting place that I was not available for picnics or any other outing. I was an obedient child, mostly, and did as they said. In the next year of my adolescence, my parents would tell this story to guests at our home who would hoot with laughter in my presence. I used to blush with shame and leave the room. My parents and no one else had ever told me about homosexuality; nor did my parents ever explain to me their reasons for forbidding my going on a picnic with the man who had approached me in the Civic.

For the purposes of this argument, I want to define a lie as a deliberate untruth, told to another with the purpose of deception. I would also extend this definition to include a truth that is deliberately withheld from another person with the intention to deceive. I call these lies of omission. My parents, for reasons of their own, deliberately withheld from me the reasons for forbidding an action on my part. The result for me was a state of unknowing that was both shameful and humiliating. I was also disillusioned, because I felt in a vague way that I had not been trusted with information to which I was entitled.

Lies of omission are commonplace in our society. Often when a couple splits up, you hear people remark that one or other partner was "living a lie." What this usually means is that one of the partners has been having an affair and concealing it from the other. In my own experience, and I have had many conversations with women in particular about this, the hurt these women feel is less directed at the offence than at the deception itself. It is the loss of trust that is truly disillusioning.

Should we have a different standard for truthfulness around children than we do for adults? You often hear it said that when children don't understand the issue at hand because they are too young, it can be necessary to lie. Lies like this are often termed "white lies." I guess that the word "white" indicates a kind of purity of intention, as if the well-being of the deceived party is being seen as paramount. However, from my perspective, the whiteness metaphor is better related to the term "whitewash," used in public affairs to deceive the populace, or the term "whiteout," to describe a weather condition which reduces seeing to zero.

My parents probably considered that because homosexuality was a taboo topic and reserved for adults, I did not deserve to hear the truth of their reservations. However, in my view, this defence is a kind of mental laziness. The information they failed to convey to me was not a method for dealing with quadratic equations. It was information that, had they thought about it, could have been shared with me in a way that I was able to understand. They could have told me that there are people who are attracted to people of the same sex and that there are also adults with a sickness that leads them to want to do harmful things with children of the same or different sex. They could have told me that they feared that the person who had picked me up was such a person and that adults found this a difficult topic to talk about. Such a sharing would have built trust and a foundation for future sharing of other difficult subjects related to human relationships. However, because they chose *not* to be upfront with me about their reasons, I decided that my parents were not an option for me when I was in need of a listening ear for my doubts and confusions about aspects of my life.

Note

1. In fact, after reading my observation she wrote: "Sorry about that—I do it all the time—it's come about from being involved in many aspects and having to talk 'on the hop'. I'm also involved in a lot of meetings where everything gets minuted!"CCC Com

Further Reading

Professionalism and Writing

- Ivanič, R. (1998). *Writing and identity: The discoursal construction of identity in academic writing.* Amsterdam, The Netherlands: Benjamins.
- Sachs, J. (2003). *The activist teaching profession.* Buckingham, UK: Open University Press.

Argument

- Andrews, R. (1995). *Teaching and learning argument.* London, UK: Cassell.
- The Toulmin model of argument. Retrieved from http://www-rohan.sdsu.edu/~digger/305/toulmin_model.htm

Fables

- Aesop's Fables: Retrieved from http://www.aesopfables.com/

Position Statements

- CCCC Committee on Assessment. (1995). Writing assessment: A position statement. *College composition and communication, 46*(3), 430–437. (This is a good example of a position statement that has been fully developed and relates to the subject of Chapter 12.)

6

WRITING AS DESIGN

This chapter focuses on written text as visual artifact. It enlarges the concept of "writer" to include such terms as "composer" and "designer" and explores the implications of this renaming for "writing" practice. It offers examples of teachers exploiting the affordances of digital technology to produce multimodal texts and hypertexts, but also confirms that the "visual" has always been with us.

Multimodality

> O for a life of sensation rather than of thoughts!

The epigraph is taken from a famous letter from poet John Keats to his friend Benjamin Bailey on November 22, 1817, where he explores the relationship between the imagination and truth. Words such as "sensation," "the senses" (sight, hearing, touch, smell, taste), "sensory" and "sensuous" connect with the process whereby the human organism interacts directly with the environment to make sense of it. A poetic expression of this process can be found in Charles Olson's essay, "The Human Universe," where he exclaims:

> If unselectedness is man's original condition. . . . but if likewise, selectiveness is just as originally the impulse by which he [sic] proceeds to do something about the unselectedness, then one is forced, is one not, to look for some instrumentation in man's given which makes selection possible. And it has gone so far, that is, science has, as to wonder if the fingertips, are not very knowing knots in their own rights, little brains (little photo-electric cells, I think they now call the skin) which, immediately, in responding to external stimuli, make decisions! It is a remarkable and usable idea. For it

> is man's first cause of wonder how rapid he is in taking in what he does
> experience.
>
> (1973, pp. 167–168)

Olson is reflecting here on the way human beings make meaning from sensory data. If we fast-forward 25 years, we arrive at neuroscientific attempts to explain the same phenomenon. One such attempt is Antonio Damasio's book, *The Feeling of What Happens* (2000). I have no space to summarize Damasio's theory here, but I can give you something of a taste of what he has to say:

> By the term images I mean mental patterns with a structure built with the tokens of each of the sensory modalities—visual, auditory, olfactory, gustatory, and somatosensory. The somatosensory modality . . . includes varied forms of sense: touch, muscular, temperature, pain, visceral, and vestibular. The word image does not refer to "visual" image alone . . . the process we come to know as mind when mental images become ours as a result of consciousness is a continuous flow of images many of which turn out to be logically interrelated.
>
> (p. 318)

> Images are constructed either when we engage objects, from persons and places to toothaches, from the outside of the brain towards its inside; or when we reconstruct objects from memory, from the inside out, as it were. The business of making images never stops. . . . One might argue that images are the currency of our minds.
>
> (pp. 318–319)

> The images you and I see in our minds are not facsimiles of the particular object, but rather images of the interactions between each of us and an object which engaged our organisms, constructed in neural pattern form according to the organism's design. The object is real, the interactions are real, and the images are as real as anything can be.
>
> (p. 321)

In Chapter 4, I used the term "concrete language" to refer to language that deliberately appeals to this wonderful sensory apparatus we are all equipped with and which we sometimes shut ourselves off from. Andrews and Smith (2011) make that point that "Writing is inescapably visual, and always has been. From the first mark made on a wall or on the ground, to highly sophisticated typographical creations and computer generated verbal text, writing has visual identity" (pp. 100–101). However, when we read texts which utilize concrete language with a "sensory alertness," we will be aware that the senses will be brought into play in our response in at least two ways. I call the first of these *evocation*—the process whereby a reader's sensory memory is stimulated by the use of concrete language. Here is an example from Keats' ode "To Autumn":

> And sometimes like a gleaner thou dost keep
> Steady thy laden head across a brook;
> Or by a cider-press, with patient look,
> Thou watchest the last oozings hours by hours.

Here the season of autumn is personified in various figures (the "gleaner," the cider-maker), both of whom we can imagine sharply. While the imagery is visual, there is also a tactile quality in "steady thy laden head" and "last oozings." We can call such writing *multisensory*.

A second way in which a sense other than the visual inhabits written verbal text is through *audible voice*. I borrow this term from Peter Elbow (2000) who claims that it is normal to hear a text, and that "most people, when they encounter a text—a set of words that just sit there silently on the page with no intonation, rhythm, accent, and so forth—automatically *project aurally* some speech sounds onto the text" (pp. 196–197). Texts vary in their ability to encapsulate audibility, of course. A newspaper column, where the writer is passionately arguing a case, will contain more audible voice than a piece of legislation or a concrete poem (i.e., a poem whose meaning is conveyed by its visual shaping on the page).

REFLECTIVE JOURNAL TASK 6.1

Select a poem or prose fiction extract that you would describe as making extensive use of concrete language. Write a journal entry which describes vividly the kinds of sense impressions that were evoked as a result of your reading. Pay particular attention to the senses that this writing appealed to in you.

I have begun this section on multimodality with the sensory because I believe that human meaning-making can occur in ways that are *not* mediated by semiotic systems (e,g., tossing up a blade of grass to establish wind direction). As discussed in Chapter 2, a semiotic system is a socially constructed system of signs which allow for *decoding* (interpreting meaning) and *encoding* (embedding meaning). The writing system is an example of a semiotic system. *Modes* are ways of categorizing different semiotic resources that have the potential for cultural systematization into codes. (A mode needs to be distinguished from image "modality" as used by Damasio above.) Written language is one type of semiotic or representational resource—something we can use to make meaning. Other modes include sound (as in music), the visual image (e.g., icons), color, dress, dance, and so on. People differ in how they categorize modes. For example, Cloonan, Kalantzis, and Cope (2010) have developed a multimodal schema, which categorizes meaning-making resources as linguistic, visual, audio, gestural and spatial.

Multimodality is a characteristic of a text or textual event that utilizes more than one mode in the production of meaning. I want to stretch the meaning of "text" in this book beyond a printed artifact (such as a book) to include films and performances of various kinds. In fact, I think of a text as an assemblage of representational resources that is capable of being read. Imagine you come across a group of bikers parked outside a restaurant. The word "biker" (the signifier) will already have a cluster of meanings in your mind. You will expect bikers to talk, move, speak and act in certain ways. As you come across this group of people, you will read such signifiers as dress, body ornament (e.g., tattoos), modes of address, body posture and so on, as you interpret your encounter with them.

In an important work on multimodality, Kress and Van Leeuwen (2001) make the point that while the potential for multimodality has always existed in human meaning-making (think of Greek theatre, with its complex assemblage of spoken text, mask, movement and music), monomodality has dominated the semiotic landscape. However, partly under the influence of digitization, this dominance is changing.

> The different modes have technically become the same at some level of representation, and they can be operated by one multi-skilled person, using one interface, one mode of physical manipulation, so that he or she can ask, at every point: "Shall I express this with sound or music?", "Shall I say this visually or verbally?"
>
> (p. 2).

Consider your own experience with such software as PowerPoint, and the range of possibilities it offers in terms of image and sound inserts, and animation.

For some time now, Kress has argued that different modes offer different *affordances* for making meaning. (The word "affordance" relates to the idea that particular modes and technologies *allow for* particular sorts of meaning-making.) He remarks, for example, that "Information that *displays* what the world is like is carried by the image; information that orients the reader to that information is carried by language" (1997, p. 65). He further argues that

> Speech-based cultures, oriented to the world through the deep logic of speech, are thus likely to differ distinctly from the image-based cultures: their engagement with the world is different, their habitual modes of representing the order of that world are different: and these differences become, over time, normal and then "natural."
>
> (1997, pp. 70–71)

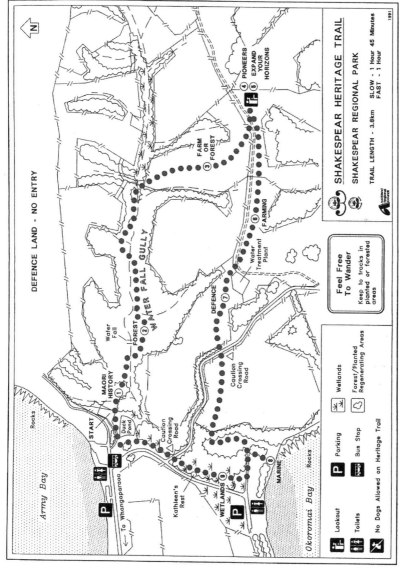

FIGURE 6.1 Nature-trail pamphlet: "Inside" face

Credit: Printed with permission by the Auckland Council. This brochure/map style is no longer used by council.

For Kress, written language as mode shares in the affordances of both the visual *and* speech. More recently, Andrews and Smith (building on Kress's concept of affordance) argue that users of written text see the world in a particular way. Compared with other modes, "Writing has the affordance of sequence, multi-leveled logical connections through linguistic hierarchies, explicit argumentation as well as narrative drive. It can convey nuances of abstract meaning" (2011, p. 108).

Pamphlets are contemporary examples of multimodal texts. Pamphlets as small, unbound texts without covers came into existence as a genre in the 17th century and were originally used for political debate. Nowadays, however, they have manifold uses—marketing, propaganda or the dissemination of information—are often folded, and often combine written text and graphics. Figure 6.1 is an example of the "inside" face of a nature-trail pamphlet, which we have been given permission to reproduce here, even though this brochure/map style is no longer used by the Auckland Council. (Shakespear Regional Park is located on the end of a peninsula near where I live.) This pamphlet was made available to park visitors to help them enjoy a "heritage trail." This side of the folded sheet contains a number of features: a map of the trail itself with numbered "stations" (particular places of interest are numbered on the map); text-blocks pointing out interesting aspects of each station; and a text-block which offers an overview of the Shakespear Heritage Trail.

Something you will notice about this text is the separation between elements. The map has a border and so does the trail overview. The station descriptions (on both sides of the pamphlet) are self-contained text-blocks with titles. Within the map border, we find further bordered elements: a key to the map, an instruction about wandering, and some trail information (length, time for completion). Even within the latter, there are three logos, which are separated off by being placed, one below the other, to the left of the written text. At work here is a multimodal design principle called *framing*. In relation to visual communication, Kress and Van Leeuwen (2001) describe framing as "the way elements of a visual composition may be disconnected, marked off from each other, for instance by framelines, pictorial framing devices (boundaries formed by the edge of a building, a tree, etc.), empty space between elements, discontinuities of colour, and so on" (p. 2). In their view, the concept of framing also embraces ways in which elements in a composition are connected. Like Andrews (2011), they regard framing as an important principle in a multimodal text such as a pamphlet. The principle can also be applied to "time-based modes," in texts such as musical composition and spoken-word poetry. (Think of the pauses which occur between the movements of a symphony.)

In their multimodal approach to representation and communication, Kress and Van Leeuwen (2001) identify "four domains of practice [or *strata*] in which meanings are dominantly made" (p. 4):

1. *Discourse:* Their understanding of this term reflects my usage of it in this book (see Chapter 2). The nature trail pamphlet in Figure 6.1 can be thought of as instantiating the discourse of environmentalism. (On the reverse of Figure 6.1 is the injunction: "Please RECYCLE paper.")

2. *Design:* This is another word that has been used regularly in this book. According to Kress and Van Leeuwen, "Design stands midway between content and expression. It is the conceptual side of expression, and the expression side of conception. Designs are (uses of) semiotic resources, in all semiotic modes and combinations of semiotic modes. Designs are means to realize discourses in the context of a given communication situation. But designs also add something new: they realize the communication situation which changes socially constructed knowledge into social (inter-) action" (2001, p. 5). In the case of the nature trail pamphlet, we can see it as realizing an environmental discourse in the context of a *context of situation,* where there is a defined audience (visitors to the park), and a particular kind of relationship set up *with* this audience (the authors of the pamphlet assume the role of "guide").

3. *Production:* Kress and Van Leeuwen call this the "actual material articulation of the semiotic event or the actual material production of the semiotic artifact" (2001, p. 6). When I have young students make nature trail pamphlets, the medium has been paper and the inscribing tools pens and colored pencils. Sometimes they do a mock-up of their design on paper, often using borders (framing) and pasting completed elements within them. (I should emphasize that framing, as used here, needs to be thought of as a creative function of the rhetor and determined by his or her "designs" on the audience. It is not a predetermined feature of a rigidly prescribed genre. There is nothing fixed about how frames should be utilized in the production of a nature trail pamphlet.)

4. *Distribution:* The local authority that commissioned the Shakespear Regional Park nature trail pamphlet (published in 1991) no longer exists as an entity. However, at the time of writing, the pamphlet was still in print and available in this form to park visitors. It was also distributed through the authority's

---

REFLECTIVE JOURNAL TASK 6.2

Write a letter to a distant ancestor telling them about the place of pamphlets in your own life and the life of your society. (You may find the subheadings for describing a genre used in Chapter 4 useful.) Be aware of the kind of language you use to describe various types of pamphlets and their use. Are there particular design features these pamphlets have in common? How are these pamphlets distributed?

website as a pdf, where it was described as a "map." Did this alternative form of distribution affect the meaning of the pamphlet? I'd argue it did. The folds, for example, had disappeared, leading to a loss of the tactile feel of the printed object and the way its folds generated frames.

WRITING TASK 6.3

Rhetorics of Place: The Pamphlet

In this task, you will be exploring through a number of steps the construction of a text: a pamphlet that provides potential visitors an enticing glimpse into the place that you wrote about in Writing task 5.4: "Wish you were here." You may find it particularly enjoyable if you can engage in this task with one or more other people, but I will describe the steps as if for one person.

Step 1: Scoping pamphlets: Visit a site where you would expect to find pamphlets about places, for example, a visitor's bureau, information center, travel center or hotel lobby. Collect a range of pamphlets that appear to be celebrating the virtues or qualities of a particular place. Choose your favorite and reflect on these questions:

- How is this pamphlet folded? How many "panels" are produced by the folds?
- Does one panel serve as a "cover" or "face" for the pamphlet? What kind of work does this cover do?
- What are the distinct elements that have been *composed* to create this pamphlet? Is there a sense of flow through the different panels? Try making a "mock up" on a piece of paper where you "block out" the various elements that compose this particular pamphlet.
- What function is each element (visual and written) serving? Is there overlap between elements in terms of function? (Are different elements performing the same function?)

Step 2: Discourse: What *kind* of story do you want to tell about the place you wrote about in Writing task 5.4? You could begin by listing the *values* that this place represents for you and the kinds of *appeal* it might have for a particular kind of person.

Step 3: Design: As rhetor, you need to decide on an audience for your pamphlet. Complete the following: "I imagine my audience to be . . ." Now engage in the following:

- Take a common-sized piece of paper from your own region (e.g., U.S. letter, foolscap [8½ × 13½ inches], A4) and experiment with folding it until you have settled on your preferred option. Note the number of panels you have arrived at.

- Write yourself a "production brief." In other words, identify the different text elements (visual and written) that you want to include in your pamphlet (e.g., pictures, headings, borders, text-blocks, slogans, logos, maps).
- Make a mock-up on your folded sheet showing as precisely as you can the location of each of your text elements. Think about *flow*—the order you might expect your readers to engage with the different panels as they unfold your pamphlet. Think about framing: what is the degree of connectedness and unconnectedness between various elements?
- Decide on the kinds of pictorial content you might use to *represent* the values and/or appeals contained in your discursive story.
- Similarly, decide on appropriate written content for your text-blocks. How do you intend to connect the visual content with the content of the text-blocks?

Step 3: Production. There are other decisions to be made in relation to design, but let's move on. You could stay with your mock-up (using paper as medium) or you could set up a file in a word processing or desktop publishing program. I invite you to begin the task of producing your pamphlet *prototype* with the following:

- A slogan is a short, catchy, memorable verbal formula (from the old Celtic word for "battle cry"). Try writing a slogan that suits the discourse you are drawing on for your place. Once you have decided on a slogan, try inserting it on your prototype in a way that connects (framing) with another element, for example, by superimposing the slogan on a photograph, or spreading it across two panels.
- Find an image (a photograph perhaps) that exemplifies somehow the discourse of place you are communicating. Insert this image in the appropriate place in your prototype. (You may want to scan the image and crop it or adjust it in some way before you do your insertion.)
- Write a text-block using the following formula. Begin with a topic sentence which states in abstract terms *one* appeal of your place. Complete the text-block with predominantly concrete language that supports the topic sentence with specific examples (sights, sounds, tastes, smells).

The following examples of slogan and text-blocks were written in a Writing Workshop by a teacher, Phillipa Grace:

KARANGAHAKE GORGE

The perfect resting place between Tauranga and Auckland. Karangahake welcomes you.

Venture through history while exploring the abandoned mine site and tunnel. Relics of New Zealand's mining history: old stamping batteries and building foundations. Railway lines, tunnels and bridges, stand testament to the region's past industry.

A rugged landscape is traversed by crystal waters tumbling over rapids providing an adventure sport heaven.

Enjoy a gentle adventure. Indulge your senses in birdsong or a leisurely ramble beside the pristine river. Rejuvenate with a plunge into an exhilarating river pool. Then indulge your palate at the café or winery.

Depart with a feeling of accomplished adventure.

The Digital Revolution and Hypertext

The digital is not the same as the multimodal. However, we can confidently say that the Digital Revolution has vastly expanded opportunities for us to engage in multimodal text production. Digitization is the process of converting information into digital format, which involves measuring the original event at frequent intervals and storing those measurements as a string of digitally encoded numbers (binary data that computers can process).

Andrews and Smith (2011) identify three phrases in the ongoing relationship between various advances in the Digital Revolution and writing:

1. 1980s: The rise of the personal computer and its affordances in terms of word processing and desktop publishing;
2. 1990s: Networked communication via the Internet;
3. 2000s: Web 2.0 technologies with their affordances in terms of social interactivity and social mediation (p. 114).

By way of illustrating this relationship, they argue that word processing programs impact the writing process by collapsing the stages (e.g., between planning, drafting and editing). They suggest (drawing on Snyder's 1994 research), for example, that word processing facilitates the writing of argument because it affords easy "structural re-arranging" (p. 116).

As I write this book, using a word processing program, I am acutely aware of two features of this form of technological mediation. The first of these is the *fluidity* of the character surface. Had I written the last sentence with a pen on a

---

REFLECTIVE JOURNAL TASK 6.4

Write a journal entry where you reflect on *how* your practices as a writer have changed as a result of digitization. What are some technologies you are using now that you didn't use 10 or more years ago? In what ways are these technologies allowing you to do things differently? Are these differences positive or is there a downside to their use? Explain.

---

sheet of paper, it would have been almost impossible to change it because the marks would have been relatively *fixed*. However, because of the affordances of the software technology I am using, it is an easy matter for me to select this sentence and change its character entirely in respect of such things as font, style, color, location and so on. Indeed, if you send me a digital text such as an email, then you are putting into my hands a text that I can alter in all sorts of ways that are beyond your control.

The second is the *impermanence* of the text. If your computer has crashed before you saved a document, you will know the dismay. In general, unless I make a point of saving drafts periodically, there will be no accessible record of the changes I have gone through in processing this book. Both the upside and the downside of digitization are illustrated by the First World War Digital Poetry Archive. The link (http://www.oucs.ox.ac.uk/ww1lit/collections/document/5215/4631? REC=1) will take you to a scanned image of Wilfred Owen's famous poem "Dulce et Decorum Est." Digitization has made this pencil on paper text available with the click of a mouse. However, had Owen been writing on a digital device, it's unlikely we would have a record of its composition process and the changes he made between drafts.

In Chapter 2, I discussed writing as a sign system. In my view, the most far-reaching aspect of the Digital Revolution has been the invention of hypertext markup language, best known as "html." Developed by Tim Berners-Lee in the early 1990s, html is the main "markup language" for composing web pages, and is made up of elements called "tags," which are like coded instructions enclosed in angle brackets. Go to any website, click on "View Source" and you will see the sign system which underpins web authoring.

Since the early 1990s, it has become progressively easier for you and me to write webpages and develop websites for a range of purposes and using a range of media (wikis, blogs, and so on). In all likelihood, you participate in some kind of web-based composition, via a Facebook page, through Twitter, through a website you have set up, or via an interactive platform such as a blog or wiki (the list could go on!).

The fact that html allowed for web-based composition is important enough. But there is another aspect of html which has the potential to radically alter our thinking about composition. This aspect is *hypertext* itself. What makes hypertext different from *text*? One way to think about hypertext is as a multi-layered composition with any one layer linked by diverse pathways to other layers. While we still call these layers "pages," they are clearly different from the pages which make up this book, not just because they are not fixed in terms of "length" but because they are linked in a non-linear way to other pages (within or beyond the site where the "step-off" page is to be found).

Burbules (1997) makes the following distinction between printed texts and hypertexts:

> Printed texts are by their nature selective and exclusive. Any page, any volume, can contain only so many words; it can refer to other texts, but accessing those involves activities such as reaching to a shelf, purchasing the book, going to a library, and so on; activities that are not themselves reading, activities that require energy, time, and sometimes money that a reader may not have to spare. Hypertexts on the Web are by nature inclusive: texts can be almost any size one wishes; any text can be linked to a virtually unlimited number of other texts online; the addition of new links does not in any significant way detract from the text at hand; and accessing any of these textual links requires little time or effort.
>
> (p. 103)

Burbules emphasizes the *link*, because the link is the key element in hypertextual structure. On the face of it, hypertexts put *navigational* control in the hands of readers because the reader can *choose* which links to activate. In reality (as with twist-a-plot novels), the reader's choice is circumscribed by the way links are managed by site designers. As Burbules puts it, "someone else has made a series of navigational decisions for us" (1997, p. 105).

Is hypertext a mode in the sense that I used the word earlier in this chapter? In my view, hypertext is a resource for meaning-making that provides for both monomodal *and* multimodal text production, but which has structurally non-linear affordances. I agree with Burbules' (1997) argument that this non-linearity invites a particular kind of meaning-making. Traditionally, written texts ". . . assume a fundamentally linear and hierarchical organization of information, with passage following passage in a sequence governed by (a) relative importance, formalized in the discipline of the Outline, and (b) the narrative structure of argument, formalized in the discipline of the Syllogism" (p. 106). Hypertext expands the possibilities for textual organization. While it does not rule out linearity, it allows for such organizational principles as *bricolage* (the creative or spontaneous construction of a work from diverse and readily available resources) and *juxtaposition*, thereby expanding the ways in which texts or text components can enter into relationships with one another. A hyperlink, as you know, can allow a reader to arrive at another location within the same webpage or at a location in another webpage. In relation to the earlier discussion of framing, a hyperlink can be thought of as a time-based framing device.

Gordon (2005) offers a number of reasons why a 21st-century writer might use hypertext. First, hypertextual writing has become a major part of our cultural milieu through the Internet. Many teachers, as part of their professional work, produce web-based texts as part of the way they interface with their students and with their school communities. Second, learning to compose hypertexts encourages writers to "engage problems of visual rhetoric directly and intensively" (p. 49). A rhetor is constrained to think through the way various textual elements (written text, visual items and sound) cohere in order to support his or her purpose and design. Third, hyperlinks allow for an active exploration of the concept of manifest intertextuality (discussed in Chapter 4).

You may have noticed that I've been using the terms "composer" and "composition" lately, rather than "writer" and "writing." That is because "composition" is a more appropriate term for the making of multimodal texts. Composition has a range of meanings; here I'm using it to refer to the placement or organization of various elements or components of a text in accordance with the rhetor's design. Multimodal, hypertextual composition challenges the usefulness of traditional, written-text based grammars (see Chapter 11). In Chapter 4, when discussing the features of a memoir (a traditional written genre), I used the following headings for features: layout, diction, punctuation, syntax and structure.

What categories might serve for the "grammatical" features of a hypertext? I would suggest:

- *Architecture* (for three-dimensional aspects of design, for example, patterns of intra-page and extra-page linking);
- *Composition* (for two-dimensional aspects of design, for example, the nature of the template and the relationship of word-based and graphic-based elements within a page);
- *Verbal diction and syntax* (for aspects of diction and syntax within word-based elements on a site);
- *Graphic diction and syntax* (for aspects of diction and syntax within graphic elements on a site);
- *Sound elements:* voiced word language, sound effects and music;
- *Thematic organization and cohesion* (for ways in which elements on a page and across pages within a site are organized thematically).

WRITING TASK 6.5

Experimenting with Hypertextual Composition

Rather than prescribe a genre and suggest steps you might follow to complete it, I'd like you to consider a variety of options that allow for hypertextual composition and to experiment.

It may be that you are already practiced in working in some kind of hypertextual environment. You may be one of millions of people who have a Facebook page. Or, you may have a blog or wiki. Perhaps you have made use of an inexpensive platform such as WordPress to set up a website. In all likelihood, you will be making use of a web template, which has already established the compositional arrangement of a number of text and graphic components on a page. Questions you might ask are: Does this template fit my purpose(s)? How much flexibility does it give me? What sorts of relationship are set up between the various elements on the page and how are these elements framed? (A site like wordpress.com will provide you with the ability to browse the web for countless templates.)

Another question to ask yourself as you experiment is the rhetorical function of your page or site. Who is your audience? What purpose do you want your site to fulfill? The term "architecture" relates to the relationship between pages through the use of hyperlinks. Hyperlinks are sometimes to be found in *menus* of various kinds. WordPress is an example of a software platform which enables webpage creators to establish drop-down menus from a menu bar which might be located directly beneath the page *banner.* A question you will be regularly asking yourself is: How can I best enable my site visitors to *navigate* their way around this site?

Another set of questions relates to the way in which written text is composed. The prevalence of surfing has led to a resistance among Internet visitors to read large stretches of text. Your challenge as a writer of web-based text is to be clear, succinct and purposeful.

Further Reading

Multimodality and Framing

- Kress, G., & Van Leeuwen, T. (2002). Colour as a semiotic mode: Notes for a grammar of colour. *Visual Communication, 1*(3), 343–368.
- Andrews, R. (2011). *Re-framing literacy: Teaching and learning English and the language arts.* New York, NY: Routledge.

Digitization and Its Impact on Writing

- Curriculum Corporation (n.d.). What is digitization. In *Video Research Project*. Melbourne, AU: Education Services Australia. Retrieved from http://www1.curriculum.edu.au/videoresearch/digitise.htm. This provides an excellent explanation of digital and analogue media
- Andrews, R., & Smith, A. (2011). *Developing writers: Teaching and learning in the digital age*. Maidenhead, UK: Open University Press/McGraw-Hill.

Hypertext and Writing

- Snyder, I. (1997). Beyond the hype: Reassessing hypertext. In I. Snyder, (Ed.). *Page to screen: Taking literacy into the electronic era* (pp. 125–143). St. Leonards, New South Wales, Australia: Allen & Unwin.
- Gordon, J. (2005). Teaching hypertext composition. *Technical Communication Quarterly, 14*(1), 49–72.

PART II

The Teacher of Writing

7

BEST PRACTICE OVERVIEW—
WHAT THE RESEARCH SAYS

This chapter provides an overview of writing pedagogy, particularly in school settings, and offers a map of the various approaches one might find in classrooms, usually in combination. It draws on a number of reviews of the research into the teaching of writing and draws some conclusions in respect to what works, in terms of activity design, the sequencing of learning, and the modeling of identity, both to improve the writing of students and to increase their motivation and self-efficacy as writers.

Teacher Professional Knowledge

A claim I bring to this book is that there is no *one* way of thinking about writing and writing pedagogy. In other words, there is more than one story (discourse) to be told about what writing *is* and *how* it is best taught. Having an overview of these different discourses of writing and writing pedagogy can empower you as a professional. As Wohlwend (2009) remarks, "A clear understanding of our simultaneous positioning across multiple discourses will allow teachers to see options and to act strategically with greater awareness" (p. 350). In saying this, she is suggesting that what we believe and how we practice as teachers are likely to be influenced by more than one discourse. Knowing where we stand in relation to the range of discourses out there enhances our choice-making ability.

In an influential paper written in 1986, Shulman suggested that a teacher's knowledge fitted into three categories, *content knowledge, pedagogical content knowledge* and *curricular knowledge*. The first part of this book has focused on content knowledge, specifically knowledge about writing itself. The second part of this book, beginning with this chapter, focuses on pedagogical content knowledge, specifically *how* to teach writing.

The third category, curricular knowledge, has a number of dimensions. Let's start with Eisner's (2002) definition of a curriculum as "a series of planned events that are intended to have educational consequences for one or more students" (p. 31). Eisner makes a further distinction between the "intended" and "operational" curriculum. The former is planned and open to inspection, revision, dissemination, and so on. The official curriculum—what a national or state government mandates should be taught in schools—is an example of an intended curriculum. I am writing this book in the knowledge that different readers will be accommodating their teaching to such mandated curriculum requirements. Another example of an intended curriculum is a school's scheme of work: its documented curricular intentions for a year level, or class, or subject. Sometimes an intended curriculum at school and class level exists in an uneasy relationship with the official curriculum as school and teachers attempt to address the context-specific needs of their students.

According to Eisner, the operational curriculum is "the unique set of events that transpire within a classroom. It is what occurs between teachers and students and between students and students" (2002, p. 33). It is in the operational curriculum that a teacher's pedagogical content knowledge manifests itself.

I would like to suggest a fourth category of professional knowledge: *strategic knowledge* or "critical savvy" (Locke, 2004b). This kind of knowledge enables a teacher to engage in the self-reflexive identification of the assumptions that underpin his or her practice, to allow these assumptions to be questioned and to be prepared to reconsider them. It also enables a teacher to reflect on the discursive underpinnings of aspects of educational policy, or of particular approaches to teaching and assessment, that impact on his or her work. Strategic knowledge is crucial if a teacher is to be a critically reflective practitioner. One of the aims of this book is to enable teachers to reflect critically on their practices as writers and teachers of writing.

REFLECTIVE JOURNAL TASK 7.1

How is the intended curriculum for writing established in your own teaching context? Who has contributed to the development of this curriculum? Do some people have more say than others? To what extent is this intended curriculum shaped by the need to comply with an official curriculum of some kind? To what extent would you say that the intended curriculum in your teaching context is responsive to the needs of the students?

A Writing Pedagogy Overview

One approach to a view of writing as discursively constructed is to identify the elements that have a (potential) role to play in constructing it. While recognizing the non-exclusive nature of the following elements, I suggest that they offer us a useful set of key words and concepts that we need to grapple with when thinking about literacy and specifically the teaching of writing:

- writer,
- reader (or audience),
- text,
- meaning-making mind,
- meaning,
- language (and other sign systems),
- technological mediation,
- and social context.

I suggest that *how* we view these elements and the relationships between them has a central role in the discursive construction of literacy, and therefore the act of writing. There are different ways of *thinking about* the above words or terms. Different ways of thinking about them, I hope to show, lead to different ways of thinking about writing and the teaching of writing. Like Ivanič (2004), I think of discourses of writing as "constellations of beliefs about writing, beliefs about learning to write, ways of talking about writing, and the sorts of approaches to teaching and assessment which are likely to be associated with these beliefs" (p. 224).

A number of writers have come up with ways of categorizing discourses or versions of English, literacy and writing. Ivanič developed a set of categories for discourses of writing which distinguish between: "a skills discourse," "a creativity discourse," "a process discourse," "a genre discourse," "social practices discourse," and "a sociopolitical discourse" (2004, p. 225). The following categorization is one I have used and found useful over the years. The discourses (in brief) are as follows:

- *Cultural heritage:* There is a traditional body of knowledge (including a canon of precious texts and specialist literary, disciplinary and grammatical knowledge) which is to be valued and inculcated as a means of "rounding out" learners so that they become fully participating and discriminating members of a discipline or culture.
- *Personal growth:* Related to what is sometimes called "progressive" English, this discourse argues that it is valuable to engage with literary (canonical *and* popular) and other texts because this facilitates the personal, individual growth of learners, for whom the acquisition of certain cognitive, cultural

and linguistic competencies will play a central role in their ongoing task of making sense of their world.

- *Rhetorical or textual competence:* At its worst, this version promotes decontextualized skills acquisition. At its best, however, the discourse puts a value on the mastery of the forms and conventions of a range of textual practices or genres, including but not privileging literary genres. Pedagogically, it can be connected with various genre approaches (see, e.g., Cope and Kalantzis, 1993) and with rhetorical framings of the literacy and writing (see, e,g,, Andrews, 2011; Bakhtin, 1986).

- *Critical practice:* Often called "critical literacy," this discourse puts a value on encouraging language-users to see themselves as engaged in textual acts which are part of a wider set of discursive practices that actively produce and sustain patterns of dominance and subordination in the wider society and offer members of society prescribed ways of being particular sorts of people. Critical literacy and critical language awareness "involved such things as explicitly identifying how particular linguistic and semiotic choices position writers and readers in terms of their views of the world, social roles and social relations" (Ivanič, 2004, p. 238).

Each of these discourses, I would argue, offers teachers of writing a particular position or stance in respect to what writing and writing pedagogy are about. These positions (schematized in Table 7.1), if they are taken up by teachers, can be expected to impact upon both understandings of what writing is or should be, and pedagogical practice (including formative and summative assessment).

In what follows, I elaborate, in respect of each of these orientations, a view of what happens in the act of writing, and the sorts of beliefs we might expect teachers working out of these orientations to hold.

TABLE 7.1 Versions of English and writer orientation

Cultural heritage	*Personal growth*
Writer orientation: • Appreciation and emulation • Deference • Acculturation	*Writer orientation:* • Self-realization through meaning-making • Creative exploration • Personal integration
Rhetorical or textual competence	*Critical literacy*
Writer orientation: • Formal mastery of textual practices • Pragmatic competence • Social adeptness	*Writer orientation:* • Critical linguistic analysis • Detachment • Social transformation

Cultural Heritage

In their classic "New Critical" text, *Understanding Poetry,* Brooks and Warren (1976) assert that "literature is the most sophisticated example of the process by which we come to grasp out own environment, especially our human environment, with its complex and ambiguous values." (p. 9). Such a statement, in harmony as it is with a cultural heritage view of English, explains why for years writing was the poor cousin of reading (especially literary reading) in the English classroom. In a cultural heritage discourse, literature was the product of the best human minds (usually male) putting the best words in the best order. How could merely mortal school pupils ever hope to emulate the feats of the great writers!

The Brooks and Warren (1976) statement also explains why certain kinds of non-fiction, "real world" texts such as editorials, newspaper columns, feature articles, reports, submissions, and media texts, have had to wait patiently for admission to the English Language Arts classroom. Somehow these genres were non-canonical, second-rate and therefore unworthy of emulation. Meaning-making, in the grandest sense, was performed by the individual, creative genius on a literary stage. Language was the raw material for this act of meaning-making, and something to be wrestled with and shaped. Meaning, with a capital "M," was something to be enshrined in the text to be elicited by the humble reader trained in the art of explication. Technology did not come into it. A text was a text was a text, whether produced by quill, pen or word processor. If poetry was best words in the best order, as Coleridge claimed, then grammar was the key to the order itself, and being able to identify types of subordinate clauses was a rite signaling admittance to the inner sanctum of syntax.

Teachers operating out of this discourse tend to believe that

- Literary texts are more important than non-literary texts.
- It is more important for students to read literary texts than to compose them.
- The meaning of a text is in the text.
- It is individuals who produce texts.
- Genius has a bigger role than craft in the production of texts, but craft is still very important.
- Literature has an important role to play in the way a culture expresses itself and is passed on.
- Technology is just a tool for doing things and not especially relevant.

Personal Growth (Progressive English)

The discourses that underpin the progressive English classroom are not a radical departure from those underpinning the cultural heritage discourse of English. In a telling phrase in *Growth through English*, John Dixon (1975) refers to "the acceptance of pupils' work as embryonic literature" (p. 55). Literature has not been knocked off its pedestal. Rather the category has been enlarged to encompass the propensity of all human beings to create meaning through language in their engagement with experience. The meaning-making mind is still an individual one; creative genius has simply become democratized.

This discourse is very attached to the idea of writing/composition as a process, as in the expression "process writing." Donald Graves' approach (1983), with its emphasis on "conferencing," dovetailed with the discourse of personal growth. Teachers of writing, in terms of this discourse, are constructed as sympathetic listeners and facilitators. As with the cultural heritage discourse, language is a means whereby inner meanings are communicated—a medium providing a clear window to the world and the possibility of shared meanings between human beings.

The 1966 Anglo-American Dartmouth Seminar was perhaps the first and last time English Language Arts teachers reached a consensus on the nature of their subject—with a few problems glossed over, it was a progressive consensus. Herbert Muller (1967) reported general agreement at the conference with the view that grammatical knowledge did little to improve speaking and writing and that ". . . the teaching of grammar has been chiefly a waste of time" (p. 68). However, the seminar was split on the question as to whether knowledge about language should be taught explicitly and, if so, at what stage. Linguists, on the back foot, found it hard to argue for the utility of linguistic knowledge but wanted to defend it as a humanistic study. Almost overnight, the teaching of grammar disappeared from many English classrooms. After all, if language was an instinct (Pinker, 1995), and human beings were born with an encoded blueprint that allowed for the generation of an infinitude of correct sentences according to need, as the transformational grammarians insisted, then "grammar" could be considered caught and not needing to be taught.

Teachers operating out of this discourse tend to believe that

- Creativity is an individual human capacity and everyone can write/compose texts requiring creative shaping (such as literary texts).
- Texts for modeling and exploration need to connect with the "world of the student."
- The meaning of a text is in the text.
- It is individuals who produce texts.
- Craft is important, but so are such things as exploration, experimentation and process; process is more important than product.
- Writing has a key role to play in a person's individual growth: writing is a way of making sense of the world.
- Literary texts, even when these are popular literature, have a bigger role to play in individual growth (self-realization) than non-literary texts.
- Technology can be a way of connecting with the world of the student.
- Teaching grammar formally is a waste of time.

Rhetorical or Textual Competence

In terms of this discourse, the classroom writing focus switches to the achievement of a range of textual competencies, at word, sentence, paragraph and whole text level—and sometimes beyond. In its worst manifestation, this discourse is utilized by skills acquisition advocates—educators who favor discrete and often decontextualized learning outcomes, which are viewed as non-problematically describable and measurable. In terms of this narrow skills discourse, meaning is relatively unproblematic so long as a writer has mastered a range of skills at sentence and text level. At its best, this discourse recognizes the socially constructed demands for "literacy" of a particular sort in a range of contexts. In one expression of the discourse, the Australian-based genre theorists turned their attention to the context of the school and declared that the pathway to empowerment lay in the mastery of six "genres": report, explanation, procedure, discussion, recount and narrative (Cope & Kalantzis, 1993, p. 9, see also, Knapp and Watkins, 2005).

In another expression of this discourse, proponents of the "new" rhetoric looked to the wider social stage and associated writing mastery with the ability to utilize knowingly and cunningly the language necessary to achieve a desired effect in a particular social context on a particular audience. The old triangle of text-maker, audience and purpose—what Richard Andrews has termed the "classic communication triangle" (1992, p. 2)—was back. Arguments about genre were central to this discourse. But I think proponents of it would agree with Cope and Kalantzis (1993) that any definition of genre entails a recognition that textual form varies according to social purpose. "Texts are different because they do different things. So, any literacy pedagogy has to be concerned, not just with the formalities of how texts work, but also with the living social reality of texts-in-use. How a text works is a function of what it is for" (p. 7).

Accompanying the rhetorical/textual competence discourse is a rationale for the overt use of grammar, or more broadly, knowledge about language, in the classroom. In the American context, Martha Kolln and others have followed this rationale, arguing for a rhetorical grammar, used for a different purpose ". . . from the remedial, error-avoidance or error-correction purpose of so many grammar lessons. I use rhetorical as a modifier to identify grammar in the service or rhetoric: grammar knowledge as a tool that enables the writer to make effective choices" (1996, p. 29). In the Australian context, we find Jim Martin and others defining a genre as "a staged, goal-oriented social process" (Eggins & Martin, 1997, p. 243)—a view which was highly influential in the Genre School's challenge to the progressive discourse during the early 1990s. Even those within the Genre School who questioned certain aspects of the approach (for example, its emphasis on product rather than process, its rigid formulation of schemata,[1] its tendency to slip into a transmission model of education) advocate the place of grammar in the classroom.

> We believe it is absolutely essential that teaching grammar must be a fundamental part of an effective genre-based approach to reading and writing. Without grammar, we will not be able to deal with the language issues which are so much a part of the concrete-abstract knowledge continuum. Grammar also enables us to break out of the reductiveness of the genre as end-product problem. Finally, it gives both teachers and students a way of talking about and dealing with language as an object that can be manipulated and changed to do particular things both in communication and expressing and organizing knowledge.
>
> (Callaghan, Knapp & Noble, 1993, pp. 201–202)

Traditional, decontextualized grammar teaching separates form from function. At their best, "Genre" and other skills-based approaches to writing view the formal qualities of a text, at whatever level, as related to textual function, and understanding of and mastery of textual function as central to a wider sort of pragmatic, social competence.

Teachers operating out of this discourse tend to believe that

- Literacy is a social practice as well as an individual one.
- The writer/composer is inevitably socially situated, with a need to be rhetorically oriented, that is, to have a keen awareness of audience and purpose.
- Students need to master a range of text-types or genres in order to be successful in the world; product is as important as process.
- Teacher modeling is vital in helping students negotiate mastery of new genres.
- Students need to be exposed to good examples of particular genres which can be used for study (breaking the generic code) and imitation.
- Individuals produce textual meaning, but in social contexts.
- There is a place for grammar in the classroom.
- It is important that students understand how language functions—at word, sentence and whole-text levels—and have a meta-language to express that understanding.

Critical Literacy

If the Genre School put the focus back on the production of texts, it is arguable that *critical literacy* (e.g., Morgan, 1997; Janks, 2010) and *critical language awareness* (e.g., Fairclough, 1992a; Janks, 1994) put the focus back on reading and away from writing. The reader who took center-stage was a somewhat different sort of reader from the relatively stable entity of the other three discourses I have described. This reader was to be viewed as a cultural product, "inscribed" by a range of discourses (not necessarily compatible with one another) and positioned by his or her discursive frames to respond in one way or another to the "preferred" position offered by a text. The text was also destabilized. It was no longer a container of meaning (as per the New Criticism), nor a constrainer of meaning (as per the progressive discourse), but rather a space within which a play of meaning might be enacted by the deconstructive, "writerly" reader. Meaning became a function of discourse (always with a capital "D"), and individual texts lost their discreteness and became meaningful only in an infinitely complex network of intertextual relationships between utterances (Bakhtin, 1986). The cultural context had become pre-eminent. So, increasingly, had technological mediation. The notion that "literacy is a social practice" became a slogan, and then a mantra. And with the increased presence of ICTs as mediating textual practices, a growing emphasis was put on literacy, in all its forms, as technologized.

Key concepts in a critical writing pedagogy are "ideology" and "hegemony"—both contested terms. I define an ideology as an elaborate story told about the ideal conduct of some aspect of human affairs. As I see it, its power lies in its "truth" value, which is determined by the size and nature of its subscription base as much as by some notion of "explanatory force." In short, the truth of an ideology is determined by the number of people subscribing to it. The related term, "hegemony," can consequently be defined as the state of affairs which exists when the subscription base of an ideology is broad in terms of numbers and reinforced "vertically" by the social status of its subscribers (Locke, 2004a). Or to put it more stridently, "Hegemony is secured when the virulence of oppression, in its many guises (e.g., race, gender, class, sexual orientation) is accepted as consensus" (Kincheloe & McLaren, 1994, p. 141).

One aspect of the job of the writing teacher in the critical literacy classroom is to draw young writers' attention to the social consequences of privileging in their own writing particular discourses or "stories." As the critically literate reader is also a writer, so the critically literate writer is also a self-reflexive reader of the position(s) he or she is inviting a prospective reader to take up. A second aspect of the job is to ensure that writers are aware that the language they use *is not* a transparent medium of communication, but rather an opaque instrument that inevitably constructs its "object" in a particular way. What Allan Luke (1992) says about the relationship between reading and metalanguage (or grammar) for critical readers, applies equally to critical writers.

> By "critical competence" then, I refer to the development of a critical metalanguage for talking about how texts code cultural ideologies, and how they position readers in subtle and often quite exploitative ways. My argument is that in order to contest or rewrite a cultural text, one has to be able to recognize and talk about the various textual, literary and linguistic, devices at work.
>
> (p. 10)

So, "grammar" retains its place in the critical literacy classroom, but with a different kind of justification, not so much to support pragmatic writing competence as to serve the purpose of linguistic analysis in the service of a critical awareness of the job all texts do in positioning readers to see the world in particular ways.

Teachers operating out of this discourse tend to believe that

- Reality (for readers and writers) is socially constructed by human sign systems;
- As readers and writers we are very much social products (individual genius doesn't have much place here);
- A text does not have a single meaning. Different readers read texts differently and texts *mean* things only in relationship to other texts;
- Texts reflect one or more discourses and are inherently ideological;
- Texts have powerful roles in representing the world in particular ways to advantage some groups and disadvantage others;
- Technological mediation impacts on the meaning of a text;
- Literacy is multiple (multiliteracies);
- There are ethical implications for the way we read the word/world as writers/ composers of texts;
- Metalinguistic understanding is vital to our understanding of the textual work we do as writers.

REFLECTIVE JOURNAL TASK 7.2

Check out the sets of beliefs for each of the discourses of writing instruction discussed above. For each set, lightly tick a belief that you subscribe to. What kind of picture of yourself emerges as a teacher of writing? Is there anything surprising about this picture?

What the Research Says About Best Writing Practice

In this section, I will offer an overview of what researchers suggest as effective practices in the teaching of writing. I begin by distinguishing between school-wide practices and classroom-situated practices, while acknowledging that the former is likely to impact on the latter and vice versa. Unsurprisingly, most research into effective writing practice focuses on classroom practice.

School-Wide Practice

In Chapter 1, I referred to the Writing is Primary project undertaken in three clusters totaling 19 schools in England during the 2007–2008 school year (Ings, 2009). This group of projects generated a number of findings related to whole-school practices, which were bulleted in the executive summary as "Essentials for sustaining improvement in writing." I draw on these essentials in listing the following whole-school practices likely to have a positive impact on the teaching of writing:

- An up-front commitment, supported by the principal, to a whole-school approach to writing, enshrined in formal school policy and planning, and subject to ongoing review;
- Encouraging and resourcing action research related to the teaching of writing;
- Encouraging staff to take on the role of a writing leader;
- Providing ongoing professional learning (especially peer-led professional learning) for all staff;
- Supporting teachers to develop a "principled and personal" (i.e., critical) response to national or state curriculum and assessment demands;
- Developing programs tailored to the school's strengths and weaknesses and reflective of its culture;
- Encouraging collaborative networking with neighboring schools;
- Fostering whole-school and community awareness of the importance of writing, including its pleasures; for high schools, this would mean enhancing subject teachers' awareness of the metalinguistic demands of their respective subjects;
- Ensuring change is undertaken at a realistic pace and is sustainable (p. 12).

INQUIRY TASK 7.3

Identify a school which has a school-wide policy on the teaching of writing. (It could be your own school.) After studying this policy, write down the school-wide practices this policy advocates. Appraise this policy. What are its strengths? How might it be improved?

Effective Classroom-Situated Writing Practice

According to the available research, what classroom practices appear to enhance student writing performance and motivation? I say "appear to" because it is not a simple matter to separate out a single practice from the complex world of the writing classroom and to assert confidently that it is effective per se. Nor, as we shall see, is there a commonly agreed understanding of what each of these practices *means* or *entails*.

In order to generate Table 7.2, I have drawn on three writing research overviews, two from the United States and one from the United Kingdom.

In *Writing Next*, Graham and Perin (2007) produced a report to the Carnegie Foundation outlining "the results of a large-scale statistical review of research in to the effects of specific types of writing instruction on adolescents' writing proficiency" using meta-analytical methods (p. 4). In a review described by Myhill, Fisher, Jones, and Lines (2008) as "extensive and robust," these American reviewers outlined 11 teaching strategies ("instructional elements") that, through meta-analysis, had been shown to be effective in the teaching of writing. The review focused on 176 experimental or quasi-experimental studies, and resulted in a ranking of teaching strategies from strongest to weakest effect sizes, a kind of "hit parade" of effective practices. In Table 7.2, I have retained Graham and Perrin's ranking on the left-hand column. ("Writing strategies" had the highest ranking in their review.)

Myhill and colleagues' review (2008) built on and constitutes a commentary on the work of Graham and Perrin (2007). These reviewers drew on a database of 400 publications, with a global reach and employing a wide range of research methodologies and conceptual frameworks. While the scope of their review was wider, their focus was more narrowly on what they described as "complex expression in writing," which they define as "the ability of writers to make sophisticated decisions which can accurately and effectively match writing choices to purposes and intentions" (p. 5). What is immediately evident, here, is that complexity is viewed as less a matter of syntax than an aspect of the writer's decision-making in respect of the demands of a rhetorical situation. In the second column of Table 7.2, I have listed the effective practices identified, sometimes cautiously, by Myhill and colleagues.

The third column of Table 7.2 lists practices identified in a literature review conducted a little earlier by Hillocks (2006) and largely based on U.S. studies. Hillocks was also interested in effect sizes, but his article also includes references to qualitative studies and explores topics other than effective classroom practices, for example, the impact of testing regimes on the quality of classroom teaching and writing across the curriculum. In column three, I have put "Strategy instruction" in square brackets because Hillocks does not mention it per se, though it is implied in sentences such as: "The treatments with the largest gains for sentence combining, scales, and inquiry all focus on systematically teaching procedural knowledge, knowledge of how to do things" (p. 45).

Potentially, "Writing strategies" is a broad category and embraces specific instructional elements such as "prewriting" and "sentence combining." That is why it is important that when you study Table 7.2, you don't read these practices as discrete. Rather, they are an attempt to highlight aspects of a complex picture of what is currently thought of as effective writing pedagogy. Graham and Perrin make this very point:

> The elements should not be seen as isolated but rather as interlinked. For instance, it is difficult to implement the process writing approach

TABLE 7.2 Effective writing practices

Graham & Perrin (2007)	Myhill et al. (2008)	Hillocks (2006)	See chapter . . .
Writing strategies/ strategy instruction	Writing strategies	[Strategy instruction]	9
	Self-regulated, meta-cognitive and rhetorical use of writing strategies		9
Summarization	Summarization		
Collaborative writing	Collaborative writing	Collaborative writing	8
	Writing-related talk and metacognitive understanding	Writing-related talk and metacognitive understanding	8
Specific product goals	Specific product goals		9
Word processing	Word processing		11
Sentence combining	Sentence combining	Sentence combining	10
Prewriting		Prewriting	9
Inquiry activities	Inquiry activities	Inquiry activities	8
Process writing approaches	Supporting the writing process	Supporting the writing process	9
Study of models	Study of textual models	Study of models	9
	An apprenticeship, workshop approach to writing: teacher modeling		8
Writing for content learning	Writing for content learning		10
		Teacher and peer written and oral response to drafts and final products	8
		Fostering student autonomy and choice	8
		High expectations of students	8
		The use of evaluative criteria (writing scales)	12

(element 9) without having peers work together (element 3) or use prewriting supports (element 7). A mixture of these elements is likely to generate the biggest return.

(2007, p. 11)

Column 4 of Table 7.2 references the chapters where I will be exploring these practices in some depth. However, to conclude this overview, let me offer some brief comments on a number of practices listed in the table.

Writing Strategies/Strategy Instruction

As defined by Graham and Perrin (2007), "Strategy instruction involves explicitly and systematically teaching steps necessary for planning, revising, and/or editing text" (p. 15). It is clear that the potential range of such strategies is enormous and can include such things as mind-mapping, modeling ways of offering peer response and demonstrating how a particular genre might be structured. Beyond explicit instruction, however, is the goal of having students assimilate these strategies into their own repertoires of writing practice for later independent use. For Myhill and colleagues (2008), this involves an additional focus on self-regulation and metacognition (developed thinking about task requirements), and task design that renders the focal strategy meaningful in relation to a set of rhetorical constraints and opportunities (text audience, purpose and function).

Summarization

Summarization is a good example of a skill involving strategies that lend themselves to explicit instruction. As a writing focus, it has more relevance to the United States than to other countries. It illustrates the relationship between reading and writing, in that good summarizers can identify topic sentences. They also have the sentence-combining skills that allow chunks of information to be combined in relatively complex sentences.

Collaborative Writing

Collaborative writing will be a major focus of Chapter 8, but in the context of the classroom as a community of writing practice. This is Graham and Perrin's (2007) third-ranked instructional element (with an effect size of 0.75) and suggests strongly that it is effective to foster a classroom culture where students work together rather than independently on processing their writing. As both Myhill and colleagues (2008) and Hillocks (2006) point out, a key ingredient of the success of this strategy is likely to be an emphasis on writing-related talk and the consequent development of metacognitive understanding. The former cite a British study by White (2000), who reported a high degree of motivation in students in a class where writing was viewed as a social activity and where they received regular feedback from both teacher and peers. White compared these primary students to craftspeople "serving their apprenticeship in a complex creative activity under the guidance of an expert" (p. 21).

Setting Product (and Process) Goals

The research suggests that providing students with specific, attainable goals related to the writing task (including goals related to audience and purpose) is an effective teaching strategy. Though Graham and Perrin (2007) emphasize specific "product" goals, there is an argument for emphasizing "process" goals also. In studies with U.S. fourth- and fifth-grade students, Schunk and Swartz (1993) engaged their treatment subjects in three experimental conditions: product goal (focused on outcome), process goal (focused on strategies aimed at facilitating an outcome) and process goal plus feedback, with students in all three experimental conditions and the control setting receiving the same strategy instruction. In the third of these conditions students were exposed to two kinds of procedure: (1) *process goal-setting*, where they were offered specific strategies for improving their writing; and (2) *progress feedback,* where researchers gave students feedback on how well they were applying a particular strategy in their own writing. Children exposed to these two procedures were found to out-perform other groups in respect of self-efficacy, writing skill and strategy use. The researchers explained their findings by noting that "a process goal highlights strategy use as a means to improve writing. Students who believe they are learning a useful strategy may feel efficacious about improving their writing and motivated to apply the strategy. . . . Progress feedback conveys that the strategy is useful and that students are becoming skillful" (p. 351). You will see that there is a direct connection between process goal-setting and progress feedback, and strategy instruction.

Word Processing

Having less able writers use word processors has been shown to be a helpful strategy in terms of both performance and motivation. However, the place of digital technologies and the best conditions for their use in the writing classroom is a big topic and will be addressed in Chapter 11.

Sentence Combining

Sentence combining can be thought of as a teaching strategy aimed at developing syntactical fluency and increasing mastery of a range of sentence types. It guides students in finding ways of combining two or more simple sentences into a longer, more complex one. As Graham and Perrin (2007) point out, most studies of sentence combining compare this "treatment" with traditional, formal grammar teaching, with sentence combining shown to be more effective, if modestly so, in its effect. Lurking here, of course, is the bigger question of the effectiveness of grammar teaching in the context of the writing classroom. This is a big topic, which will be addressed in Chapter 10, where we will see that the question involves a good deal more than sentence combining.

Supporting the Writing Process: Prewriting

Graham and Perrin (2007) identify both prewriting and writing process approaches as effective teaching practices. I will be focusing on the writing process (including prewriting) in Chapter 9, so will make just a few brief points here:

- A focus on process needs to recognize that not all genres are produced with the same process. Different genres require different steps.
- Teachers need to recognize that different writers process the same genre in different ways. It is not a good idea to impose the same process steps rigidly across a class.
- Different discourses of writing view process in different ways. A *personal growth* discourse is more likely to focus on the individual and the cognitive processes required to produce a piece of writing. A *rhetorical skills* discourse is more likely to focus on the audience and the steps required to produce a particular text-type suited to purpose.

We encountered Flower and Hayes' (1981) cognitive writing model in Chapter 2. From a cognitive psychological perspective, there are three distinct aspects of the writing process: *planning* (generating content fit for purpose and situation); *translation* (expressing this content in textual form as words, sentences, paragraphs and so on); and *revision* (re-visioning and editing text in accordance with rhetorical purpose). What teachers need to bear in mind is that this process is not linear. In different ways, all writers move between these three processes in the course of producing a piece of writing.

Inquiry Activities

According to Graham and Perrin (2007), "Involving adolescents in writing activities designed to sharpen their inquiry skills improves the quality of their writing" (p. 19). They also note that this instructional strategy was last studied in 1986! My own response to this comment is that inquiry-based learning as an approach has gained prominence in the last 30 years; it is likely that it has had positive effects on student writing and motivation, especially when it is linked with prewriting. I would argue that involving students in inquiry-based learning sharpens the focus of their prewriting. One instance is Spence (2009), a teacher-librarian working collaboratively with a second-grade teacher on an inquiry-based project using a range of non-fiction texts. These young writers became highly enthusiastic about the choices provided to them in respect of their topics. The two teachers worked collaboratively to construct a writing workshop, where the specific writing needs of students were addressed via specially tailored mini-lessons on such research-related strategies as paraphrasing.

Modeling

In Graham and Perrin's (2007) review, the use of models is confined to the use of exemplary texts, often by published authors, that students study in order to "emulate the critical elements, patterns, and forms" (p. 20). However, there is far more to modeling than this suggests. In a workshop approach to writing, the teacher and sometimes peers model various aspects of the writing process, perhaps using think-aloud protocols. Think-aloud protocols occur when the person demonstrating a writing strategy, for example revision, shares their thinking about the task as they go with the class as audience. In Chapter 8, I will be advocating the idea of the class as community of writing practice, where the teacher herself models the identity of writer and where students can be thought of as apprenticed to the collective expertise of teacher and peers.

Writing for Content Area Learning

In Graham and Perrin's (2007) review, this instructional element is the one with the least effect size. Because this strategy is about the assigning of written tasks for content-area learning (a kind of writing to learn), it cannot be viewed as teaching writing per se because it does not involve explicit writing instruction. There is a link between this practice and content-based instruction (CBI) as an approach to second-language learning (see Brinton, Snow, & Wesche, 1989)

In the next four chapters, I make a case for an approach to the teaching of writing that builds on this overview and develops in some detail some of the themes foreshadowed here.

REFLECTIVE JOURNAL TASK 7.4

Revisit Table 7.2. Use it as a kind of self-review by putting two ticks next to the practices you consider to be a real strength and one tick next to the practices which you consider yourself as having *some* strength in. On the basis of this self-review, write a self-appraisal setting out what you consider to be your strengths as a writing teacher and the areas where you would like to improve.

Note

1. In fairness to Martin, while earlier work (1993) refers, for example, to "the canonical structure of the report genre" (p. 122), later work (with Eggins, 1997) emphasizes that the "relationship between context and text [as reflected in an unfolding of stages] is theorized as probabilistic, not deterministic . . ." (p. 236).

Further Reading

Discourses of Writing Instruction and Research

- Ivanič, R. (2004). Discourses of writing and learning to write. *Language and Education, 18*(3), 220–245.
- Hyland, K. (2002). *Teaching and researching writing.* London, UK: Longman.

Overviews of Effective Writing Practice

- Hillocks Jr, G. (2006). Research in writing, secondary school, 1984–2003. *L1—Educational Studies in Language and Literature, 6*(2), 27–51.
- Graham, S., & Perin, D. (2007). *Writing next: Effective strategies to improve writing of adolescents in middle and high schools—A report to Carnegie Corporation of New York.* Washington, DC: Alliance for Excellent Education.
- Myhill, D., Fisher, R., Jones, S., & Lines, H. (2008), *Effective ways of teaching complex expression in writing. A literature review of evidence from the secondary school phase* (Research Report No. DCSF-RR032). London, UK: The Department for Children, Schools and Families (DCSF).

8

BUILDING A COMMUNITY
OF WRITING PRACTICE

The starting point for this chapter is that writing is a socialized practice. I explore the implications of this assumption in respect to the identification of roles in the writing classroom, notions of authenticity in relation to the meaningfulness of the writing task, and the primacy of audience. I also examine the kind of fluidity in identity that occurs when the writing classroom is thought of as a community of writers where expertise is distributed among members. In particular, I discuss ways in which response to text can be taught and fostered, and the place of talk and metacognition.

A Social View of Learning to Write

In Chapter 2, I discussed how a view of writing as anchored in an individual's skillset and his or her cognitive processing became challenged in the 1970s by a view of writing as socially constructed. One of the challenges to a model of linguistic knowledge anchored in cognitive psychology came from the discipline of ethnography, with Dell Hymes' espousal in the mid-70s of the concepts of "communicative competence" and "speech community" (1974). The concept of *communicative competence* suggests that appropriate (correct) usage is not fixed but is context dependent. An ad writer, for example, has more scope to use colloquial language than an editorial writer. Communicative competence, then, is not just about how to use certain language features but *when*.

The concept of a *speech community* suggests that the linguistic resources a writer has available are a property or characteristic of the community itself. This is in line with the discussion in Chapter 4, where I drew on Bakhtin's work to suggest that all of us are socialized into the acquisition of a repertoire of genres. Faigley (1985) has argued that "within a language community, people acquire specialized kinds of discourse competence that enable them to participate in specialized groups" (p. 238). That is, depending on the speech or language community we belong to, we acquire a degree of competence in particular forms and genres (their typical content, structure, style and so on).

Our primary speech community, of course, is the family or extended family we grew up in. If our family encouraged the practice of writing thank-you letters to show appreciation for gifts, then it is likely that we learned to write such a letter from an early age. As we enter the world of formal schooling, we undergo a kind of induction into a secondary speech or writing community. For some of us from middle-class backgrounds, this process will be managed relatively comfortably because of the practices we learned in our primary speech communities. For others of us, for a range of reasons, the writing community of the school will feel very strange indeed. Effective teachers of writing are keenly aware that not all students find the process of induction into the language community/ies of formal schooling straightforward. Then, as we grow older, we find ourselves joining other speech communities: churches, lobby groups, professions, occupational groups and so on.

In his influential book on *Communities of Practice,* Etienne Wenger (1998) noted that a social theory of learning views it as a characteristic of practice. By way of illustration, he contrasted two scenarios. The first is characterized by the belief that "knowledge consists of pieces of information explicitly stored in the brain" (p. 9). According to Wenger, this belief justifies approaches to learning that package information in discrete units and deliver it to recipients (e.g., students) in specific locations (e.g., classrooms). You can see how this belief fits in with a transmission view of education. In the second scenario (consistent with a social theory of learning), it is believed that "knowing involves primarily active participation in social communities" (p. 10). From this perspective, scenario one appears unproductive. Rather, this second theory proposes, it makes more sense to engage students "in meaningful practices" with "access to resources that enhance their participation" and which enlarge their "horizons so that they can put themselves on learning trajectories they can identify with . . . involving them in actions, discussions, and reflections that make a difference to the communities that they value" (p. 10). In terms of this second scenario, the student is a participant rather than a recipient.

Framing the Writing Task

Sociocultural theory views writing as a social practice, or rather sets of social practices, since different language communities foster the acquisition of different *ways* of doing writing. The meaning of a piece of writing derives from the function it fulfils in terms of the community's way of life. Different communities offer different purposes for writing, have a say in the typical content of texts and determine the kinds of audience readily available to a writer. In short, a sociocultural view of writing impacts on the way writing teachers need to think about texts, author and audience.

While this chapter advocates for the writing classroom as a community of practice, it also argues that teachers need to recognize the part played by the language communities to which each student belongs. Work by Luis Moll and others in the United States makes use of the term "funds of knowledge" to signify the premise "that people are competent and have knowledge, and their life experiences have given them that knowledge" (Gonzalez & Moll, 2002, p. 625). Funds of knowledge research shows that effective instruction (including writing instruction) needs to be linked with students' lives—to their "local histories and community contexts" (p. 623). By the same token, writing instruction is likely to be less effective if it attempts to impose standardizing agendas on diverse students, either in terms of task design or assessment practice (see Chapter 12). Bruning and Horn (2000) define as authentic "activities that involve children in the immediate use of literacy for enjoyment and communication" as opposed to "activities where literacy skills are acquired for some unspecified future use" (p. 30).

Thinking About the Text

Prior (2006) argues that according to sociocultural theory, writing needs to be seen as "chains of short- and long-term production, representation, reception, and distribution" involving a dialogic process of invention" (pp. 57–58).

> Texts and moments of inscription are no more autonomous than the spray thrown up by the white water in a river, and like that spray, literate acts today are far downstream from their sociohistoric origins. . . . Seeing writing as distributed and mediated means recognizing that all writing is collaborative, involving divisions of labor and forms of coauthorship.
>
> (p. 58)

This is rather dense writing, so I'd like to unpack it a little. We have encountered the metaphor of the *chain* in Chapter 4, where Bakhtin (1986) refers to an "organized chain of . . . utterances" (p. 69) to encapsulate his concept of intertextuality—the idea that texts are not isolated, discrete entities but rather derive their meaningfulness in part from the way they enter into a relationship with texts (utterances) that precede them as well as those which are yet to be written. The word "dialogue" emphasizes the way in which writers, in producing texts, enter into dialogue with what has been written previously and with an anticipated audience. In this sense, all texts are "co-authored," since, when we write, the voices of other "authors" impact on the act of production, though they have a different role in the "division of labor." For instance, if I write a letter to the editor of a newspaper in response to an editorial, there is a sense in which the voice of the editorial writer impacts the way I frame my response.

For teachers of writing, the message is clear. For a writing task to be meaningful and motivating, the chosen text needs to be relevant to the student's world in terms of:

- its genre;
- previously written texts the task may reference (in the prewriting stage, for example, or as part of a process of inquiry);
- the purpose for which the text is to be written, and
- the anticipated audience of the text.

Thinking About the Author

A sociocultural view of writing encourages us to think of all texts as in a certain way co-authored, even though in terms of a division of labor, only one person is assuming responsibility for *prewriting*, *translating* and *revision* (terms we've met in cognitive approaches to writing). When Prior uses the term "distributed," he is suggesting that many hands are at work in the construction of a single piece of writing.

An issue to be confronted in any classroom, of course, is the establishment of power relations. Traditionally, teachers have power *over* students, but this inequality has been shown to have a detrimental effect on students' ownership of their learning. The following statement from Prior (2006) should give us all food for thought:

> One important corollary of this view is the recognition that teachers in schools are always coauthors (often dominant ones) in students' writing as teachers take up many roles in the authorship function (deciding to write, setting deadlines, specifying style and topic, structuring the writing process, offering specific words and phrases). The fact that students are typically held fully accountable as authors is thus an interesting cultural practice (pointing to both power and the subject-producing dimensions of writing in school . . .).
>
> (p. 58)

As I will discuss below, there are constructive ways of addressing the issue of teacher "dominance" in the context of a community of writing practice, particularly in maximizing the degree of choice our students have in respect of the writing tasks we set for or negotiate with them. When this occurs, we are validating their identities as authors of their writing and enabling them to develop their voice (a concept discussed in Chapter 3). There is no voice without choice!

Thinking About the Audience

Research suggests a strong relationship between task meaningfulness and student motivation, which as Boscolo (2009) suggests, needs to be seen as something characterizing the learning environment itself. For a writing task to be meaningful, there needs to be a sense of audience. Without a sense of audience, there can be no social purpose for the writing. Without a sense of audience, there can be no basis for the development of a rhetorical strategy, that is, the construction of a text in accordance with the rhetor's designs in relation to the context of production. Without a sense of audience, terms like *formal* and *informal* have no meaning. Without a sense of audience, it is impossible to develop a contextually appropriate, argumentative strategy.

Magnifico (2010) argues strongly for the importance of audience as a motivating factor, particularly in a digital, web-oriented age. I will never forget the excitement generated back in 1996 when a tenth-grade (14-year-old) student of mine discovered a website that published student poetry, had her poem accepted for publication and then found herself "editor's choice" for that particular month (Locke, 1997). After reviewing a number of studies on the impact of having students write for authentic audiences, Magnifico concluded that

> direct engagement with the performative aspects of writing for an audience seem [sic] to enable students of many ages, grades, achievement levels, and social backgrounds to imagine what an effective writing performance might be, to set goals for achieving that performance, and to motivate themselves to achieve to that level.
>
> (2010, p. 177–178)

REFLECTIVE JOURNAL TASK 8.1

What kinds of writing did you do as a child in the context of your own family or extended family? Who encouraged you to write? Did you have a role model for writing within your family? What sorts of purpose did writing serve in your family? Did the writing that was encouraged have particular audiences? Write an account of one occasion where you wrote a text with some kind of family encouragement or complicity.

Communities of Practice

As indicated earlier, a social theory of learning focuses on the acquisition of knowledge through participation in communities of practice (Wenger 1998) or discourse communities. In such a view, participation in a range of socially constructed writing practices helps make us particular kinds of writers. According to Wenger (1998), there are three dimensions that constitute a community of practice as coherent and therefore powerful in respect of learning and identity formation: (1) the mutual engagement of participants; (2) the "negotiation of a joint enterprise"; and (3) the "development of shared repertoire" (pp. 77, 82). I will discuss the first of these below ("Roles and relationships in the writing classroom"). Learning to write might be thought of as the *joint enterprise* that all participants in a writing classroom have signed up to. However, the question of *negotiation* will be explored further in the section on "Negotiation and choice." The *development of a shared repertoire* will be explored in the section on "Modeling and feedback" and later chapters in this book.

It is unsurprising that Gallagher, Penuel, Shields, and Bosetti (2008) found Writing Project practices to be consistent with a social view of learning, identifying the uniqueness of the NWP in "the strength of the combination of approaches it uses to bring about deep changes in teachers' understanding and practice" (p. 5). In their view, at the heart of the Writing Project philosophy was community building, which invited teachers to take risks to improve their teaching by, for example, "overcoming isolation and building community through collegial critiques of their work" and "becoming part of a culture in which they are active learners rather than passive recipients of expert knowledge" (pp. 5–6). Teachers of writing, influenced by such a philosophy, are likely to commit themselves to the implementation of such community-building in their own classroom.

Identities, Roles and Relationships in the Writing Classroom

Identity is a concept I discussed at length in Chapter 3. For now, let me state simply that our identity is who we are and what we stand for and is best seen as multiple and subject to change over time. As a reader of this book, it is likely that you identify as a teacher. We might call this your professional identity. You'll be aware that I have been arguing in this book for the value of teachers identifying as writers. You don't have to be a teacher to identify as a writer, of course. When teachers identify as writers, they are assuming an additional identity. As we walk through our classroom doors, there will be other identities we bring with us, related to our family ties and membership of various cultural groups. As we shall see, it is important that we keep these identities distinct from one another.

Likewise, our students bring with them multiple identities, all demanding recognition from us as teachers. Students also have the potential to develop a writer identity. This is *not* the same as being a student who is required to *do* writing. In the latter case, the motive comes from without and above. For a student to identify as a writer, "writer" needs to be an aspect of his or her identity that is willingly subscribed to and intrinsically meaningful. Recently, I studied the impact of a poetry competition on junior English students in a rural school, where most teachers also viewed themselves as writers. Following an intensive unit of work on the writing of poetry, teachers reported changes in student relationships—no put-downs, a willingness to share work and have work read aloud—in part effected by the development of a writing community at class level. One teacher couched his sense of the collective transformation in terms of self-identity, as a shift from *not* seeing themselves as writers to a "turn around," where at the end of the unit, students would say, "Now I am a writer" (Locke, 2013, p. 288).

In a hierarchical arrangement, we are teachers and our students are learners. However, this typical sense of hierarchy is modified when as teachers we also assume the identity of learner. You may recall that in Helen's story (Chapter 1), a turning point occurred in her relationship with her class, when she shared with them a poem she had written for her daughter and invited their response. Helen's action challenged the typical power structure of the writing classroom by reversing roles; she became the learner, sharing a draft with her students and inviting them to give *her* feedback and ask questions. By flattening the hierarchical structure, Helen had taken a huge step towards establishing a *community* of writing practice. She was also opening a door and admitting identities other than teacher to enter and occupy the teaching space—identities of mother and writer.

While this book makes a case for the effectiveness of teachers assuming identities as writers, it does not pretend that such a shift is without its challenges and tensions. In a British study, Cremin and Baker (2010) highlighted the "tensions and difficulties . . . associated with the two professionals' positions as teachers and as writers" (p. 13). In one illustrative vignette, the teacher, Elaine (a pseudonym), struggled to assert and maintain "authorial agency" (p. 15) while demonstrating the writing of a description based on a visit to a local church. A range of factors intruded to distract her from exercising a role as writer, including suggestions from the children themselves, an awareness of the school's program demands, and dissatisfaction with the task itself. Cremin and Baker concluded that

> The teachers' relationship with their unfolding compositions, their emotional engagement, degree of authenticity and authorial agency were identified [by them] as significant intrapersonal strands. These operated in a dynamic relationship with interpersonal and institutional influences [determined by the classroom, school and policy context].
>
> (2010, p. 20)

They expressed this relationship in a diagram (Figure 8.1), which represents a kind of continuum, showing how teachers might position themselves in relation to texts they might produce in the classroom. At one end of the continuum, authorial agency, personal authenticity and engagement are maximized (teacher as writer) as the role of instructor is put on hold. At the other end of the continuum,

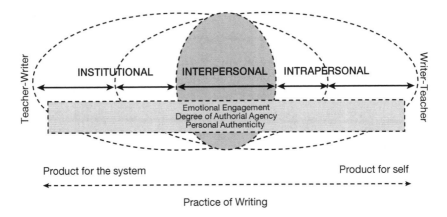

FIGURE 8.1 A diagram to represent a teacher–writer, writer–teacher continuum

institutional pressures and professional demands are to the fore, and the writing becomes a kind of strategy modeling with little personal investment (teacher as instructor). The challenge for teachers is to manage the required fluidity in how they position themselves moment by moment in terms of the roles on offer: writer, facilitator, instructor, accountable professional and so on.

Negotiation and Choice

Choice of topic has been shown by a number of researchers to impact student motivation. Topic is related to the concept of *interest*, which can be either *situational* or *individual*. Situational interest is aroused by something in the immediate context of the learning situation; it might be a particular text shared with the student, for example, or an anecdote. In contrast, the individual interests of a student are a characteristic of that student and are relatively enduring. As Boscolo (2009) points out, a topic can potentially be a source of situational or individual interest, and a topic of situational interest may, for some students, develop into individual interests.

In some ways, Helen's success with her unpromising students (see Chapter 1) was in part because their engagement in poetry potentially maximized opportunities for choice and experimentation. The tasks Helen designed allowed for choice, that is, they spoke to students' individual interests. They allowed students to develop a personal or authentic voice, in the sense that Elbow (2000) talks about it. This permission-giving practice was endorsed in the student evaluations. Hone's statement perhaps put it best: "It was good to be able to write freely about things that are special to us . . ." (Locke & Kato, 2012, p. 74). The provision of choice allowed students space to integrate genuine, emotional responses into their writing.

In the real world (including communities of practice), choice is always circumscribed by various sets of constraints. Effective teachers of writing ensure that students are aware of the constraints they operate within and help them, through their own practice, to make choices while negotiating these constraints.

- Not all topics are suited for treatment in the school context because of their subject matter and the risk of offence. All genres put constraints on the choice of subject matter.
- Because genres themselves can be thought of as sets of linguistic constraints and affordances determined by context and purpose, students need to be taught what they can and can't do in relation to them. Some genres are more tightly constrained than others, for example, a letter to the editor is more tightly constrained than a lyric poem.

The key principle for effective writing practice is to ensure that the scope for choice-making is made explicit to students and that choice-making is always related to rhetorical purpose.

REFLECTIVE JOURNAL TASK 8.2

Drawing on either your own experience or on your observations of other teachers, describe the classroom that, in your view, best fits the description of a community of writing practice. Identify the distinct features or practices that characterized that classroom.

Modeling and Feedback

I want to restrict my use of the word "modeling" here to the demonstration of a skill or set of skills for the purpose of instruction. What is assumed in the act of demonstration is some kind of expertise on the part of the demonstrator. In the context of a community of writing practice, the sharing of expertise through the process of demonstration is crucial to the development in its members of a repertoire of effective writing practices—first through observation, then by discussion, imitation, feedback and ongoing practice. In a community of writing practice, where the hierarchy is flattened, all members are regarded as having expertise to offer to some degree and in some form. While students are usually thought of as apprenticed to the teacher, it is perhaps better to think of them as apprenticed to the community itself, since it is the way the community acts in consort that will finally determine what an individual student learns and how motivated they will be *to* learn.

Structures for Feedback

When Helen shared her poem about her daughter with her class, she was taking a risk by inviting their response without any assurance that they were going to be either respectful or have the resources to offer her comments that were either helpful or insightful. It was an act of trust!

The centrality of response as an element in writing instruction is a feature of Writing Workshop practice everywhere. You will find it operating in professional learning settings for teachers, and you will find it encouraged in the classroom as writing community. One way of understanding why this should be so is to think of *response to writing* practices in relation to the concept of *self-efficacy*. As mentioned in Chapter 1, self-efficacy pioneer, Albert Bandura, defined "Perceived self-efficacy [as] concerned with judgments of how well one can execute courses of action required to deal with prospective situations" (1982, p. 122). This is a broad definition, which can be applied to a large range of human competencies. More specifically, teacher efficacy can be defined as "the confidence teachers hold about their individual and collective capability to influence student learning" (Klassen, Tze, Betts, & Gordon, 2011, p. 21). Because a range of practices impact on student learning, you could argue that overall, a teachers' self-efficacy is likely to be affected by the extent to which they feel confident in respect of these practices, including the ability to write per se.

Where does self-efficacy come from? Bandura (1997) posited four *sources* which have stood the test of time in the literature. Here I relate them to the potential offered by having one's writing responded to in a helpful and productive manner.

1. *Mastery experiences:* We can have our sense of competence enhanced when our writing is confirmed by others as meeting certain success criteria.
2. *Physiological and emotional states:* Sharing one's writing is likely to be accompanied by feelings of tension and anxiety (hopefully) followed by feelings of contentment and release.
3. *Vicarious experiences:* Witnessing our peers manage to write a particular genre with success can give us confidence to emulate what they have done.
4. *Social persuasion:* When others affirm a number of features of our writing, applaud our risk-taking and offer us constructive critique in terms of what we might do differently, we are likely to feel our self-confidence increase.

However, there is a caveat I must offer at this point. It is important to recognize that the potential for these sources of information to enhance self-efficacy is affected by *how* individual teachers interpret it in terms of both the *task* and their sense of their own *competence*. According to self-efficacy researchers, Tschannen-Moran, M. Hoy, and W. Hoy, "In making judgments of self-efficacy, teachers weigh their self-perceptions of personal teaching competence *in light of* the assumed requirements of the anticipated teaching task" (1998, p. 231). The availability of response, however sympathetic, is not a magic bullet. As my own research has shown, a teacher with a low view of her writing capability may not have her self-efficacy enhanced simply by involvement in a response group (Locke, Whitehead, & Dix, 2013). All of this is true for our students. There will be students in your class who may find response groups a daunting challenge, whatever their potential benefits.

That said, I agree with Pritchard and Honeycutt (2007) in their contention that the use of peer groups offers a range of social benefits.

> These include a nonthreatening audience, immediate feedback, experience of a wide range of writing abilities, reduced writing apprehension, development of positive attitudes about writing, increased motivation to revise, increased quantity of writing, more teaching time for individual attention, and development of cooperation and interpersonal skills.
>
> (p. 35)

In what follows, I discuss three kinds of response structure, commencing with response groups, then working with partners, and then concluding with some comments on whole-class response.

Response Groups

As a teacher of writing, you have probably already made the decision whether or not to include the use of response groups as a feature of your classroom practice. Before embarking on their use, I suggest that you address some of the emotional issues related to writing and share these with your students.

- Writing, especially about topics that are close to our hearts or which we feel strongly about, can feel risky. We are putting ourselves out there. It is natural to feel somewhat apprehensive about sharing in this way with others. On the other hand, this kind of sharing is an opportunity for us to develop our relationships with others. (You can see how powerful it is for you as a teacher to model risk-taking with your own students, as Helen did with her poem about her daughter.)
- Even the most accomplished writers experience a degree of writing apprehension. It is natural to feel apprehensive about sharing our writing, especially for those of us who have received negative messages over the years from teachers and others. You might mention that there are still teachers out there whose immediate response to a piece of student writing is to get out the red pen and begin correcting some surface error or other. Tell your students that response groups are *not* like this. Some teachers encourage their students to confront their apprehension by having them complete writing apprehension

questionnaires—not for sharing with others but as a way of keeping a record of their own sense of growing confidence through sharing.

As Pritchard and Honeycutt (2007) point out, the rules for ensuring that response groups operate effectively have developed over a number of years. The following basics have been adapted from these authors, and are the ones that I have encouraged in research projects I have been involved in and with students I have taught:

1. Through a process of negotiation, assign students to a group. These groups may be friendship-based, but there is an argument to be made for random groups that allow for a spread of abilities (this is how the real world operates). Four is a good size.
2. Ensure that students have copies of each other's writing. Having a script allows for notes to be made while students read their work.
3. Ensure the students are comfortably seated and can make eye contact with one another.
4. Student 1 reads his or her piece of writing *without* any kind of self-deprecation or other comment that might influence the peer response. The piece should be read *without* interruption.
5. Once the reading is finished, the respondent on Student 1's right makes a single comment, then the next, then the next, around the circle until a kind of saturation is reached, perhaps after each respondent has made 2–3 responses.
6. Initial responses are to be positive, indicating an idea or way of expressing something that the respondent likes. Encourage respondents to say *why* they like something, "I like your use of the verb 'stroll' because it helps me see clearly how John was walking."
7. Later comments can come under the category of "constructive critique," for example, asking for more information ("I'm curious about what Stella was wearing.") or expressing difficulty in relation to a particular language feature ("I felt confused about your use of present tense in the second and third paragraph.").
8. Student 1 remains silent throughout the response process, perhaps making notes on his or her script.
9. When the process for Student 1 is completed, it is now Student 2's turn, and so on until all group members have had the benefit of the process.

I can't emphasize strongly enough the importance of teaching modeling in relation to response to writing in all its forms. Something I have done with my own students is to work with a student volunteer one-on-one who has agreed to us having a "writing conference" (Graves, 1983) with other students as spectators. I have the student read their piece to me, just as would happen in a response group, while I take notes on their script. (This could be done digitally on some kind of pad and shown to the class on an interactive whiteboard.) I then offer the student various kinds of feedback, focusing on both their ideas and their written expression.

Response groups can be used productively with relatively young writers. In a case study, Dix and Cawkwell (2011) report on an elementary school teacher, Jasmine (a pseudonym), who had begun to think of herself as a writer as a result of positive, response-group experiences in the context of Writing Project professional development:

> It wasn't that scary, we learned to listen to each other and not feel threatened. . .and I appreciated that others made me think about my writing. . . . They commented positively on things I hadn't really thought about.
>
> (Interview, June, 2011, p. 48)

Jasmine taught a class of six-year-old students in a large, rural school. Her pupils exhibited a range of writing abilities but generally felt positive about writing and themselves as writers. Naturally, Jasmine wondered whether her children were mature enough or able to respond adequately to one another's writing? Could they listen, make helpful, evaluative judgments, and suggest other possibilities?

She knew that she would need to teach these skills and proceeded to explore ways of doing this. Her solution was to have a student occupy an "Author's Chair" (McCallister, 2008) and read their writing to her. She responded by what she called a *star* and a *wish*. A *star* was a positive response; a *wish* was a suggestion that the child do something different with their writing. Following this demonstration, she put students in groups of three, each with their own scripts (a picture accompanied by text). "Full of new possibilities and thoughts about making changes to their writing the students revisited and wrote, knowing they had the choice to add in, change words or add on" (Dix & Cawkwell, 2011, p. 51). Jasmine's fears were allayed, as she witnessed the positive effects of these young children's engagement with the response group process.

Working with Partners

Response to text can also be modeled and encouraged in paired learning situations. However, the use of pairs can serve other productive purposes in the classroom writing community. For instance, more able and less able students can be "buddied up" over a period of time in collaborative writing pairs, while working on their own texts. This is a kind of informal peer tutoring arrangement. I say "informal," because it would be giving an unhelpful and incorrect message to suggest that all of the expertise resides with the more able writer. Rather, each pupil becomes a resource for the other, contributing ideas, affirming risk-taking, listening responsively and making constructive suggestions for changes in each other's writing.

In a case study, Barrett (2013) decided to use paired learning with an English class of 13-year-olds in an all-girls, urban high school. One of her study questions was: "How can paired groupings be utilized to provide productive formative feedback on syntactical fluency?" (p. 2). In the course of an eight-week unit of work on "Relationships," the class with their teacher negotiated the task of writing a *scaffolded story* in the romance genre. Barrett decided to pair students with unfamiliar partners of contrasting ability. (In only one instance, there was a clash that needed sorting out.) She wrote of her aims as follows:

> The idea was to promote experimentation, with sentence variety and enjoyment whilst working closely with a peer. These activities began with sentence-combining exercises, developed further with such tasks as changing the order of a sentence, adding adjectives, adverbs and phrases, and later explored changes in tense through a process of re-writing sentences and paragraphs. Often the activities generated a degree of competition between writing pairs, vying with each other to come up with original and innovative sentences.
>
> (p. 6)

Mini-whiteboards were used to encourage this experimentation. To facilitate the feedback process, the class co-constructed a feedback sheet (see Chapter 10), which could be used as a basis for written feedback or to prompt oral comment.

A comparison of pre- and post-intervention writing scores showed that students improved in their ability to deliberately construct sentences for effect. Questionnaire and interview data indicated increased self-efficacy as writers and increased enjoyment of writing, especially among less able students. A number of students expressed positive feelings about the writing they had produced, taking on identities as proficient writers in ways they had not done previously.

Some students shared feelings of initial embarrassment about the paired arrangement, but also indicated that they had overcome this once they began experiencing benefit. Students saw a single partner as offering "more on-going and detailed response" than one would get in a group (Barrett, 2013, p. 95). Students also liked the availability of differing perspectives on their writing as a result of the relationship. Barrett summed up the paired arrangement in the following way:

> In the main, they saw themselves as benefiting from working closely with another student, receiving and giving feedback. This dynamic helped to reinforce learning already undertaken in class exercises. The pair partnerships encouraged them to examine their work closely and consider different ways of expressing their ideas.
>
> (p. 99)

The Whole Class as Audience

In a rhetorical view of writing, audience and context become prime determinants of written expression. While pairs and groups offer writers opportunities for response and feedback in small-scale, relatively safe settings, the whole class offers an opportunity for writers to share a relatively polished piece of writing with a large, perhaps diverse audience. The risk is greater, of course, but so is the potential reward.

Many teachers who have been influenced by Writing Workshop practices have made use of the "Author's Chair" (Graves & Hansen, 1983). For Graves and Hansen (1983), the "Author's Chair" is "where the reader sits" (p. 176) and where professional writers or class members (including the teacher) read texts and, on completion, are asked questions by audience members. These researchers originally conceived of this practice to develop students' awareness of what it means to be a reader as well as a writer, since it introduces them to the sense of what "author" means by having them experience being *read to* by the *actual* writer of a text. Then, through undergoing the process of writing themselves, "They gain the understanding that authors have options through exercising topic choice, revising by choice, being exposed to different types of composing across the range of diverse interpretations of texts" (McCallister, 2008, pp. 456–457).

McCallister (2008), reviewing her experience of using the "Author's Chair" over many years, wrote that it was a daily highlight for her and her students. In keeping with Graves and Hansen's (1983) original contentions, she writes:

> The Chair invited my students to view themselves as authors and helped them understand their options as writers. . . . Not only did the Author's Chair assist in the children's developing sense of what an author (including themselves) does, it strengthened the classroom learning culture by fueling a collective sense of engagement and motivation, enhancing the children's intentions as writers, and developing group cohesion.
>
> (p. 457)

Talk and Metacognition

Back in 1976, British educator Douglas Barnes famously asserted the "learning floats on a sea of talk." This chapter has drawn attention to the key role played by dialogue, especially oral dialogue, in the learning process. As Dyson (2004) asserted, "our written voices are quite literally linked to the oral voices of others" (p. 159). This is especially true for the classroom as a community of writers, which is designed to provide opportunities for each student to become apprenticed to the expertise of others. Collaboration is essentially talk-mediated, though other kinds of mediation are available, for instance, where a student is offered written feedback. But even written feedback is likely to be more effective if accompanied by an oral conversation (or a quasi-oral conversation conducted via some form of digital chat medium).

Vygotsky's (1978) theorizing around the role of social interaction in the learning process has drawn attention to the ways in which collaborative talk contributes to the development of a range of competences, including enhanced competence in writing. Vygotsky's concept of a *zone of proximal development* refers to the gap between what learners can do unassisted and what they achieve with the help of more expert others. For him, language was "the container holding and passing thoughts from one individual to another" (Vanderburg, 2006. p. 375). In a collaborative classroom, where reciprocal assistance is the norm, there are regular instances where students help one another overcome this gap. This kind of scaffolded learning happens informally and also when a teacher has formally identified the nature of this gap for one or more students and deliberately designs a step-by-step learning process to ensure that this gap is bridged (see Chapter 9).

Vygotsky also developed the concept of *inner speech* to refer to a socially triggered process whereby external oral speech is transformed or internalized as mental images (written symbols)—a kind of internal linguistic resource to be drawn on in the translation process, where ideas become articulated as words. From this perspective, learning is dependent on the process of internalization. As Vygotsky said, the development of inner "speech and reflexive thought arise from the interactions between the child and persons in her environment, these interactions provide the source of development of a child's voluntary behavior" (1978, p. 90), that is, behavior they can exercise independently.

Another term for "reflexive thought" is "metacognition." Metacognition occurs when we reflect on our own thinking and learning. For example, if I say, "I have an issue with run-on sentences," I am engaging in metacognition. In Chapter 7 the importance of metacognition as improving students' writing performance was noted. Verbalizing our thinking in talk with others is a powerful means of developing metacognition, since it forces us to draw attention to and sometimes justify our own thinking processes. In interaction with others, we have opportunities to reflect on our thinking, as Jasmine noted, when she commented that I appreciated that "others made me think about my writing." Indeed, Bakhtin would suggest that in the course of this kind of dialogue, our thinking becomes a shared property of the interaction itself and is inevitably changed by it, if only in small ways.

Most of the reflective journaling tasks in this book are invitations to metacognition. In the classroom as writing community, there is no more powerful demonstrator of metacognition than the teacher herself. There is no aspect of the writing process that does not benefit from metacognitive reflection. You might share with your pupils:

• How you identify and address the demands of the target audience of your writing;

- How you decide on topics;
- How you go about structuring an argument;
- The checklisting procedures you use when you revise your writing, and so on.

As mentioned previously, think-aloud protocols are a powerful way of modeling metacognition. When I visited Helen's class during the project reported on in Chapter 1, I used an overhead projector to model the process of revising a draft of a poem I had written about my niece, sharing with them as I went the reasoning I brought to bear on the revision process. I will be returning to this important topic of metacognition in Chapter 10, when I deal at length with the important topic of "metalanguage."

REFLECTIVE JOURNAL TASK 8.3

Think back over the many occasions when you have received either oral or written feedback on a piece of your own writing. First, identify an occasion when this was a positive experience for you. What made it so? Second, identify an occasion when this experience had negative consequences for you, perhaps making you feel bad about yourself as a writer. What happened exactly to make this a negative experience? On the basis of these two experiences, what resolutions would you make in relation to responding to your students' writing?

Further Reading

Building a Writing Community

- Sperling, M., & Woodlief, L (1997). Two classrooms, two writing communities: Urban and Suburban tenth-graders learning to write. *Research in the Teaching of English, 31*(2), 205–239.
- McCarty, M. (2006). How can I as a teacher encourage my students to become a community of writers? *Ontario Action Researcher.* Retrieved August 14, 2013, from http://oar.nipissingu.ca/PDFS/V913E.pdf

Writing and Motivation

- Boscolo, P., & Gelati, C. (2007). Best practices in promoting motivation for writing. In S. Graham, C. MacArthur, & J. Fitzgerald (Eds.), *Best practices in writing instruction* (pp. 202–221). New York, NY: Guilford.

- Bruning, R., & Horn, C. (2000). Developing motivation to write. *Educational Psychologist, 35*(1), 25–37.
- Locke, T., & Kato, H. (2012). Poetry for the broken-hearted: How a marginal year 12 English class was turned on to writing. *English in Australia, 47*(1), 61–79.

Peer Response Strategies

- Dix, S., & Cawkwell, C. (2011). The influence of peer group response: Building a teacher and student expertise in the writing classroom. *English Teaching: Practice and Critique, 10*(4), 41–57.
- Dyson, A. H. (1990). Talking up a writing community: The role of talk in learning to write. In S. Hynds & D. L. Rubin (Eds.), *Perspectives on talk & learning* (pp. 99–114). Urbana, IL.: National Council of Teachers of English.

Author's Chair

- McCallister, C. (2008). "The author's chair" revisited. *Curriculum Inquiry, 38*(4), 455–471.

Vygotsky and Metacognition

- Vanderburg, R. M. (2006). Reviewing research on teaching writing based on Vygotsky's theories: What we can learn. *Reading & Writing Quarterly*, 22(4), 375–393.
- Cremin, T., & Myhill, D. (2012). *Writing voices: Creating communities of writers.* London, UK: Routledge (Chapter 6).

9

WRITING AS PROCESS

This chapter revisits writing as a process, both as involving a range of cognitive operations and as a sequence of tasks determined by the sociocultural context and rhetorical situation. It spells out the implications of what we know about the writing process for the development of learning strategies and shows how an instructional sequence can be constructed using the example of travel writing.

Thinking About Writing as Process

In Chapter 7, I referred to a research consensus that suggests that students are likely to become better, more motivated writers when supported in the writing process. In relation to writing, the word "process" can have a number of meanings, and at the outset, I would like to keep three of these meanings distinct. They are:

1. *A sequence of cognitive operations:* This view of process focuses on the individual and the range and sequencing of tasks required to complete the production of a text, from initially conceptualizing the task and its requirements (including some sense of audience and purpose), to locating appropriate content, transforming that content into language fit for task and finally ensuring that the finished product meets task requirements. Two points need to be made here:

   - Writers differ in the way they manage the sequence of tasks required to produce a text. This is as true of the world of professional writing as it is of the classroom.
   - While this view suggests an overall linear sequencing of tasks, in fact, writing is very much a *recursive* or non-linear activity. Recursiveness refers

to the way in which writers are *not* locked into a set of rigid stages but go back and forth between operations such as content generation, translating, revision and so on (see below). As we will see in Chapter 11, the development of word processors has revolutionized the ease with which writers can work recursively.

2. *A set of steps determined by the contextual demands on a particular genre:* This view of process takes the emphasis away from the individual and puts it on the social context and the genres that characterize textual practice in that context. This is a rhetorical view of process. In terms of sequence, there is an overall logic in the steps required in the production of a particular genre. It begins with a wide-view consideration of a social context, the relationships that occur between participants, and the kinds of textual practice these participants engage in that lead to the emergence of certain types of text or genres. It then moves to the study of a particular genre—a process of familiarization—where the novice begins to develop an awareness of the specific requirements that have to be fulfilled for the successful production of the genre. Finally, it focuses on the systematic mastery of the skills required to meet these requirements and which will ensure that when the text is published and disseminated, it fulfills the functions/purposes appropriate to its intended audience. The additional points made in relation to the sequence of cognitive operations apply here also. The further point needs to be made that different genres lend themselves to differences in the steps required for their successful production.

3. *A sequence of instruction:* This view focuses on the way in which instruction/learning is sequenced in the writing classroom. A premise of this book is that the sequence of learning you plan for your students when you set a writing task will reflect your understanding of process in terms of a sequence of cognitive operations and the steps determined by the contextual demands on a particular genre. As Pritchard and Honeycutt (2007) assert:

> An overall finding of research on the process approach is that all the stages [of the process] must be fully implemented if students are to build a repertoire of writing strategies. Students need structure and sequence and do not benefit from a pick-and-choose approach to teaching writing.
>
> (p. 28)

Avoiding pick-and-choose is not the same as being inflexible about how you sequence instruction. The following is a general guide for planning a unit of work with a writing focus:

• Adopt the *less is more* principle. Writing is a complex, recursive process and takes time.

- Be guided by your understanding of the overall sequence of operations or steps required for the successful completion of a writing task. This understanding will help shape the overall direction of your teaching and ensure that you "cover all bases."
- Make some decisions about productive ways of sharing your *own* writing practices with your students as a way of helping them understand various task requirements.
- Be guided by your understanding of the steps required for the successful completion of a writing task in identifying the writing strategies and skills your students need to apply and eventually master.
- Remember that just as writing is a recursive process, so also is the teaching of writing. Be prepared to revisit certain kinds of strategy instruction, either with the whole class or with small groups, and to use mini-lessons. (Mini-lessons are discrete lessons within lessons, which are highly focused and specific, and which may be spontaneous responses to an immediately perceived learning need (see Weaver et al., 2006.)
- Use formative assessment (see Chapter 12), based on ongoing dialogue with your students, to guide you in identifying their learning needs, in planning ongoing strategy instruction and helping your students in goal-setting and self-regulation (see below). Tell yourself that you won't be able to address *all* of your students' learning needs in a single unit of work.

In what follows, I will begin by discussing a cognitive view of process and its relationship to strategy instruction, and then move to a rhetorical view of process. In doing so, I am not suggesting that these views are radically opposed. Rather, I am suggesting that they bring with them different emphases, and that an understanding of both views serves to deepen a writing teacher's understanding of how her students might be helped through this complex business of composing a successful written text.

INQUIRY TASK 9.1

Using your favorite search engine, enter key words such as: "writing process," "writing as process," and "process approaches to writing." Identify some of the webpages that you discover as a result of your search and the ones you think may reward reading. Skim-read them. What view of writing as process emerges from your reading? Does a single view dominate? Or do there appear to be a range of views? If the latter, how do these views differ in their emphasis?

A Cognitive View of the Writing Process

The view of writing as a process propounded by cognitive psychologists Flower and Hayes (1980, 1981) has been the model that has been most influential for writing researchers and educational practitioners alike (Vanderburg, 2006). As discussed in Chapter 2 (see Figure 2.2), Flower and Hayes identified three distinct processes in their cognitive model: *planning, translating* and *reviewing.* In broad terms, "Planning is concerned with the generation and organization of ideas and with determining the purpose of the text, translation with the forming of these ideas into words and sentences, and revision with the correcting of errors with the improving of text in line with the writers' purpose and intention" (Myhill, Fisher, Jones, & Lines, 2008, p. 15).

Pre-Writing and Planning

As Flower and Hayes (1981) pointed out, the term "pre-writing" became popularized in the 1960s in the work of Rohman (1965) and others who introduced the notion of a staged process of writing (pre-write/write/re-write). When these authors developed their tri-partite view of the writing process, they shied away from the suggestion of rigid sequence in the word "stage," and subsumed the concept of pre-writing under the broad term "planning." I adopt the same stance here. In what follows, I draw on the work of Flower and Hayes (1981) to explore what planning, translating and reviewing mean. I will be using the opportunity to identify as I go the kinds of strategies associated with each aspect of the process (see Table 9.1).

So, what is the difference between a strategy and a skill? A *strategy* is a means of achieving a particular end or goal and is characterized by intentionality or conscious deliberation. In relation to reading, Afflerbach, Pearson, and Paris (2008) contend that

> Control and working toward a goal characterize the strategic reader who selects a particular path to a reading goal (i.e., a specific means to a desired end). Awareness helps the reader select an intended path, the means to the goal, and the processes used to achieve the goal, including volitional control . . . that prevents distractions and preserves commitment to the goal. Being strategic allows the reader to examine the strategy, to monitor its effectiveness, and to revise goals or means if necessary.
>
> (p. 368)

In terms of a writing task, a number of means can be called upon to ensure that the task is successfully completed. A *skill* or *competence* is the ability to do something, habitually and often without thinking, and with speed and efficiency. While the ability to strategize is a skill, a skill is not always a strategy. Knowingly deciding what level of formality to adopt in a piece of writing is a strategy. Being able to avoid excessively colloquial language is a skill.

From a cognitive perspective, the planning process involves writers in forming "an internal *representation* of the knowledge that will be used in writing" in visual or verbal form (Flower & Hayes, 1981, p. 372). They identify a number of sub-processes, which I discuss below.

Generating Ideas

Generating ideas includes the retrieval of information from long-term memory. "Schema activation" is a term used for a strategy for accessing prior knowledge and experience of a topic or task. Teachers can assist in schema activation by the use of prompts of various kinds. In Chapter 3, for example, we have seen how Carolyn Frank used a neighborhood map as prompt for her teachers to help them access childhood memories to feed their writing of personal narratives. Another kind of prompt makes use of *inventories*. An inventory is a list of categories, which allows a process of itemization (and hence content generation). For example, in preparing students to write a memoir, you might have them make an inventory with the following categories: memorable events, important individuals, places, decisions and consequences.

Another kind of strategy is the use of visual stimuli (including evocative prose and poetry) and guided fantasies. I have used the fantasy below with junior high school students as a stimulus for "mythic" writing:

> I want you to imagine that you are standing on the edge of a great forest. Before entering, picture as clearly as you can the shape and color of the trees.
>
> Is there much undergrowth? Is there a path to follow? Can you hear anything? Smell anything?
>
> As you enter the forest, try to keep imagining things sharply in your mind. How are you feeling? Do you notice anything unusual? Are you aware of any animals, birds or insects?
>
> After some time, you are aware that you have travelled deep into the forest. What thoughts are passing through your mind?
>
> Suddenly, you become aware of a person. What does the person look like? Eyes? Facial features? Clothing? Are they carrying anything? Do they speak to you? If so, what do they say?
>
> After a moment, the person beckons you. You follow. Willingly or unwillingly? Where do they take you? Picture the place you are taken as clearly as you can.
>
> The person asks you to do something. What is it? How do you feel about doing it?

Suddenly something unexpected occurs. A danger of some kind is threatening. Imagine in detail where the danger is coming from.

Fortunately, however, you obtain an object that gives you special power against the danger. What is the object? How did you get it? Did someone give it to you? If so, what kind of creature gave you the special object?

Imagine in detail how you use the special object to free yourself from the danger.

I ask students to put their heads on their desks and close their eyes, while I take them through this fantasy, with frequent pauses. I then have them engage in sustained silent writing for around 50 minutes.

As a strategy for generating ideas, *inquiry* has the opposite starting point from the retrieval of information from long-term memory. Rather, it starts from gaps in the known—gaps which in some way trigger curiosity, a wanting to find out. (Having said that, schema activation *can* help identify gaps in existing knowledge.) An early advocate of inquiry-based learning, Wells (1995) illustrated its benefits by describing the learning experiences of a student: (1) The boy's "intense engagement"—the fact that he *cared* about the question; (2) The fact that the impetus for inquiry was *not* a "clearly formulated statement of the problem" but rather a "puzzlement" or "wondering about something observed"; (3). "the way in which a *real* question transforms the manner in which one deals with new information" [italics mine]; and (4). The role played by "communication with others" which takes various forms, including consultation with more expert others and dissemination (pp. 241–242).

As Wells and others have pointed out, inquiry as a strategy calls on teachers to guide students in this content generation process while maximizing independent and negotiated decision-making. Students need to master a range of investigation skills or techniques. These include brainstorming, mind-mapping formulating questions, selecting key words, accessing and retrieving information, skimming, scanning, analyzing, and so on.

REFLECTIVE JOURNAL TASK 9.2

Reflect on your own planning practices. What texts do you write *without* making any kind of notes or plan? What is your attitude to planning? What texts do you plan most for before you start writing? What form does this planning take? What would you say to your class if you were telling them about your own planning practices?

Organizing Ideas

When Flower and Hayes (1981) discuss organizing ideas, they are referring to ways of structuring content fit for audience and purpose (the "current rhetorical task," p. 372). (I will have more to say about audience, purpose and appropriate form in the second part of this chapter, where I focus on a rhetorical view of process.) As a process, organizing ideas has the potential to generate new content, as well as to address issues related to the structuring of content in the text itself.

To some extent, all of us as writers begin the process of shaping our ideas in our heads. However, for a number of text-types, the deliberate use of graphic organizers (see Figure 9.1) is an effective way of organizing our ideas. The box plan organizer that I discussed in Chapter 5 (Figure 5.2) is another example of a graphic organizer. Students need to learn the strategy of tailoring the use of a graphic organizer to a particular kind of text. For example, a "Series line" lends itself to the planning of narrative, where events are set out in chronological order. A "Venn diagram" lends itself to any kind of writing that involves *compare and contrast*. A Venn diagram is a good example of how the use of a graphic organizer can prompt new ideas. Suppose you are demonstrating the use of a Venn diagram to compare and contrast two characters from a story. You will soon find that as similarities and differences are recorded on the Venn chart, the *basis* for these will become clearer.

Goal-Setting

Flower and Hayes (1981) distinguish between *procedural* goals, that is, goals related to the steps to be undergone in order to manage the successful production of a text, and *substantive* goals, that is, goals related to shaping of the text in relation to audience and purpose. Other researchers, for example, Schunk and Swartz (1993) use the term "process goals" for strategies aimed at facilitating an outcome and "product goals" for text to be produced. If your students were working on a letter to the editor, a process goal might be to improve paragraphing by ensuring that each paragraph addresses just one point. A product goal might be deciding on the best way of sequencing the points to be made so that your argument is effective.

In Chapter 7, I referred to Graham and Perrin's (2007) research review, which indicated a strong effect for the strategy of product-goal setting. Additionally, the work of Schunk and Swartz (1993) highlights the effectiveness of process goal use coupled with feedback on progress as a means of improving writing. The researchers explained their findings by noting that: "Students who believe they are learning a useful strategy may feel efficacious about improving their writing and motivated to apply the strategy. . . . Progress feedback conveys that the strategy is useful and that students are becoming skillful" (1993, p. 351).

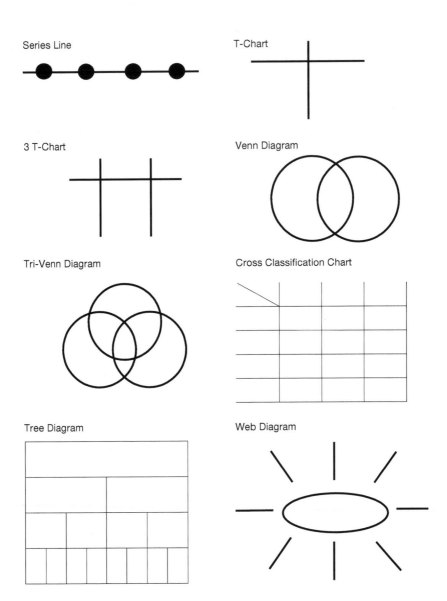

FIGURE 9.1 A selection of graphic organizers

As a strategy, *self-regulation* has a close relationship with goal-setting, though it is better conceived as an aspect of the writing process as a whole. Self-regulation is a kind of self-monitoring, where a writer becomes a reader of his or her own writing, even when it is in draft form, and reflects on the progress they have made in achieving their goals. It is, then, a form of metacognition. A point we should make, in relation to the focus of Chapter 8, is that self-regulation is likely to be more effective when undertaken in the context of a collaborative setting, where others are invited to respond to a writer's text.

Translating

For Flower and Hayes (1981), this is "essentially the process of putting ideas into visible language" (p. 373). In using the word "translation," they are highlighting the gap between the forms language take in the planning stage, either as mental representations or as material texts such as a box plan, list or set of pros and cons. My preferred word is *composition*, since it draws attention to the way in which text production always has a design aspect to it. While some texts rely predominantly on linear prose (a short story, for example), others rely on the juxtaposition of design elements—words, pictures, captions, and so on.

We know that this process is cognitively demanding, putting big burdens on short-term (working) memory—writing is hard work. Words have to be selected, spelled correctly, and incorporated into syntactically appropriate and correctly punctuated sentences. These sentences in turn need to be incorporated into text sections such as paragraphs, and linked to one another cohesively. These sections then need to be sequenced coherently in bigger structures called texts, each with its own layout conventions and rules about appropriate content. It's over-whelming, isn't it!

Myhill and colleagues (2008) draw on the work of Bereiter and Scardamalia (1987) to show how automating various cognitive processes is linked to the development of writing ability, because it frees the working memory to attend to larger textual considerations such as structure and fitness for purpose and audience. Bereiter and Scardamalia described novice writers as *knowledge tellers,* who jump from one idea to the next without establishing much relationship between them. They saw more expert writers as *knowledge transformers.* Expert writers have automated a number of writing skills—words come more easily to them and they have mastered a variety of sentence shapes—and are in a much better position to shape as well as generate content.

What can be done to help novice writers, for whom many skills are yet to become automated. I suggest two strategies:

*   *Using writing frames:* A writing frame might be thought of as a skeleton outline given to students to scaffold various types of writing. Barrett's (2013) scaffold for a "romance story" (see Chapter 8) is an example of a frame. Providing

it to her students freed them from certain structural demands to focus on syntax.

- *Prioritizing:* This is a strategy which can be modeled to students, and involves recognition that in producing a piece of writing, not *all* skills have to be applied at the same time. A simple example of prioritization is to suggest to students when they are writing a poem not to worry about spelling when they are beginning to develop their ideas.

JOURNAL REFLECTION TASK 9.3

All of us have skills that we have not yet automated. Imagine yourself engaging in a writing task. What are some skills that you would consider that you have yet to automate? It might be some aspect of punctuation, or a type of sentence linkage, or the spelling of a particular sort of word. To what extent does this lack of automaticity hinder you when you write?

Revision

Flower and Hayes (1981) associate two sub-processes with revision, *evaluating* and *revising.* As our repertoire of writing skills enlarges and becomes automated, the likelihood increases that we will evaluate and revise our writing as we go, and without too much thought. (I am writing this on a word processor, and the program I use is kind enough to put a red line under misspellings for me and even auto-corrects.) For young or novice writers, however, revision has to be taught and can be a tedious business. (But again, word processing is making it less tedious than it once was.)

Evaluating

Let me begin by distinguishing between two terms, *correctness* and *appropriateness.* The term "correct" suggests that a particular usage (how a word is spelled, how a sentence is constructed or punctuated) conforms with a particular standard that has been prescribed and to some extent standardized. While there are some people who challenge the use of the apostrophe, most of us observe the convention that apostrophes must be used to show possession (e.g., *Tom's* bicycle). To say that a particular usage (e.g., colloquial language in an advertisement) is *appropriate* is to suggest that it is conventionally acceptable and even desirable, given the function of the text and its intended audience. It will be clear from this distinction, that it is very difficult for young writers to learn appropriate usage when they are not engaged in authentic writings tasks, related to real contexts, purposes and audiences.

The concept of appropriateness can be applied at all levels of language use:

- Word level (use, choice and spelling);
- Sentence level (tense, word order, phrase/clause construction, linkages, punctuation);
- Paragraph/text-block level (topic identification, focus, cohesion);
- Whole text level (structure, sectioning, composition, layout);
- Context level (choice of genre, tone, voice, stance, pitch, purpose, function).

There is a lot to learn, so how can we apprentice our student writers in ways that develop their understanding of appropriateness and thereby foster their evaluating skills? Here are a few suggestions, some of which build on previous chapters:

- The use of teacher modeling and demonstration. (Chapter 8)
- The use of teacher and peer response. (Chapter 8)
- The use of exemplary texts. We all learn, often unconsciously, by imitation. Exposing students to excellent examples of the genre they are writing can help develop criteria of evaluation. (Chapter 7)

TABLE 9.1 A cognitive approach to the writing process: some key strategies

Planning	Translating	Reviewing
Generating ideas • Schema activation (use of prompts such as inventories, pictorial stimuli and guided fantasy) • Inquiry (brainstorming, mind-mapping formulating questions, selecting key words, accessing and retrieving information, skimming, scanning, analyzing) Organizing ideas (use of graphic organizers) Goal-setting • Using substantive/ product goals • Using procedural/ process goals Self-regulation	Knowledge transforming Using writing frames Prioritizing	Evaluating • Reviewing appropriate usage • Teacher modeling and demonstration • Teacher and peer response • Exemplary texts • Grading scales (including the co-construction of rubrics). Revision • Revisioning • Checklists

- Have students work with grading scales or rubrics. While there is a downside to the use of rubrics (see Chapter 12), their strategic use can help students develop their evaluative skills. Some teachers who commit themselves to fostering a community of writers engage their students in co-constructing rubrics collaboratively, often based on the study of model texts (Skillings & Ferrell, 2000).

Revising

To reiterate points made earlier, as writers mature, revision is likely to coincide with composing, will be affected by an understanding of appropriateness, and will be enhanced when writers share drafts with a responsive other. Some teachers find the distinction between revision and re-visioning useful. *Re-visioning* can be thought of as a rethinking of one's overall writing strategy. It is focused on macro issues, such as selection and organization of content, rhetorical strategy, overall tone, and so on. Using this term may be useful for students who equate revision with micro-level corrections to spelling, punctuation and syntax.

Is there an argument for locating revision at the completion of almost-finished draft? I think there is. A strategy I employ with my own writing is the creation of an ordered checklist. For me and for other writers, this is a metacognitive strategy, since I (more than anyone) have a sense of the *sorts* of errors I tend to make and which I want to check for systematically. A useful metacognitive task for students is to have them compile such a list for themselves.

REFLECTIVE JOURNAL TASK 9.4

Reflect on your own revision practices. Do you tend to revise as you go or once you have completed a draft? Are there certain kinds of revision you do early on in the composing process and other kinds you postpone until you are almost ready to publish? In sharing with your students your own "philosophy" of revision, what would you say to them?

Situating the Writing Process Rhetorically

Flower and Hayes (1981) did not downplay the importance of situating the act of writing rhetorically. Indeed, they stated that "defining the rhetorical problem [audience, purpose, situation] is a major, immutable part of the writing process" (p. 369). However, because such authors consider writing to be "best understood as a set of distinctive thinking processes which writers orchestrate or organize during the act of composing" (p. 366), they are predisposed to be largely interested in how writers *represent* the rhetorical problem internally.

A rhetorical approach to writing as process moves the emphasis from writing as a set of thinking processes to an emphasis on how writing functions as a socially constructed practice. In this approach (see Chapter 4 and particularly Figure 4.2), I suggest that in understanding and undertaking a writing task, it is helpful for students to think in terms of four levels of consideration. Issues related to a particular level can only be resolved or made meaningful when issues related to levels above it have been resolved. These four levels in descending order are:

1. Context of culture;
2. Context of situation;
3. Macro features (intended audience, purpose(s), language functions(s), typical content);
4. Micro features (including layout, structure, diction, syntax and spelling).

Each of these levels poses particular challenges to a writer and requires different writing strategies (and associated skillsets). Because the levels form a hierarchy (e.g., context of culture needs to be addressed in order to make sense of context of situation), they suggest both an instructional sequence and also a sequence that individual writers can follow when undertaking a writing task.

By way of illustration, I will use the example of travel writing. I have a number of reasons for this choice. Travel writing has broad appeal and in various forms has been around for centuries and can be found in diverse cultural settings. It can accommodate a range of writing styles and functions. It can be attempted by writers of all ages. You don't have to be a professional writer to write about a visit to a place that was new to you and which you enjoyed (or not) for a range of reasons.

Context of Culture

As explained in Chapter 4, the context of culture is the broad socio-cultural milieu in which any text is produced and which constructs practices related to production, reception and dissemination. In this chapter, I referred to the rhetor as the purposeful text-maker or designer, who is aware of the semiotic resources available to him or her as means for achieving the best possible outcome in a communicative situation.

Adopting inquiry as a strategy, and with a focus on travel writing, how might you stimulate student curiosity about cultural factors that impact on such writing? Here are some possible prompts:

*   Have people always traveled? (How do you know?)
*   How have people traveled?
*   For what reasons do people travel?
*   Have people always written accounts of their travels? (How do you know?)

- What sorts of things did they write about? (How could you find out?)
- What form did this travel writing take? (How could you find out?)
- Why do you think some people decided to write about their travels?
- In what ways do you think that traveling has changed over time?

The overall aim here is to invite students to explore *connections* between travel writing as a social practice and the context within which it occurs. At this stage in the process there is, of course, large scope for teachers and students alike to share their own travel experiences. Have the pupils themselves ever written about their travels or a journey they undertook? Are any of them prepared to share travel anecdotes? (You can see how an inquiry strategy like this one will quickly generate ideas.)

Context of Situation

The context of situation refers to the immediate environment within which the production of a text occurs (see Chapter 4). The term "rhetorical situation" generally refers to the immediate situation that prompts the production of a text and addresses such questions as: What drives the act of textual production? What kind of intertextual dialogue is this text participating in? What is the purpose of the text and what means does it adopt to achieve this purpose?

The best way of helping students develop an understanding of the relationship between a text and its context of situation is to select examples (in this case, of travel writing) and to engage students in a relevant line of inquiry, with such prompts as:

- What prompted the author to write this?
- Was the author responding to something that happened to him/her?
- Was the author asked to write this?
- What was the intended audience?
- Are there clues in the way this text was written that can tell us about the author's purpose?

Again, there is scope here for the teacher to model aspects of inquiry as a strategy. For example, students might be invited to consider ways of answering some of the above questions by engaging in an investigation that goes beyond the text under consideration. More importantly, however, teacher modeling is a key strategy for helping students to learn how answers to the above questions can be established on the basis of *internal* textual evidence. (Here we see a clear instance of the productive relationship between reading skills and the development of understandings about writing.)

Rhetorical Unit Planning: A Diversion

When planning units of work, teachers have many different starting places. Some teachers like to plan units around a theme; others may base units of work around a particular kind of text (a novel, memoir, a laboratory report). Rhetorical unit planning (Figure 9.2) is based on principles I discussed in Chapter 4, including:

1.   People construct texts with a view to achieving a desired result with a particular audience.
2.   Text is a product of function (form follows function).
3.   Texts are generated by contexts. Social/cultural contexts call forth texts.

The starting point is to establish, in negotiation with students, a social situation which features, for example, a crisis, a widespread problem of some kind, a proposal that is dividing a community, a campaign of some kind, or a community enterprise. Possible scenarios might be:

*   Developers wanting to build a resort in a location rich in wildlife;
*   A school where a number of students are being bullied;
*   A school deciding to showcase its talent in a cabaret evening;
*   A neighborhood which has seen a spate of attacks on people of a certain cultural group.

Scenarios can be real or imaginary. For any scenario, certain people and groups are identified as typical participants. For example, in the bullying scenario, participants might be bullies, victims, parents, teachers, concerned students, counsellors, mobile phone companies, and so on. There is considerable dramatic potential in many of these scenarios and the potential for students, as they *commit* to the scenario, to take on roles appropriate to the social situation that has been established. When this happens, there is potential for a drama-in-education approach to be adopted, within which writing expertise in relevant genres can be developed *in role* (see O'Neill & Lambert, 1991).

Context of Situation: Travel Writing

The purpose in establishing a context of situation for writing is to motivate students by designing authentic writing tasks and ensuring that issues of audience and text purpose are foregrounded. What kind of scenario might be developed that is relevant to a focus on travel writing? Here are two (I'm sure you can think of others).

1.   You are a member of an expedition that is traveling to a place (real or imagined) that is very different from your own. As an expedition member,

you are charged with recording your experience of this place and its inhabitants in a journal, which you will submit to the expedition-funders on your return.

2. You are a citizen of a town or city (real or imagined) that is experiencing economic hardship. As citizens, you are keen to have tourists come to your town in order to experience what it has to offer: scenic beauty, its unique history, its cultural life and attractions, and so on. At a certain point, you take on the role of a travel writer who is invited to visit your town, savor its attractions, and write an article that will be published in a number of magazines around the world.

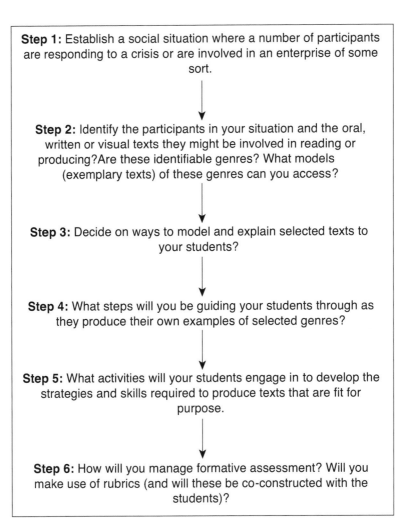

Step 1: Establish a social situation where a number of participants are responding to a crisis or are involved in an enterprise of some sort.

Step 2: Identify the participants in your situation and the oral, written or visual texts they might be involved in reading or producing?Are these identifiable genres? What models (exemplary texts) of these genres can you access?

Step 3: Decide on ways to model and explain selected texts to your students?

Step 4: What steps will you be guiding your students through as they produce their own examples of selected genres?

Step 5: What activities will your students engage in to develop the strategies and skills required to produce texts that are fit for purpose.

Step 6: How will you manage formative assessment? Will you make use of rubrics (and will these be co-constructed with the students)?

FIGURE 9.2 Rhetorical unit planning steps

In what follows, I am going to imagine that we have adopted Scenario 2 with our class, and that we will be focusing on a *travel story* text. We will be positioning ourselves as travel writers, who have visited Ashville (substitute your own destination name) and have gathered enough information to write a travel story about our visit.

Macro Features

Now that a context has been established for our writing task, we need to make another set of strategic decisions if we are to be successful. We have not finished with our examples of travel writing models, since they can offer us strategies for addressing issues of intended audience, purpose(s), language functions(s) and typical content.

Audience

As travel writers, we have been asked to reach as many people as possible with our travel story. However, there are some prompts that we and our students need to address in order to clarify for ourselves who our audience is, such as:

- What kind of people read travel stories?
- Where do they find them?
- What income bracket are these people in?
- What kinds of pastimes do these people engage in?

As we develop a view of our audience, we can make use of the concept of "appeal." An appeal is a fear or desire that typifies a particular audience and hence influences the way we pitch our writing to achieve our purpose. For example, if we decide that our audience has a desire for a "wilderness experience," we can ensure that when we write our travel story about Ashville, we refer to wilderness opportunities in the vicinity.

At this point, if you are interested in a critical literacy approach to writing, you might take a break and reread the material on this approach in Chapter 7. What strategies might a critical literacy teacher bring to bear in addressing the issues of audience, especially with older students? By now, you would have brought a particular kind of questioning to bear in having students study examples of travel stories:

- Who is likely to benefit from this travel story?
- Whose voices do we hear and not hear in this travel story?
- What view of the location visited are we being encouraged to have, and how is this reflected in the way language has been used in this text?
- Are their ethical issues raised by the way this writer has written about this location?

Teachers using a critical literacy approach will want their students to ask similar questions as they orient themselves to the task of writing. In terms of our scenario, it is clear that the good citizens of Ashville would like a very positive view of their town to emerge in the travel story we have promised to write. How truthful are we prepared to be in our portrayal?

Purpose

The study of a range of models will enable students to identify the sorts of purposes served by travel writing. These will vary across texts, but I suggest that in general, travel writing sets out to:

- Vividly evoke a setting;
- Relate in an entertaining way a range of incidents and encounters that the writer has experienced;
- Cover a range of features of a place that are deemed of interest to the target audience;
- Offer a personal, yet balanced appraisal of a place, and recommending it (or not) as a place to visit.

Language Function

Language function refers to the *work* that is being done by a text. Two points need to be kept mind: (1) most texts are multifunctional and (2) the function that the language is serving at one point in a text may be different from the function it is performing at other points. This is important for writing teachers to know, because different skills are required to ensure that different functions are being served. For example, abstract argumentation is likely to require skills in writing complex sentences. Setting the scene in a novel requires skills in descriptive writing, for example, the use of concrete content words such as nouns, verbs, adjectives, and adverbs of manner (see Chapter 10).

A travel story is a good example of a multifunctional text. We are likely to find in it language that functions as:

- *Description:* Passages evoke the place through lively description of its sights and sounds.
- *Narrative:* Accounts of arrivals and departures, events and encounters, with narrative features such as past-tense storytelling and direct speech.
- *Argumentation:* Writing which makes points extolling the virtues of the place or alternatively suggesting reasons for *not* visiting it.

Thinking about language function is important for writers of all ages. All students can be taught how to address the question: "What job do I want this piece of writing to do?"

Typical Content

All genres are characterized by typical content, which relates to purpose and audience. There is scope for choice for a writer setting out to produce a travel story. All the same, one would expect to find settings, incidents, encounters, places of interest and recommendations. Travel stories often contain graphic material such as photographs and maps. How, as a teacher, can we help students generate content for a travel story? If Ashville is an imaginary place, then schema activation prompts can be used. If a real location has been selected, then it is timely to facilitate students in undertaking a process of focused inquiry.

Micro Features

Thus far, in this account of a rhetorical approach to writing as a process, I have discussed strategies for addressing considerations related to the context of culture, the context of situation and textual macro features. In adopting such an approach, we are helping young writers to develop what I term "orientation strategies," that is, strategies that help students orient themselves to the contextual demands of a particular genre. Such strategies are an example of pre-writing, a term that has been associated with the teaching of writing as a process for a number of decades.

We have now reached the "business end" of the process, where the job of composition starts. At this point, our writers (including ourselves if we are writing alongside our students) need to set goals (adopt strategies) related to layout, structure, diction and syntax. While this part of the chapter has set out a rhetorical view of the writing/instructional process, it is here that the strategies outlined in the first part of the chapter (on a cognitive view of the writing process) come into play. Rather than repeat this material, I will make some brief comments about these micro concerns from a rhetorical point of view.

Layout

Travel writing is a "real world" genre. In part our choice of such a genre has been motivated by a desire to engage our students in an authentic task. In my view, having them engage in the production of such a genre while ignoring the way in which travel stories are formatted in the real world undermines this aim. The widespread availability of word-processing and desktop publishing software means that our students are in a position to format their texts in ways that resemble the "real thing." For this reason, I would invite the students to identify some of the formatting features of the model they like most for its visual appeal, making decisions around the use of columns, font style and size, guttering, borders, text-blocks and so on.

Structure

Because students have already studied some examples of travel stories, they will have gained a sense of how professional writers have structured their content. Prompts such as the following can help students develop strategies for addressing considerations of structure and begin developing a range of *structural competencies*:

- Have you noticed a typical structure in the travel stories we have read? For example, are they all organized chronologically?
- Can we use organizers for our research findings in ways which assist us in structuring our material when we begin writing?
- Are there identifiable components in the travel stories we have read, for example, journeys, accounts of first impressions, encounters, historical sites, places to shop, and so on.
- In view of our purpose and audience, what is the best way to sequence the components we have decided to use?
- How can we most effectively plan our travel story *before* we start writing?

I have used the term "component" above to denote a discrete structural element in a text that can be treated independently when thinking about composing it. For instance, an anecdote may be used as a component of an argument, but may also be a component of a travel story. Some components of a travel story can only occur once (e.g., first impressions). Some can occur more than once (e.g., encounters).

Texture

If structural competencies address questions related to the organization of a text as a whole, textural competencies refer to questions of *style*, which is here taken to denote the typical diction (selection of words), syntax and punctuation that characterizes a text at a particular point. Though Coleridge was referring to poetry when he talked about "best words in the best order," such a description could be applied to any style that does its job well.

The following prompts touch on strategies related to the development of *textural competencies*:

- How much can we bring ourselves into this travel story? Can we overdo the use of first-person pronouns?
- In the travel stories we have read, is the diction mostly concrete or abstract? Is there a place for metaphorical (figurative) expression?
- Are there certain sentence shapes that we have found and enjoyed in the examples we have read? How much syntactical variety did we find? Do we want to experiment with different kinds of sentence shape?
- Is there a place for the use of direct speech to make our writing more lively?

As far as revision is concerned, the points made in my discussion of the cognitive view of writing as process apply here. Table 9.2 provides an overview of the strategies alluded to in the second half of this chapter.

TABLE 9.2 A rhetorical approach to the writing process: some key strategies

Context of culture	Context of situation	Macro features	Micro features
Orientation competencies			
Inquiry	Inquiry	Constructing an audience for the task text	Deciding on layout features
Making connections between genre and social context	Identifying aspects of the context of situation of textual models		Identifying typical structures and components
Exploring how genres change over time	Finding evidence in textual models for textual purpose and intended audience	Deciding on appeals fitted to chosen audience	Using organisers for experimenting with organization
Reflecting on one's own exposure to a particular genre		Exploring ethical implications of the stance adopted with the chosen audience	
	Constructing a scenario to provide a context of situation for the writing task	Identifying appropriate purposes for the task	Addressing issues of style in terms of textual function and audience appeal
	Adopting a role as a means of committing to a writing scenario	Deciding text functions	Revising
		Assembling suitable content	

INQUIRY TASK 9.5

Investigate instances in your own setting in which teachers have set up a scenario with their class in order to contextualize and give meaning to a writing task. How did they go about this? Did it appear to make a difference to their students' motivation and achievement? What lessons do you take from your findings in relation to your own future practice?

Further Reading

The Writing Process

- Pritchard, R., & Honeycutt, R. (2007). Best practices in implementing a process approach to teaching writing. In S. Graham, C. MacArthur & J. Fitzgerald (Eds.), *Best practices in writing instruction* (pp. 28–49). New York, NY: Guilford.
- De La Paz, S., & Graham, S. (2002). Explicitly teaching strategies, skills, and knowledge: Writing instruction in middle school classrooms. *Journal of Educational Psychology, 94* (4), 687–69.

Self-Regulation

- Zimmerman, B. & Risemberg, R. (1997). Becoming a self-regulated writer: A social-cognitive perspective. *Journal of Contemporary Educational Psychology, 22*(1), 70–101.

Writing Frames

- Subramaniam, K. (2010). Integrating writing frames into inquiry-based instruction. *Science Educator, 19*(2), 31–34.

Process Drama Strategies for Learning

- Fraser, D., Aitken, V., & Whyte, B. (2013). *Connecting curriculum, linking learning.* Wellington, NZ: NZCER Press.

10

ADDRESSING (AND ANSWERING) THE "GRAMMAR" QUESTION

The chapter begins with a brief account of the issues that lay behind the so-called grammar wars. It then draws on current research and theorizations of practice, to suggest a range of ways that the explicit use of grammatical knowledge can contribute to the writing process. Underpinning this chapter is a recognition that acts of reading are intimately bound up with acts of writing and an assumption that the use of metalanguage is rendered most meaningful and productive in the context of a rhetorical approach to writing and writing instruction.

Beyond the Grammar Wars

In Chapter 7, I suggested that teachers who adopt a personal growth approach to writing often view teaching grammar formally as a waste of time. Before we write off this position as irresponsible, let's reflect on the way we all *acquire* various kinds of language competence *without* the intervention of formal schooling.

We know that our brains are "wired" for syntax and that, before we arrive at school, we can already produce correctly formed, complex sentences as unique instances of the deep, sentence-related grammar of our mother tongue. We can do this because our brains interact with the mostly oral language we hear in our immediate environment. The richer this oral language environment, the more advantaged we are as language acquirers, in terms of our developing vocabularies and our sentence-producing competence. As discussed in Chapter 2, reading and writing practices are acquired outside of formal schooling, and from a young age. These practices include the particular repertoire of genres, which characterize the particular language community we grow up in.

Wherever language acquisition and learning (including learning to write) take place, in home or in school, there is a developmental aspect which has been investigated by many researchers. In a comprehensive review of this literature, Myhill, Fisher, Jones, and Lines (2008) suggest that

> It is evident that many linguistic constructions appear to increase in length or complexity with age, including sentence length, clause length, and the noun phrase. A less pronounced, but nonetheless significant trend, is for there to be an increase in diversity, whether that be through greater use of the passive, variety of vocabulary, or an increasing ability to use an alternative to the personal pronoun in the subject position.
>
> (p. 9)

In considering writing development, however, a number of points need to be kept in mind.

- It can be more useful to think of development in terms of competence than age, comparing mature and novice writers, rather than older with younger ones.
- Using complex syntax should not be equated with writing effectiveness, since mature writers know how to tailor the degree of syntactical *variety* to the genre they are writing.
- However, less effective writers are likely to experience difficulties with subordination and clause linkages.
- A focus on whole-text competence (e.g., in relation to cohesion) is as important as a focus on sentence-writing ability, when considering issues of writing development.

As writing skills are acquired and learned, a *tacit* or *implicit* understanding develops around language usage (van Gelderen, 2006). We can *know* we are writing a correct conditional complex sentence without being able to "name" the construction as containing an adverbial clause nor the various word classes and their function. The "grammar wars" which have raged for more than a century have been fought over two questions:

1. Do teachers need an explicit knowledge of language to teach writing?
2. Are students likely to become better writers if they have an explicit knowledge of language?

You will notice that I have shifted from the term "grammar" here to the phrase "knowledge of language." I have done so because there is a tendency to equate grammar with syntactical competence and explicit knowledge of terms related to syntax. As I will be arguing, *knowledge of language* or *metalanguage* (having a language to talk about language) needs to extend to the four levels of consideration I discussed in the second section of Chapter 9: Context of culture, context of situation, macro levels and micro levels.

Explicit Knowledge of Language for Teachers

Do we as teachers need to have an explicit knowledge of language to teach writing? The blunt answer is "Yes." The argument goes like this. Teachers need to think about the writing process in order to plan an effective, instructional sequence. In order to think about writing (metacognition) a language is required (meta-language). The specific questions, then, for all teachers become: "What kind?" and "How much?"

As a teacher of writing you may be aware that there are different "grammar" schools. Some schools develop their systems from the "bottom up," that is, they start from small units of language such as morphemes and words, then move to combinations of words in phrases, clause and sentences, and then to a consideration of how sentences become combined in larger units like paragraphs and other kinds of text section. If you are a teacher in the United Kingdom, the United States or New Zealand, you are likely to be mostly exposed to bottom-up grammars. If you are an Australian or South African teacher, then you may well have adopted for your own use systemic functional (or Hallidayan) grammar, which can be described as "top down," because it begins with the text/context relationship and derives its description of language features at various levels in terms of how these function in terms of this relationship. In this book, I am not advocating exclusively for one of these.

What I do argue, however, is that the way you understand the writing process and how you build your instructional sequence on this understanding will determine the kind of metalanguage you use to think about your teaching. So will the curriculum area that you teach. As Figure 10.1 suggests, a teacher's professional knowledge of his or her subject includes knowledge of the genres his or her students need to master. Conversely, his or her knowledge of the genres related to his or her subject enhances overall professional content knowledge. Similarly, a teacher's professional knowledge of subject-related pedagogy (e.g., how to teach Science) enhances and is enhanced by his or her professional knowledge of the writing-related pedagogy of his or her subject (e.g., how to teach laboratory reports and write these reports themselves). A teacher's knowledge of his or her subject area includes its content-specific terminology (e.g., photosynthesis, electron, inertia and so on). A teacher's professional knowledge of writing-related pedagogy will also include knowing a metalanguage that is tailored to the specific genres that are relevant to his or her subject.

What will have emerged, I think, is that teachers who are influenced by cognitive approaches to the writing process, build up their metalinguistic knowledge by focusing on such processes as planning, translating and reviewing. This metalinguistic knowledge relates to the strategies outlined in Figure 9.1. In my work with teachers, however, I encourage them to take a wide, rhetorical view of the development of a personal metalanguage, because such a view accommodates but goes beyond the considerations that apply in a cognitive view of the writing process.

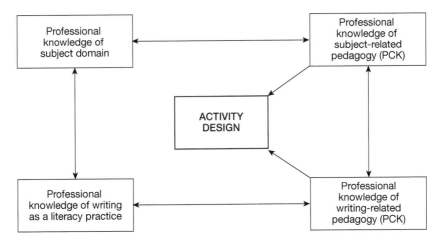

FIGURE 10.1 Professional and metalinguistic knowledge

INQUIRY TASK 10.1

Take this opportunity to turn back to Chapter 9 on writing as a process, as it provides an overview of two approaches to the writing process, one with a cognitive emphasis and the other with a rhetorical one. You will be aware that Chapter 9 uses a considerable amount of metalanguage. As you skim through this chapter, note the instances of metalinguistic use you come across. Do you notice any differences between metalinguistic usage across the two approaches? What are they? How would you explain this difference?

While teachers don't need to have the *same* mastery of language, it can be very useful to map one's own metalinguistic knowledge and use. Be assured that you probably have a wider metalinguistic knowledge than you give yourself credit for. The following are some useful headings to think about the terms and concepts you know and perhaps use with your students.

• Words in relation to the relationship between texts and their social context;
• Words in relation to the overall structure of texts;
• Words in relation to sentence-level structures;
• Words in relation to the words used in texts (diction);
• Words in relation to the prosodic and kinesic (body language) features of oral or audio-visual texts;
• Words in relation to the visual/pictorial aspects of texts.

Table 10.1 shows the terms identified by a high school English teacher, whom I'll call Bronwen, in relation to the different textual levels suggested by the headings above. Bronwen had been involved in a project on teaching literature in the multicultural classroom, and you will see this reflected in the terms she identified. When asked how confident she felt about her own "technical" vocabulary, she had written in a reflective profile: "I don't worry when I don't know. I explain to students that we're in a changing world with changing language. So sometimes I discover new words only when they do."

REFLECTIVE SELF-STUDY ACTIVITY 10.2

Use the headings above and Bronwen's example to map your own meta-linguistic profile. I suggest that you set up a table with the same headings as Table 10.1, using the same textual levels. Write as many terms as you think of immediately. For example, a level 1 term might be "genre," a level 2 term "rhyme scheme" (for a poem), a level 3 term "complex sentence," a level 4 term "noun" or "metaphor," a level 5 term "intonation," and a level 6 term "close-up." If a term is one you make a practice of using with your students, put it in bold or color it. Return to this activity from time to time as you recall other terms you know or terms you have learned.

Explicit Language Knowledge in the Writing Classroom

In the remainder of this chapter, my focus will be the place of metalinguistic knowledge (grammar in the widest sense) in helping students become better writers. I will be returning to a question raised earlier: Are students likely to become better writers if they have an explicit knowledge of language? In what follows, I argue that the answer is yes, particularly if the explicit use of metalanguage is framed by a rhetorical view of writing instruction (see Chapter 9).

To begin laying the foundations for this argument, let me make a number of points based on the research and professional literature:

1. The decontextualized teaching of a formal, traditional, school grammar with an emphasis on error identification and correction does not improve student writing and is likely to be demotivating (Andrews et al., 2006). Such teaching is likely to characterize the practice of teachers who adopt a narrow, skills-based version of the rhetorical or textual competence discourse.

2. Strident opposition to the incorporation of "grammar" into writing instruction has impeded productive professional debate around the kinds of instructional models that would be enhanced by use of a metalanguage. This

TABLE 10.1 Textual levels and metalinguistic terms

Textual level	Metalinguistic term
Text in relation to social context	Cultural context, context of situation, discourse, story, genre, position (as noun and verb), version of reality, representation, partial, rhetoric, function, purpose, audience, intention, novel, stage-play, lyric poem, ballad, short story, biography, autobiography, review, hyperfiction, literary, literature, literary non-fiction, tragedy, comedy, absurd, existential, fate, theme, hero, anti-hero, concrete poetry.
Text structure	Script, structure, plot, form, exposition (or orientation), rising action, suspense, initial incident, problem, complication, predicament, dilemma, choice, conflict, resolution, turning point, climax, catastrophe, denouement, foreshadowing, motif, point of view, first person, second person, third person, restricted access, omniscient, composition, architecture, meter, stanza, paragraph, coherence, cohesion, setting, character, characterization, mood, atmosphere, hypertext, hotlink, animation
Sentence-level	Syntax, sentence (various types), phrase (various types), clause (various types), rhythm, meter, iambic, non-metrical, non-syntactical pause, lineation, indent, dialogue, indirect speech, reported speech, punctuation, run-on sentence, semi-colon, full stop, capital letter, tone, exclamation, question-mark
Word-level (diction)	Figures of speech, metaphor, simile, symbol personification, oxymoron, hyperbole, metonymy, figures of sound, assonance, alliteration, onomatopoeia, synaesthesia, sound coloring, formal, informal, literal, figurative, concrete, abstract, image, visual, aural, tactile, olifactory, gustatory, rhyme, redundant, tautology, synonym, antonym, word class, noun, verb, adjective, pronoun, determiner, conjunction, pronoun, preposition
Prosodic and kinesic (body language) features	prosodic features, transcription, pitch, pause, pace, volume, intonation, emphasis, tempo, paralinguistic features, kinesic signals, body language, body movement, gesture, facial expression, stance
Visual/pictorial features	Symbol, icon, index, composition, layout, border, font, size, bold, italic, plain, point, gutter, text block, autoflow, highlight, perspective, disposition, point of view, close-up, medium shot, long shot, establishing shot, distance, angle, objective, subjective, element, relationship, mock up, mise-en-scène, costume, make-up, lighting, pagination, justification, alignment, tabulation, bullets

opposition has sometimes come from teachers who adopt a personal growth discourse of writing, because, they argue, that any preoccupation with "grammar" wastes time, is demotivating, and is a distraction from the real business of fostering creativity in students (Locke, 2009).

3. Explicit knowledge of language facilitates writing development when it enhances a writer's ability to make informed choices around usage, particularly in relation to audience and purpose. This is the point of view adopted by Martha Kolln (1996), who has long advocated the use in classrooms of what she calls a *rhetorical grammar*, for different purposes "from the remedial, error-avoidance or error-correction purpose of so many grammar lessons. I use rhetorical as a modifier to identify grammar in the service of rhetoric: grammar knowledge as a tool that enables the writer to make effective choices" (p. 29). This view is likely to characterize the practice of teachers who adopt a broad, contextually oriented, rhetorical or textual competence discourse.

4. The task of translation (turning ideas into text) is cognitively demanding. Expecting a focus on metalanguage during translation is probably unreasonable. It is best to encourage such a focus in the pre-writing/planning stage and as much as possible view the translation process as utilizing skills which have been automated and as focused on the shaping of content at sentence and text section level.

5. Reference to a metalanguage has particular value when the writer becomes the reader of his or her own text, either as an audience, or as sharing texts with others in response groups/pairs or when conferencing with a teacher. Having a metalanguage empowers a writer to reflect on his or her language choices in relation to audience and purpose. Teachers who adopt a critical literacy discourse of writing instruction are likely to endorse a focus on metalanguage, because they see it as enabling young writers to see that the language choices they make are central to how they position their audience to see the world in particular ways. Are they using language in ways which demean women or position them as having less power or importance than men? Does their language use suggest that a particular kind of person is inferior? And so on.

6. There is evidence that certain kinds of direct strategy instruction with a focus on syntax can foster writing ability. In their systematic review, Andrews and colleagues (2006) concluded that sentence-combining had a "positive effect on writing quality and accuracy," indicating that this strategy suggested "a pedagogy of applied knowledge—at its best, applied in situations of contextualized learning; at its worst, drilling" (pp. 52–52). This finding is an instance of the argument made by Weaver and colleagues (2006), that explicit grammatical knowledge is best taught at the point of need and that such knowledge opens up choices to writers in their acts of composition. They assert that "teachers can more successfully teach less grammar with better results by focusing on key grammatical options and skills in the context

of actual writing, throughout the writing process and over time" (p. 77).

7. The mastery of formal, standard writing discourse happens best where the vernacular usages of students are respected and treated as a resource. If these usages are manifestations of a recognizable dialect, then that dialect should be treated on equal terms with "standard English." There is research to suggest that explicit grammar-based strategies such as *contrastive analysis* and *codeswitching* are effective in teaching writing in classrooms with a large proportion of English dialect speakers (Wheeler & Swords, 2006).

8. It is hard to conceive of a writing classroom where some kind of metalinguistic talk does not occur at all! However, the evidence suggests that the effective use of metalanguage in the writing classroom depends on the teacher's knowledge of language and their confidence in using it in situations where they are modeling their own writing identities and practices and engaging in process-related strategy instruction. If, as a teacher, your ideal is a classroom as community of writing practice (Chapter 8), then you will recognize the key role of metalanguage in developing metacognition through the conversations you encourage your students to participate in. Pritchard and Honeycutt (2007) use the term "composing vocabulary" to refer to the language students use to talk about their writing. They make a number of useful points:

- This vocabulary development is inductive and accumulative, growing out of the conversations that take place related to texts students and teacher are producing.
- Students should be encouraged to build and own their *own* composing vocabularies (metalinguistic glossaries).
- A composing vocabulary can include terms that refer to affective aspects of the writing process (e.g., "fear of the blank") as well as terms that might not be found in formal grammar books (e.g., "showing not telling").
- Composing vocabularies need to be tailored to the age and stage of the students.

In Chapter 9, I outlined four levels of consideration that come into play when we situate the writing process rhetorically.

1. Context of culture;
2. Context of situation;
3. Macro features (intended audience, purpose(s), language functions(s), typical content);
4. Micro features (including layout, structure, diction, syntax and spelling).

In what follows, I focus on each of these in relation to metalanguage and writing instruction.

REFLECTIVE JOURNAL TASK 10.3

Which of the above 1–8 points speak to you as a writer and teacher of writing? As you think about your own practices as a teacher of writing, how do one or more of these points relate to what happens in your classroom?

Context of Culture and Situation

In Chapter 9 I used the example of travel writing to model ways in which students need to orient themselves to the rhetorical demands of this kind of writing. Am I a more effective writing teacher if I explicitly use the terms "context of culture" and "context of situation" with my students? The first point I would make in response to this question is that understanding these metalinguistic concepts myself has had (I would argue) a positive effect on choices I make when planning my instructional sequence. With high school students, I introduce these terms into the classroom conversations when I want my students to develop an understanding of the term "genre" (see the discussion of memoir in Chapter 4). However, if you look at my modeling of prompts in relation to contexts for travel writing in Chapter 9, you will notice that I don't actually use these terms. Particularly with young or novice writers, my position is that an understanding of context of culture and context of situation can be developed without my *actually* introducing these terms into the classroom conversation. I would resolve this apparent contradiction in my practice in the following way:

- If my aim is to have my students think about how they orient themselves to a particular type of writing, then I can do this without explicitly using the terms "context of culture" and "context of situation."
- If my aim is to have my students develop a metacognitive understanding of what "genre" is, then the explicit use of these metalinguistic terms will assist this.

The broad principle, then, is that decisions around the metalanguage to introduce into the classroom conversation are best determined by the kind of metacognitive activity you want to encourage your students to engage in.

The term "intertextuality" is another example where decision-making on its explicit use depends on your aim as a teacher. In Chapter 4, I cited Fairclough (1992a) as stating that an "intertextual perspective stresses the historicity of texts: how they always constitute additions to existing 'chains of speech communication' consisting of prior texts to which they respond" (p. 85). It is a useful strategy for *all* writers, young and old, to reflect on the way the texts they produce in some way relate back to other texts they have encountered. However, a teacher can have students engage in activities which have them engage in exactly this kind of reflection without using the term "intertextuality." However, if your aim is to have (senior) students reflect on the way texts function contextually, then you have a reason to introduce them to this term to aid their metacognition.

REFLECTIVE JOURNAL TASK 10.4

I came across the following terms in perusing my discussion of contexts for travel writing in Chapter 9: "written account," "form," "social practice," "anecdote," "inquiry," "strategy," "rhetorical situation," "intertextual," "dialogue," "production," "purpose," "textual," "context," "author," "audience," "textual evidence," "scenario," "participant," and "genre." Which of these would you expect to use *explicitly* with your students in the context of your writing program? Which of these terms are a focus of your writing instruction but not used explicitly with your students? Which of these terms are *not* a focus on your writing instruction?

Macro Features

In addressing the macro features of a text, a teacher is having her students address considerations around intended audience, purpose(s), language functions(s), and typical content. Terms such as "purpose" and "content" can be taken for granted as having a role in all writing classrooms, so I will restrict myself here to some comments on audience and language function.

Audience

There are a number of terms you will find useful in helping students develop strategies for thinking about their writing goals in relation to a target audience: "appeal," "voice," "stance," "point of view" and "position."

The word "appeal" is common in general usage. In the last chapter I referred to travel writing as having broad appeal. In relation to the practice of writing, an *appeal* is a fear or desire in the target audience, which we can "appeal" to in the way we pitch our writing in order to achieve our purpose. For us as writers, it is closely connected with how we view our audience. What are their interests? If we are constructing an argument, which points are likely to influence the particular audience we have in mind. A useful exercise you can do with students is to present them with a display advertisement, and ask them to decide, on the basis of the words and images used: who the target audience is; and what is being appealed to in this audience (e.g., a fear of not being one of the crowd, a desire to be thought of as beautiful)?

I discussed the concept of "voice" in detail in Chapter 3 and won't repeat myself here. A widespread definition of voice in the American context is:

> Voice is the writer coming through the words, the sense that a real person is speaking to us and cares about the message. It is the heart and soul of the writing, the magic, the wit, the feeling, the life and breath. When the writer is engaged personally with the topic, he/she imparts a personal tone and flavor to the piece that is unmistakably his/hers alone. And it is that individual something—different from the mark of all other writers—that we call Voice.
>
> (Education Northwest, 2014)

I suggest that you reflect on these various definitions/understandings, and decide for yourself the meaning(s) you would want to bring to the word when you use it with your students. Some teachers find the word *stance* preferable to "voice," since it enables a focus on textual features such as style, tone and point of view, rather than the "writer behind the text." DiPardo, Storms, and Selland (2011) view stance as describing, "how effectively the writing communicates a perspective through an appropriate level of formality, elements of style, and tone appropriate for the audience and purpose" (p. 178).

Point of view is another concept which is part of general usage but which has a more technical meaning, particularly in relation to the writing of narrative. If we ask someone: "What's your point of view on capital punishment?" we are using the phrase "point of view" in its general sense. This is the sense we are likely to use if our students are writing argumentative texts. However, if our students are writing a narrative genre such as a short story, then we need to consider using the term "point of view" in a more technical sense while recognizing the age of our young writers.

Point of view answers the question, "Through whose eyes or from what vantage point am I viewing the action that is being presented in this story?" When young writers engage in narrative, they tend to write from a *first person* point of view, that is, they will use the pronouns "I" and "me" to establish themselves as the point of view through which we (their audience) view the events they recount. From an early age, of course, all of us were exposed to *third person* narratives. (Fairy tales are almost always in the third person.) Here a somewhat more "objective" vantage point is established by the use of pronouns such as "he," "she," and "they." Here are some key points for your students to reflect on (metacognitively) as they decide strategically on a suitable point of view for a narrative:

- A first person narrative can offer a reader immediate access to events, but this access is restricted to what the narrator (the "I") knows either directly or via another character.

• A third person narrative can allow for more than one point of view on the action. For instance, it allows for an omniscient point of view, where the narrator is somewhat detached (an "eye in the sky") but can move rapidly from one setting to another and forwards and backwards in time. It can also restrict itself to the point of view of one or more characters who are involved in the action, and move between them, *restricting* a reader's access to what these selected characters experience or learn via other characters.

If your writing classroom is going to feature the writing of prose narrative, then you will need to find a way of engaging your students in talk around choice of point of view. It is a decision to be made by any writer of such texts *before* the act of composition begins. The decision has a huge impact on how the reader will experience the story being told. You will also notice that I have introduced some other examples of metalanguage in this paragraph, all of which have a part to play in your classroom talk: "pronoun," "access," "first and second person," "action," "omniscient," and "restricted."

We also find the word "position" in general usage. (I hope as you read this that you are in a comfortable position.) The term "position" has a key role to play in argumentative writing. In Chapter 5, I defined it (along with other important terms in relation to argumentation) as where we stand on some issue. If you are a teacher with an interest in critical literacy approaches to writing, the term "position" will occupy a key place in your classroom talk. You will find yourself using it with your students when you are having them study model texts, with such prompts as: How is this text *positioning* you to view x? As students write their own texts, you will want them in planning to think through the ways they will be *positioning* their readers to sympathize with one perspective rather than another.

Language Function

As discussed elsewhere, *language function* is the work the language is doing at any point in the text. In engaging students to think about the function of their writing, you will find yourself using verbs. Major language functions are to argue, to describe and to narrate. But there are many words that can be brought into the classroom conversation about language function: to persuade, to entertain, to amuse, to provoke, and so on. (I'm sure you can think of lots more.)

Micro Features

Textual micro features include layout, structure, diction, syntax and spelling. Most of the academic and professional literature about the use (or not) of metalanguage in the classroom focuses on syntax, which will be my major focus in this remaining sub-section. But first, some general points:

- When considering the use of a metalinguistic term or concept with your students, ask yourself whether *you* find it useful in reflecting metacognitively on your own writing process. If it *is* useful, then it is likely to be of use to your students.
- Would the use of this term help facilitate your students' strategic choice making and goal setting? If so, there is a case for using it.
- Would having this term deepen your students' understanding of a particular genre or of some aspect of the writing process? If so, a case can be made for its use.
- Finally, how many of the above grounds are relevant to the age and stage of your students? One or more? If so, consider yourself as having the green light.

These general considerations can be applied to any metalinguistic terms and concepts, regardless of whether they relate to layout, structure, diction, syntax or spelling. These categories are, of course, themselves metalinguistic and apply to any print genre. In Chapter 6, however, I made the important point that in the digital (hypertextual) age, we have to rethink categories such as these, and replace them with terms such as "architecture," "composition," "verbal diction and syntax," "sound elements," "thematic organization" and "cohesion." (Some terms related to these categories appear in Bronwen's list in Figure 10.1.)

Layout refers to the arrangement and formatting of elements on a page (see Chapter 4 and compare with the term "composition"). In engaging students in talk about layout, you will be asking them to make connections between the design of their text and their overall intentions. For some genres (e.g., a display ad or a poster), it is useful to have students produce a *mock-up* as a step in the planning process.

In contrast, *structure* refers to the relationship of elements to one another within a whole text and is the way a writer decides to organize his or her ideas (content). In my example of travel writing in Chapter 9, I have modelled some of the prompts that can be used to facilitate student thinking in relation to structuring this kind of genre. However, as you think about how you might approach the issue of structure with respect to a particular genre (let's use the example of a short story), avoid the pitfall of rigid formulas. In the case of prose fiction genres (memoirs, short stories, autobiography, potted biographies, travel writing), my advice is to think in terms of structural components or elements and to see these as susceptible to sequencing in different ways. In Chapter 4, I identify eight structural elements for narrative, all of which have a place in your conversations around story-writing with your class. While an element such as predicament is likely to occur early in a story (and often provide a "launch" for the narrative), a narrative can have a number of complications and resolutions.

In relation to argumentation, I agree with Andrews (1995) that the widespread use of the *expository essay* has had a stultifying effect on the teaching of argumentative writing. There are a number of reasons for this:

- The expository essay with its rigid structure (introduction, 5 to 6 body paragraphs and conclusion) has distracted from the lively way argumentative genres are "done" in the world outside the schoolroom via essays, columns and newspaper opinion pieces.
- These paragraphs themselves are often taught in a formulaic way, each body paragraph with a topic sentence at the beginning, followed by an explanation and example (the SEX formula).

Andrews (1995) identified from his own research an impressive list of 24 potential structural elements for argumentation, which included, for example, *statement, reason, instance, example, credo, dilemma, rhetorical question* and *analogy.* I'm not suggesting you use all these. Rather I'm suggesting you rethink the terms you use to discuss the structure of argumentative writing with your students.

REFLECTIVE JOURNAL TASK 10.5

What genres that function in some way as arguments do you use with your students? How do you generally go about modeling to your students how to think about the structuring of argumentative writing? On the whole-text level? On the level of text section (paragraphing)? If you were to rethink your practice, what would you consider doing differently?

A term which is sometimes confused with "structure" is "cohesion." Myhill et al. (2008) make the point that cohesion is a whole-text issue and "involves links between sentences rather than within sentences and is central to the principle of articulating complex ideas" (p. 9). They cite research suggesting that writing teachers have tended to underestimate the importance of cohesion in relation to the quality of writing. You may find that the grammar reference book you generally use does not discuss cohesion. If you subscribe to a top-down grammar such as systemic functional grammar, you will find that cohesion is a major topic and that you will be provided with various categories of cohesion. Whether you choose to use these terms with your students is another matter. In my own experience, an alertness to issues of cohesion is often enough for teachers to alert their students to them in their writing. In general, conversations around cohesion are likely to occur in the feedback stage and are best conducted in one-on-one dialogue between teacher and student.

Although not all punctuation is for syntactical purposes (i.e., marking relationships between elements in sentences), I will be discussing punctuation and syntax under the same umbrella. (The decision to use an exclamation, for example, is not related to syntax.) The general points made at the beginning of this section apply here. Here are some additional ones:

- Different grammars use different categories for "parts of speech" or "word classes" (my preferred term). These categories can be useful as a way of being concise in your feedback to students. ("That's a really evocative verb.") It is useful knowledge for students to realize that a word's class relates to the function it fulfills in a sentence. (Depending on function, "flower" can be a noun or a verb.)
- While user-friendly terminology can be helpful with young students, avoid using terms that are misleading. For example, calling adjectives "describing words" is misleading, because any *content word* (verb, adjective, noun or adverb of manner) can be descriptive in function.
- Different grammars use different terms for word-groups within sentences. For example, traditional grammars use terms such as "subject" and "predicate." Systemic functional grammar uses the terms "theme" and "rheme." This book is not about telling you what grammar to use. All of us begin with the grammars we were exposed to through our formal education and then diversify as we find terms that are helpful in our thinking about writing.
- You can't avoid reference to punctuation marks when you teach writing. However, in respect of punctuation, remember that your conversations without students are likely to be more meaningful if they are rhetorically focused.
- Conversely, in conversations around syntax, you may find that while you as teacher are guided by a metacognitive understanding that utilizes a metalanguage (*noun phrases, appositive phrases, coordination, subordinate clause, subordinating conjunction*, and so on), you may find that you can conduct a meaningful and helpful conversation with your students (especially young ones) that doesn't use such terms (substituting terms such as "linking words") or uses them sparingly.

In Chapter 8, I mentioned Barrett's (2013) work with paired learning. As part of this study, she taught sentence combining as a strategy to help her students master complex and longer sentences. Like other studies on sentence combining, her study suggested a modest impact on students' writing in terms of its syntactical complexity (see Chapter 7). In reviewing the literature on this strategy, Myhill et al. (2008) suggest that sentence combining "should be embedded within a writing curriculum which takes account of individual writers' developmental needs, which focuses learners' attention on the effects and impact of different sentence structures in writing, and which avoids exercise-driven strategies" (p. 40).

In Barrett's (2013) study, it is noteworthy that the teaching of sentence-combining skills was contextualized to a unit of work where students were positioned as members of a community of writers and inducted into peer response practices. Indeed, to support students into these practices, Barrett and her students negotiated a "Feedback Guide," which reflects the metalanguage she expected her junior high school students understand and use in their writing conversations.

TABLE 10.2 Feedback guide (Barrett, 2013)

Feedback Guide

Write on the story and/or make comments on sentence structure, punctuation and structure. Use the following examples as starters.

Sentence structure
- I can't understand this sentence
- There seem to be words left out here (You could suggest a word)
- This is a run-on sentence
- This sentence could be joined (and, but, or, because, etc)
- You could begin with a conjunction here
- You could invert the sentence
- Try adding adjectives before this noun
- You could use an adverb after this verb like . . .
- Try adding a phrase to give more information
- The tense has changed
- This is the wrong preposition
- Try a shorter/longer sentence for more effect

Punctuation
- Try using direct speech here
- You need a comma here
- The direct speech needs commas
- This needs a question mark
- Use a capital here
- Why does this have a capital?

Structure
- This should be a separate paragraph
- This is not ended well
- This seems unfinished
- Why did she/he do this?
- Explain (briefly) why this happened
- Add more description here

INQUIRY TASK 10.6

What categories for diction (words) are used in the grammar reference book you usually use? How do these compare with the categories used in Chapter 4 ("Selection")? Which categories are useful to you in framing your own thinking about word selection in writing? Which terms would you encourage your own students to use in their writing conversations?

The final topic under micro features is diction. In this regard, I refer you to the discussion of "Selection" in Chapter 4 under the topic of "Lyric poetry," and the Inquiry task below.

Further Reading

Grammar and Writing

- Locke, T. (2010b). *Beyond the grammar wars: A resource for teachers and students on developing language knowledge in the English/literacy classroom.* New York, NY: Routledge.

Sentence Combining

- Saddler, B., & Graham, S. (2005). The effects of peer-assisted sentence-combining instruction on the writing performance of more and less skilled young writers. *Journal of Educational Psychology, 97*(1), 43–54.

Teaching Argumentation

- Andrews, R., Torgerson, C., Low, G., & McGuinn, N. (2009). Teaching argument writing to 7- to 14-year-olds: An International review of the evidence of successful practice. *Cambridge Journal of Education, 39*(3), 291–310.

11

WRITING AS TECHNOLOGY, OR WRITING AS ICRT

This chapter begins by arguing that the term "ICT" (Information and Communication Technologies) should be replaced by the term "ICRT" (Information, Communication *and* Representational Technologies). It reviews some of the research, which has investigated the productive and not-so-productive ways in which the teaching of writing has changed through the integration of various ICRTs in classrooms. In particular, it focuses on word processing, multimodal storytelling and blogging.

Writing as an ICRT

Some years ago, I was involved with colleagues at the University of York undertaking systematic reviews into the impact of ICT on literacy (see Andrews, 2004). Over the years, however, my preferred abbreviation has become ICRT; Table 11.1 elaborates and in part justifies this decision.

These groupings in Table 11.1 are not mutually exclusive. Nor is the list of verbs in column 2 exhaustive. None of these functions is technology dependent, unless one expands one's definition of technology to regard the human linguistic and vocalizing capability as a technology. The human memory enables information storage and retrieval, the human body communicates in a variety of ways, and the human mind makes sense of the world and has ways of representing that sense to itself without the need of technology.

There are two ways we can unpack this abbreviation in words:

1. Technologies for information, communication and representation;
2. Technologies of information, communication and representation.

TABLE 11.1 ICRT functions

Broad function	Specific function
Information (processing)	• record • code • organise • store • access • retrieve
Communication	• send • receive • acknowledge • address • appeal
Representation	• shape • express • order • construct • render • position

The first of these tends to suggest a kind of separation between technology and function, and to view the function as having a kind of priority. In this view, we have a message to communicate and look for a technology to do the job effectively. The second view tends to suggest a more symbiotic (or reciprocal) relationship, with the suggestion that function and technology are mutually penetrative, with function not just simply preceding a choice of technology, but rather technology as productive of particular forms of informational, communicational and representational functioning. In this book, I adopt the second of these positions.

As we think about the place of technologies in our writing classroom, there are some broad questions we need to reflect on with our students as we approach the task of composing a particular text:

- What functions does this text serve?
- What representational resources (modalities) support these functions?
- What technologies best enable these representational resources (see Chapter 6) to be assembled in the production of this text?
- In what ways do particular technologies affect the content this text is communicating?

A useful metalinguistic term for classroom use is "affordance" (see Chapter 6), which relates to the idea that particular modes and technologies *allow for* particular sorts of meaning-making. A further question to guide our use of ICRTs, then, is: What are the affordances of this technology? What sorts of meanings does this technology allow us to make?

As an example, let's imagine that our class is constructing a nature trail pamphlet, as discussed in Chapter 6.

- *What functions does this text serve?* Primarily informational. However, there is also a function that relates to distribution? It *is* possible to put a nature trail pamphlet on a website as a pdf, thus allowing a visitor to download it and print it off. However, there is a convenience value in having a printed and folded version of a nature trail pamphlet: it can be carried around in one's hand on the trail itself and, when folded, can be easily slipped into a jacket pocket.
- *What representational resources (modalities) support these functions?* Verbal language in the form of print is particularly suited to the kind of commentary that is required for each of the trail stations. However, the visual language of the map works best to represent the trail itself.
- *What technologies best enable these representational resources (see Chapter 6) to be assembled in the production of this text?* Let's bear in mind that most texts are produced in stages. We may decide that for the mock-up stage of planning, the technologies of paper (medium) and pencil (hardware) offer suitable affordances. We can experiment with different ways of folding the paper until a final decision is made. With folds in place we can use a pencil to test locating the various components of the pamphlet. It's easy to rub out pencil lines. Once major layout decisions have been made, we may decide that for the actual production of our pamphlet, we will use a desktop publishing program such as Adobe Indesign. In this choice, we are influenced by such affordances as:

  o The ease of working with columns;
  o The ease of shaping, wrapping and flowing text (e.g. in making text blocks);
  o The range of lines that can be used for borders (framing);
  o The ease of inserting, moving and resizing pictorial components.

  While desktop publishing software is our major technology, it is likely that we will be looking to ancillary technologies affording us the ability to produce copy for the pamphlet itself: digital cameras; tools for producing graphic items such as the map and logos; scanners for digitizing hard-copy graphic items for insertion, and so on.
- *In what ways do particular technologies affect the content this text is communicating?* It is likely that both we and our students have experienced the way in which the more we explore a particular kind of software (word processing, video editing, presentational, desktop publishing), the more we become aware of the range of its affordances. Typically, when we start using certain software,

we master basic functions and then progress over time to a mastery of other features. When this happens, our realization of these other affordances provides us with increased choice about *how* to shape the content of our text. And when we *do* engage in reshaping, we will find that changes in content occur. For instance, if in a nature trail pamphlet we reduce the words in a text block and "wrap" the text around a graphic, we have moved from a reliance on verbal text to a situation where verbal text and graphic interact with each other.

REFLECTIVE JOURNAL TASK 11.1

Think of one genre that you commonly produce with your students in your classroom. Use the questions in italics in the bulleted list above to reflect on the relationship of this genre with the technologies that might be utilized in its production.

Technology and Process: Word Processing

In Chapter 9, I discussed two approaches to the writing process, cognitive and rhetorical, each with its own version of steps or stages. At this point, let me conflate these and suggest the following as broad, identifiable stages in the writing process:

1. Pre-writing (addressing issues related to context of culture, context of situation and macro features);
2. Generating and organizing ideas (through schema activation and inquiry, for example);
3. Planning (addressing micro feature such as layout and structure);
4. Translating (assembling words and other material in the making of the text itself);
5. Revising.

The key point I want to make in this section is that, for ourselves and our students, our choice of technology should be determined by the demands of *each* stage of the process. Our job is to help our students match the demands of the task with the affordances of the technology. Let me illustrate this with reference to word processing.

I am writing this chapter using Microsoft Word. That makes me part of a club of around 500 million people worldwide! Microsoft released its first version of this program, Word 1.0, in 1983. In the 1990s the software began to take its version name from a year (e.g., Word 2007) and become part of the Microsoft Office software compendium. In the 1990s, I used both Word (as a word processing program) and Pagemaker (as a desktop publishing program). These words in parentheses say much about comparative affordances. "Word processing" suggests affordances related to the ease of managing verbal text (sequencing, rearranging, correcting, enlarging, deleting, shaping) on a screen through using a keyboard and mouse. "Desktop publishing" suggests affordances related to the book-like quality of a text as product (formatting whole documents, managing columns, text-blocks, text-wrap, pagination and so on). Through the 1990s, word processing programs increasingly incorporated the affordances of desktop publishing programs. Increasingly also, word processing became an affordance of other applications (such as web authoring programs) and other devices (such as mobile phones).

The use of word processing programs has become so ubiquitous that we perhaps take it for granted. That is why you're more likely to find research related to its use in the classroom-writing program in the late 1980s and 1990s. In discussing the place of word processing in the writing classroom, I will be drawing on insights offered by the research of Snyder (1993, 1994) and Haas (1996).

Snyder's Australian research involved two eighth grade English classes, of comparable ability academically and technically, in a girls' secondary school, taught by the same teacher (Jacqui), under two conditions: one class used pens for the writing program and the other used word processors. Differences in technology aside, both classes had the same program—genre-based teaching which involved students writing a narrative, argument and expository report. Snyder had three research aims: (1) to investigate the impact of different tools on the texts themselves; (2) to compare the impact of different tools on the writing process itself; and (3) to explore ways in which these different tools appeared to impact on the classroom learning environment. Findings included:

- The demands of the genre had more influence than the technology on composing processes, with students planning least for narrative and most for argument. When revising narratives students tended to focus on surface features; when revising argument, they focused on clarity of meaning.
- Word-processed writing was generally better than penned writing, at least for argumentation and reporting.
- Jacqui's role underwent a shift in the computer room, with less expository teaching, less spontaneity and more "guide-at-the-side" facilitation.
- Talk in the computer room became progressively less over time but was generally more task-centered than talk in the "pen" class. Students appeared more engaged in the word-processing class.
- A "community of writers" began to develop in the word-processing class, with a considerable amount of peer-mediated learning occurring (1994, p. 156).

From a contemporary perspective, aspects of this study seem dated. I suspect the contemporary norm would be a classroom either with desktop computers freely available, or with students owning word processing devices (laptops or tablets) so that when they engage in writing, the use of a word processing program becomes just one choice to be made during the composing process. While students in the control class had no access to word processing tools, it's not clear from the report whether students in the word processing class ever used pencils. In terms of the writing process, my impression is that the group using the word processing program, once given their assignment, began composing straight away on a screen. There doesn't appear to have been a lot of emphasis on pre-writing, though planning is mentioned. However, it's unclear how the students using the word processing tools planned their argumentation (on computers? with paper and pencil?). There is clear evidence of the way in which revision is facilitated by the use of the word processor, with students remarking on how onerous this process is with paper and pen. It is unclear whether response groups were a feature of Jacqui's teaching. However, it is interesting to note how students in the group using the word processing program responded differently to the way in which the computer effectively put their writing *on display*. On the one hand, this appeared to prompt informal peer response and constructive feedback; on the other hand, it also appeared to prompt nosiness and unhelpful comment.

Haas's (1996) research investigated the relationship between the materiality of writing (tools and media) and composing processes. Like Snyder, she was interested in differences that seemed to emerge around pen and paper and computer-based writing. What she brought to her research was a belief that "Technology is the place where culture and cognition meet—technologies are cultural artefacts imbued with history, as well as tools used by individuals for their own motives and purposes" (p. 229). A corollary of this is that "By supporting one kind of physical writing activity rather than another, technologies can affect writers' thinking processes in very real ways (p. 115). In other words, the affordances related to a particular tool impact on the way writers think during the composition process. In Chapter 10 (on grammar), I argued that metalinguistic awareness (and metacognition) productively enter the composition process at a point where writers become readers of their own text. Related to this argument is Haas's useful concept of "sense of the text." As we write, says Haas, we develop a "mental representation of the structure and meaning" of our text, which draws on our sense of the compositional process and what the text actually looks like as an artefact in progress.

Haas's research findings included:

1.   Reorganizing a text can be difficult when a writer has only a partial view of the text on a computer screen.
2.   Some writers find it easier to proofread hard copies than text on a screen.
3.   A number of writers reported an impaired "sense of text" when they wrote on computers, that is "writers' spatial understanding of text was eroded when they read that text on a standard personal computer" (1996, p. 69).
4.   There was less planning when a word processing program was used.

5.   There was less conceptual planning and more sequential planning when a word processing program was used.

Haas makes the point that word processing programs don't make it easy for writers to engage in "spatial" planning by using boxes, arrows and other diagrammatic representations in the form of notes. She also surmises that because we compose faster with a word processor, we may be tempted to begin writing without engaging in adequate pre-writing and planning (cf. Snyder, 1994).

REFLECTIVE JOURNAL RASK 11.2

What do you find interesting about the research findings I have just reported on? Given the high likelihood that you are an experienced "word processor," do you identify with any of the strengths and limitations that this research indicates in regard to the use of word processing programs for writing? If so, what are some implications of this for you as a teacher of writing?

In light of the previous discussion, I offer a number of points to be borne in mind as you have your students use some form of word processing tool in the composition process. You will also find these points pertinent for other kinds of text-production technologies.

- Have a range of tools available and model to students why you might choose one technology over another in relation to a particular aspect of the writing process. Don't abandon pencil and paper.
- Anticipate that different stages of the writing process may call for different technologies with different affordances. Use the term "affordances" with your students as you explain your uptake of a particular technology. For example, you may decide to model the use of a box-plan for planning argument by drawing with a felt-tip on an overhead transparency and projecting it for class comment as you do it (see Chapter 5).
- Likewise, demonstrate to students how different genres are likely to call for different technologically based affordances (as per the example of the nature trail pamphlet discussed earlier in this chapter).
- Communicate an understanding that not everyone is the same in terms of *how* they view the affordances of a particular tool such as the word processor. Many people find it easier to rethink their organization and make corrections on a hard copy of their text. That's OK.
- Don't let the availability of word processing programs mean that you reduce time spent on pre-writing.

- Encourage experimentation with ancillary affordances. For example, as I write this I am aware of an application in my word processing program called "Stickies." I often use these when I write to summarize material from, say, a pdf, before incorporating it into the text I am working on. Such a strategy is easy to model with your students. (You can also, of course, use paper sticky notes as a way of making notes on hard-copy texts.)
- Think carefully about the way in which word processing and other technologies feature in your classroom environment as you work on building up a community of writers. Remember that technologies also have affordances that relate to aspects of human interaction. Seek your students' views on ways different technologies support collaborative relationships around writing.

Multimodal Storytelling

This section connects with a number of themes addressed in Chapter 3—narrative, voice and identity. At the same time, it recognizes the way in which digital technologies offer new affordances for storytelling that have implications for the writing classroom. These affordances are in two broad categories:

- *Production:* As discussed in the previous section on word processing, technologies impact in various ways on the composing process, facilitating certain tasks but also affecting the kind of thinking we engage in as we perform these tasks.
- *Genre:* Digitization is affecting our society's repertoire of genres in all sorts of ways. For example, breaking news stories in the online version of your daily newspaper may carry a link inviting readers with relevant information to email the online editor. This is a new genre feature. Animation software such as Flash has led to a new poetic genre—the animated poem.

While there is a growing academic literature on digital storytelling, I have used the term "multimodal" in the heading because it is important to recognize that a multimodal story that is composed for or largely using a digital platform such as PowerPoint or iMovie can use non-digital technologies as part of the composition process.

To highlight the value of multimodal storytelling in the writing classroom, I will use the case of Michael, the pseudonym for an African American fifth-grade student in a culturally diverse New York school located in a largely African American neighborhood. Michael was a participant in a case study based in his class, which investigated:

1. the "range and variation of literacy practices" present;
2. the "literate identities" students progressive assumed "within the context of a yearlong multimodal storytelling project"; and

3. how multimodality can lead to a rethinking of compositional practices. (Vasudevan, Schultz, & Bateman, 2010, p. 443)

Prior to the case study, he would have been described as a loud but academically disengaged student. For Michael a gulf existed between his out-of-school literacy practices and what was expected of him in the classroom context. As part of the study's sequence of writing projects, Michael:

*   wrote a "Where I'm From" poem;
*   created a "Memoir Pocket" as a prompt for oral and written storytelling;
*   participated in a neighborhood walk in a "Buildings Speak" project, photographing buildings/spaces that were meaningful to him for later use as visual content for stories told orally;
*   collected sounds from his community using an audio or video recorder to contribute to a "Sound Portrait", and finally
*   composed a multimodal story about himself as reader and writer using iMovie video editing software.

This was not a well-off school, and all these projects utilized relatively straightforward and inexpensive technologies, such as disposable digital cameras and voice recorders. What you notice immediately about this sequence of activities is the way in which Michael's neighborhood context is brought into the frame of his classroom writing program. The researchers termed this move beyond the classroom walls as "breaking the frame" (p. 453), a move which enabled Michael's community-based funds of knowledge to become a resource and motivator for his writing (Moll, Amanti, Neff, & Gonzalez, 1992). It also enabled the *space* of the classroom to expand to include those meaningful, semiotically rich places/spaces of various neighborhoods (for example, doorways and stoops). The "Memoir Pocket" also enabled the integration of personally significant artefacts into the writing program (Honeyford, 2013).

Multimodal storytelling draws on a wide range of affordances of both digital and non-digital technologies and modes, including written language, sound, visual images, color, dress, bodily movement, gesture and stance. Culminating in the composition of a multimodal story, involvement in the project enabled Michael and other students to "author new literate identities," what the researchers called "authorial stances," in their classroom writing communities (Vasudevan et al., 2010, p. 443). Our identities cannot be separated from our relationships and the contexts we inhabit. Vasudevan and her colleagues defined *authorial stance* as the "practice of taking on literate identities and claiming a presence as an author and narrator of one's own experiences" (2010, p. 461). Because the learning program enabled Michael to bring his out-of-school identities (as son, brother, concerned neighborhood citizen) into his classroom, these identities became resources to reconfiguring his authorial stance in a positive way. He became an expert on his neighborhood and the authority on his own life as "writer and raconteur" (p. 453). As a tech-savvy young person, he also became an expert for his peers.

INQUIRY TASK 11.3

Do you use multimodal storytelling with your own students? If so, what technologies do you find enable this kind of storytelling? If not, inquire whether there are other teachers in your school who do. Or, search online for examples of teachers who have introduced multimodal storytelling into their writing programs. What advantages do these teachers claim for this kind of storytelling? What are some of the challenges?

Blogs

My decision to conclude this chapter with a consideration of blogging stems in part from its popularity as a digital, Web-based genre that affords an author the opportunity to post, usually in reverse chronological order, entries which offer commentary or reflection on an issue that is important to her/him. The genre, summed up in Figure 11.1, also affords comments to be posted by site visitors, for links to be made to other sites and pages, and for other features as well.

Advocates for the use of blogs in the writing classroom (e.g., Penrod, 2007) draw attention to the fact that writing is the blogger's core skill. Penrod (2007) notes that "Part conversation, part diary, part narrative, part letter, part newspaper article, a blog performs diligently and reliably in whatever type of writing the blogger undertakes" (p. 44). The blog differs from other social media sites such as Facebook, where writing tends to be spontaneous, uncrafted and subservient to a highly regimented template with an emphasis on graphics and affordances such as chat. Having said that, the *blogosphere* still affords writers considerably multimodal potential in terms of the insertion of images and sound files. In addition, in keeping with the rhetorical focus of this book, a blogger has to consistently consider his/her audience. Therefore, the blogger as rhetor, addressing a potentially huge public, will be attentive to matters of modality, style, tone, pitch, emphasis, arrangement, and so on. Above all, they will know how to communicate their message concisely and avoid longwindedness.

Penrod (2007) notes that "Because a blog is a personalized learning environment in a real setting, it simulates a genuine writing activity" (p. 14). It also allows for students to exercise choice in terms of content. Further, because blog entries often require content to be supported by research, there is a real sense in which blogs encourage a process of writing to learn, regardless of the academic discipline the blog is related to. In this regard, it is an excellent writing-across-the-curriculum tool.

1. *Context of culture:* While journals and logs have been around for centuries, the "weblog" or "blog" emerged in the late 1990s when web authoring tools became manageable for writers who were not especially tech savvy.

2. *Context of situation:* People develop blogs for a variety of reasons, from personal diarying to raising issues publicly on particular topics.

3. *Function/purpose:* Common functions include: social commentary, topic exploration, keeping a journal of significant autobiographical events, providing an interactive site to launch a product. Whatever the function, a blogger seeks to establish a personal voice through the adoption of a particular tone or stance, but without revealing private or confidential details about themselves.

4. *Typical content:* Content can be thought of under two headings:
   a. content related to the blog function. A political blog is likely to focus on political events and provide comment on them.
   b. a range of modalities and features: written text, images, sound files and links to other websites.

5. *Features:*
   - *Architecture:* A blog is three-dimensional, allowing for links to webpages that are part of the blog itself (e.g. an events page on a band blog) and elsewhere on the Internet.

   - *Composition:* Most bloggers utilize a pre-existing template, allowing for the placement (layout and formatting) of such blog elements as a banner, menu bar, postings (i.e. the key written component of the blog), archive, graphic elements, sound links and so on. Most templates are underpinned by an arrangement of columns (three or four) in a similar way to desktop publishing.

   - *Verbal diction and syntax:* The inherently public nature of the blog demands a writing style that is plain, respectful, clear and engaging and a formatting style that effectively utilizes color, font and size. It also demands a degree of self-protection through the use of a pseudonym. Headings and subheadings are used to attract attention and signal content.

   - *Graphic diction and syntax:* Images need to be appropriate and free of copyright restrictions. In addition, the relationship of image to written text needs to be carefully thought through.

   - *Sound elements:* Recorded spoken language, sound effects and music.

   - *Thematic organization and cohesion:* While a predetermined template means constraints, effective blogs are thematically and esthetically organized in uncluttered ways that are coherent and cohesive, that is, there is a clear pattern of relationship between the elements that make up the composition of a page and a clear rationale for hotlinks that are embedded in any page.

FIGURE 11.1 The blog as genre

INQUIRY TASK 11.4

Visit the Youth Voices website (http://youthvoices.net/front), a collaborative school-based social network which commenced in 2003 and is managed by a group of National Writing Project teachers. After exploring the site, make your own list of the qualities exhibited by the student writers who have contributed to this site. As a teacher, list some of the potentials that you see engagement in blogging offering your own students. What difficulties do you foresee in introducing blogging into the writing classroom?

Further Reading

Word Processing and Writing

- Snyder, I. (1993). The impact of computers on students' writing: A comparative study of the effects of pens and word processors on writing context, process and product. *Australian Journal of Education, 37*(1), 5–25.

Multimodal Storytelling

- Vasudevan, L., Schultz, K., & Bateman, J. (2010). Rethinking composing in a digital age: Authoring literate identities through multimodal storytelling. *Written Communication, 27* (4), 441–468.
- Sylvester, R., & Greenidge, W. (2009). Digital storytelling: Extending the potential for struggling writers. *The Reading Teacher, 63*(4), 284–295.

Blogs in the Writing Classroom

- Allison, P. (2009). Be a blogger: Social networking in the classroom. In A. Herrington, K. Hodgson & C. Moran (Eds.), *Teaching the new writing: Technology, change, and assessment in the 21st-century classroom* (pp. 75–91). New York, NY: Teachers College Press.

12

WRITING ASSESSMENT AS NEGOTIATING POWER AND DISCOURSE

This chapter begins with an example of how the evaluation of writing occurs in the world beyond the education system. It then provides an overview of assessment practice in the educational setting, noting that there are a number of discourses (philosophies) of assessment. Using the metaphor of a servant to two masters, it suggests that most teachers are caught up in the dilemma of negotiating two broad discourses of writing assessment practice. The first of these, extrinsically oriented discourse, is "framed" or "constructed" by high-stakes testing or standards regimes that have been government mandated. The second, intrinsically oriented discourse, relates to the professional content knowledge of the teacher who understands the nature of writing and how it is best evaluated for the good of individual students. This second discourse favors assessment strategies that are formative in their intent, negotiated with students, task-specific and based on "real-world" texts and practices.

An Example From the "Real" World

In 1978, I received a letter from the Senior Script Editor (Drama) of Radio New Zealand who wrote:

> Thank you for OPEN AND SHUT which has been read with interest, but which I am sorry to have to reject herewith. The problem with the whole play is that it is skeletal—there is no depth in either the play or the characters. ... I think you have fallen into the trap of making your characters serve as mouthpieces for you as a writer, too often.

As you can see, the writer had evaluated my radio script writing and found it wanting. The discourse the letter writer was operating out of was, broadly, *arts criticism,* that is, the criteria of evaluation were derived from review practices in the arts. Regardless of the discipline, arts criticism operates on the basis of assumed standards of excellence, which are sometimes covert and sometimes overt, and which are often hotly debated. I could not complain that the letter-writer did not declare his hand. He informed me in no uncertain terms that plays need characters with "depth" and that they shouldn't be a playwright's "mouthpieces."

The letter is a reminder of how evaluation occurs in the world outside of the school setting when a written text is submitted to an editor or reviewer of some kind. I was not given a grade for my radio script. Nor was my writing assessed against a general standard for script-writing. However, it is clear that the editor assessed my script against specific criteria, for example, in relation to characterization. It was also clear to me that he had viewed my characters as shallow and that I was using them as mere "mouthpieces."

REFLECTIVE JOURNAL TASK 12.1

Select a written genre that can be found in the world outside of school as well as in classroom settings (e.g., a memoir, a lyric poem, a report). Without seeking ideas from somewhere else, write down some criteria that characterize an excellent example of this genre. When you have done this, reflect on *where* you got your ideas from. (Possible answers would be from: some kind of writing workshop; from participation in a community of practice related to employment; from a college course; from a book or web-based resource on writing; from criteria that have their origins in the educational system.)

Assessment in the Educational Context

Teachers at all levels engage in three types of assessment:

- *Diagnostic assessment* enables teachers to discover what students know and can do. It can be used also to identify difficulties particular students might be having and contribute to the design of activities to meet those students' needs. There are all sorts of ways diagnostic testing can be done, from nationally referenced tests to a simple question and answer session with a student.
- *Formative assessment* is integral to the teaching and learning process and is used to provide students with feedback to help them take control of their learning and set realizable goals, and to help teachers scaffold complex tasks (such as learning a new written genre). It can take a variety of forms, such as written comment on a draft, conferencing, or the use of rubrics. It can also involve peer-teaching via response groups and pairs.

- *Summative assessment* is usually carried out at the end of a block of study to provide an indication of the student's achievements. High-stakes assessment that contributes to a qualification can be thought of as a type of summative assessment.

Harlen (2006) neatly sums up the distinction between formative and summative assessment by noting that the purpose of the former is to "help learning" and the purpose of the latter is to "summarize what has been learned" (p. 103). In practice, the boundary between diagnostic and formative assessment is often blurred, since both are concerned to identify and make use of information that can contribute to the learning process.

Harlen (2006) also provides a sentence that provides a wider picture of the assessment process, because it points to conditions that need to be in place *before* decisions are made in respect of *how* "evidence" is to be used and by *whom*:

> It is generally agreed that assessment in the context of education involves deciding, collecting and making judgments about evidence relating to the goals of the learning being assessed.
>
> (2006, p. 103)

Let me translate this statement into a series of steps, which may or may not be enacted in actual classroom and program contexts.

1. Learning goals are established and agreed upon.
2. A student engages in tasks or activities which are goal-oriented, that is, which are oriented to the goals established and agreed upon.
3. A decision is made in respect of *what* kind of information/data ("evidence") will allow for a determination of how well the student has attained the agreed-upon goals.
4. This information ("evidence") is collected, often via a process of analysis, which involves the scrutiny of aspects of a document or object or behavior that the student has produced in relation to a task or activity.
5. This information may or may not be quantified for the purposes of measurement.
6. There is resort to criteria, either implicit or explicit, as a basis for ascribing value to some aspect of the evidence collected as indicating the extent to which learning goals have been attained.
7. On the basis of these criteria, one or more judgments are made (either for formative or summative purposes).
8. Depending on the use to be made of these judgments, they are communicated in some way to the student or other stakeholders in the assessment process.

This articulation of the assessment process is, of course, highly abstract. That is, it is not remotely particularized to a particular school subject or domain of knowledge.

Throughout this book, I have been using the word discourse, drawing on Fairclough (1992a), to denote "a practice not just of representing the world, but of signifying the world, constituting and constructing the world in meaning" (p. 64). These eight steps are telling a story about how assessment is to be conducted. Like any discourse, this one has its own "markers" or "traces"—words such as "goal," "evidence," "judgment," "formative," "summative," "feedback," and so on. The contributors to the book Harlen's chapter is drawn from have backgrounds and expertise in assessment in educational contexts. They are not literary critics or reviewers! Moreover, these contributors and others can be seen as belonging to or associated with a particular discourse community—the Assessment Reform Group (ARG)—which has been in existence in Britain since 1988. The group has its own agreed-upon description of "assessment of learning," namely:

> the process of seeking and interpreting evidence for use by learners and their teachers, to identify where the learners are in their learning, where they need to go and how best to get there.
>
> (ARG, 2002a, cited in Gardner, 2006, p. 2)

Like any discourse, the one this definition encapsulates tells a particular story about assessment as a kind of process with certain means and ends in relation to both teachers and students. It is a discourse I have some personal sympathy with, but it is not the only assessment discourse out there in the current social context having an impact on what happens in classrooms.

Serving Two Masters

In 1753 Carlo Goldini wrote a play entitled *Servant of Two Masters,* wherein the main character, Truffaldino, is obliged to go to extraordinary and side-splittingly funny lengths to maintain the illusion of serving one master when he is in fact serving two. I suggest that most of us teaching writing in an educational system are servants of two masters. On the one hand, we are held extrinsically accountable to an assessment regime that expects us to assess student writing in a particular way. This regime is the product of government mandate, either at country or state level. On the other hand, there is another kind of accountability—intrinsic—whereby we engage in assessment of our students' writing in terms of criteria that have another source altogether and which are a part of a teacher's disciplinary content knowledge. Many teachers experience this dual accountability in terms of a dilemma (Wohlwend, 2009).

The knowledge about writing and what makes it effective that underpins the first half of this book relates to this latter kind of disciplinary knowledge. It does not have its origins in a particular education system. Rather it derives from a range of disciplines, including cognitive psychology, applied linguistics, socio-cultural theory, literary criticism and cognitive neuroscience, to name a few.

In this chapter, I distinguish between these two masters by naming the first *extrinsically oriented discourse* and the second *intrinsically oriented discourse*. Each of these discourses can be linked to contrasting practices and tendencies in teaching (see Table 12.1). In constructing this table, I have drawn on a schema developed by Codd (1997), who suggested that advocates of the sorts of neo-liberal, market-driven reforms that have occurred in countries such as the United States, Great Britain, Australia and New Zealand since 1990 have tended to have what he

TABLE 12.1 Contrasting conceptions of teaching

	Extrinsically oriented discourse	*Intrinsically oriented discourse*
Type of teaching encouraged	Technocratic-Reductionist	Professional-Contextualist
Criterion of good practice	Competent technician who gets results	Moral integrity and a willingness to make autonomous judgments
Pedagogical aim	To produce the attainment of specific learning outcomes	To enable the development of diverse human capabilities
Altruism/making a difference	Viewed in terms of raising the standards, measured by test results, of all children and closing the gap between high and low achievers	Driven by a holistic child-centred concern to benefit children's lives
Type of motivation	Extrinsic	Intrinsic
Accountability	Mainly extrinsic (audit)	Mainly intrinsic (professional)
Goal-setting	Performance goals	Mastery goals
Assessment	Goals and criteria determined by policy-mandated regimes (for example, national standards and tests)	Goals and criteria determined/negotiated on the basis of broadly based professional knowledge
Professional development	Externally determined and designed to make teachers effectively implement government reforms	Individually determined by schools/teachers seeking to meet their own professional development needs and to find better ways of addressing a community's learning needs

called a "technocratic-reductionist" as opposed to a "professional-contextualist" view of teaching. According to Codd:

> In the technocratic view, good practice can be reduced to a set of predefined skills or competences, with little or no acknowledgement given of the moral dimensions of teaching. In the professional view, on the other hand, the good practitioner is a well-rounded person who can integrate all aspects of their prior knowledge and act in a teaching situation with moral integrity.
>
> (p. 140)

At the outset, let me make it clear that I am *not* arguing that teachers who tend to fit the descriptors in the "extrinsically oriented" column are bad teachers and those who fit "intrinsically oriented" descriptors are good teachers. Rather, as mentioned previously, the columns indicate *tendencies*—those of us who are teachers are likely to recognize that at different times we experience some kind of allegiance to qualities in *both* columns. What we *can* say, however, is that each column orients a writing teacher to a different kind of assessment practice. I explore these in the remainder of this chapter.

REFLECTIVE JOURNAL TASK 12.2

To what extent do you recognize yourself in either of the two columns in Table 12.1? In what ways do you see yourself as serving two masters? What are some dilemmas that you experience as a result of this "dual service"?

Extrinsically Oriented Assessment Practice

Standardized assessment/testing regimes have been with us since the early years of the 20th century and can be thought of as the transference of an industrial technology into the educational setting and applied to human subjects. It is easy to see why the introduction of such regimes, which has gathered pace in most Anglophonic countries since 1990, should be attractive to governments.

1. When countries view their literacy standards as linked to their economic competitiveness, developing measures that can be applied to large cohorts of students year by year are seen as a means of monitoring a fall or improvement in these standards.
2. A school's performance can be measured with reference to the performance of its students in relation to national standards.

3. Likewise, the performance of teachers can also be measured in relation to their students' test results vis-à-vis national standards, with the potential for their remuneration to be indexed to these results.
4. The use of nationally developed standards can be a way for a school to measure the success of its students compared to national norms of achievement.
5. Parents have access to a view of their children's performance in comparison to other students of a similar age and stage.

You are probably aware of some of these arguments, which I have attempted to present impartially. However, at the end of this chapter, I will be indicating some readings which critique these arguments. What these arguments have in common is that they represent a powerful advocacy for extrinsic accountability (see Table 12.1). The mandated implementation of a standards regime is a powerful regulator of a teacher's practice.

In standards-based assessment, a student's achievement is assessed against defined standards and not in reference to other students in a cohort. Assessment and reporting are then linked to specified competencies, which are described in words with more or less detail (as *descriptors*). Let's compare the national writing standards for a 10-year-old pupil across two settings, the United States and England.

The Common Core State Standards (CCSS)[1]

At the time of writing, 45 American states, Washington, DC and four territories had adopted the CCSS. Bomer and Maloch (2011), in an opinion piece written for *Language Arts,* the journal of the National Council of Teachers of English (NCTE), described the standards development as "the most sweeping nationalization of the K–12 curriculum in US history" (p. 38). By what these authors term an "indirect process," the CCSS, having their origins in the American Diploma Project, effectively became national standards. The Project rationale was to find a way of assuring that "a high school diploma across state lines could be interpreted as having similar educational value" (p. 39). Bomer and Maloch, critical of the assumptions behind the CCSS, described it as an attempt to reconcile "diverse regional and ideological perspectives. . .under a universalized, rationalized curriculum framework" (2011, p. 39). In this respect, the CCSS is similar to universalizing assessment frameworks in other countries.

The CCSS outline standardized requirements, not just for the English language arts (ELA), but also for other school subjects and are therefore multidisciplinary in their scope. They are "anchored" by so-called College and Career Readiness (CCR) standards—"cross-disciplinary literacy expectations that must be met for students to be prepared to enter college and workforce training programs ready to succeed" (CCSS, 2010a, p. 4). K–5 standards are inclusive of all subject domains in an elementary school, including ELA, and cover reading, writing, speaking, listening, and language. Six–12 standards are divided into ELA standards and standards viewed as applicable to history/social studies, science, and technical subjects.

In the United States, a teacher of a 10-year-old student is likely to be addressing Grade 5 writing standards. She will notice that there are 10 distinct standards for her students to meet by the end of their Grade 5 year, each corresponding with a CCR anchor standard as follows: Text types and purposes (3 standards); Production and distribution of writing (3 standards); Research to build and present knowledge (three standards); Range of writing (1 standard) (CCSS, 2010a, p. 18). She will note also that, like students at other grade levels, her students will be expected to write three broad categories of text: opinion pieces, informative/explanatory texts and narratives. Here is the Grade 5 standard together with its level descriptors for writing narrative:

> CCSS.ELA-Literacy.W.5.3: Write narratives to develop real or imagined experiences or events using effective technique, descriptive details, and clear event sequences.
>
> - *CCSS.ELA-Literacy.W.5.3a:* Orient the reader by establishing a situation and introducing a narrator and/or characters; organize an event sequence that unfolds naturally.
> - *CCSS.ELA-Literacy.W.5.3b* Use narrative techniques, such as dialogue, description, and pacing, to develop experiences and events or show the responses of characters to situations.
> - *CCSS.ELA-Literacy.W.5.3c:* Use a variety of transitional words, phrases, and clauses to manage the sequence of events.
> - *CCSS.ELA-Literacy.W.5.3d:* Use concrete words and phrases and sensory details to convey experiences and events precisely.
> - *CCSS.ELA-Literacy.W.5.3e:* Provide a conclusion that follows from the narrated experiences or events.[2]

Before considering how this American teacher might address the demands of the extrinsic accountability master, let's look briefly at the situation of her counterpart in England.

The National Curriculum in England

At the time of writing, teachers in England were readying themselves for a National Curriculum (NC) to be introduced into schools in September 2014. Subjects from the old curriculum would be retained as would Key Stages 1–4.[3] In its draft form, the NC moves the overt focus from standards to statutory program requirements. For grades 5–6, there are two broad requirements, "Transcription" ("spelling" and "Handwriting and presentation") and "Composition" (which includes a subsection on "Grammar and punctuation"). While the focus is on the teacher, there is a clear directive ("Pupils should be taught to") specifying the skills and knowledge these 10-year-old students are expected to master. While composition is to be internally assessed by the teacher, Year 6 students take a national grammar, punctuation and spelling test reflecting "Government's beliefs that children should have mastered these important aspects of English by the time they leave primary school."[4]

Composition includes: planning; drafting and writing; evaluating and editing; proof-reading; and performance. By way of example, "Pupils should be taught to draft and write by:

- selecting appropriate grammar and vocabulary, understanding how such choices can change and enhance meaning
- in narratives, describing settings, characters and atmosphere and integrating dialogue to convey character and advance the action
- précising longer passages
- using a wide range of devices to build cohesion within and across paragraphs
- using further organizational and presentational devices to structure text and to guide the reader (e.g. headings, bullet points, underlining). (DfE, 2013, pp. 37–38)

Compared to her American counterpart, a teacher in England appears to have more freedom in her choice of genres (text-types) and less of an imperative to teach writing-related research skills. However, she is under a lot of pressure to ensure that her pupils meet certain standards around grammar, punctuation and spelling.

Serving the Extrinsic Master

Despite differences, these extrinsic curriculum/assessment regimes have a lot in common in terms of the assessment and teaching practices they encourage. Let's look at these in terms of the eight assessment steps I discussed earlier in this chapter.

- *Step 1:* Both regimes aim to predetermine the learning goals for students on a one-size-fits-all basis, that is, all students in a particular grade (or age-group) are expected to know and do certain things. American teachers will be expected to include learning goals related to the three prescribed text-types (opinion pieces, informative/explanatory texts and narratives), while teachers in England will be expected to focus on narratives. Teachers in both countries may well feel discouraged from having their students engage in writing poetry since it doesn't appear to be a favored form.[5]

- *Steps 3 and 4:* Because both regimes determine certain learning goals and not others, they will influence the kind of information teachers' will look for in student writing. A teacher from England will look for the presence or absence of cohesive devices while American teachers can be expected to ensure that their 10-year-old students use dialogue in their narratives. There is a tendency towards *performance goals* representing a "concern with demonstrating competence to others by appearing capable or outperforming others" (Urdan & Schoenfelder, 2006, p. 334).

- *Step 5:* Both regimes are associated with high-stakes standardized tests which introduce an element of measurement. In England, Grade 6 students take a national grammar, punctuation and spelling test, while in the United States students of all ages are beginning to take standardized tests aligned to the CCSS. There is an international debate about the value of standardized tests. However, what we can say with confidence is that when they become high stakes, they have a narrowing effect on the learning goals that teachers set or negotiate with their students.

- *Step 6:* Both the CCSS and the NC (and comparable documents in other countries) impact a teacher's development and use of criteria. Indeed, much of the work of developing criteria has been done *for* teachers. For instance, an American teacher, taking her cue from CCSS.ELA-Literacy.W.5.3b might have as a criterion for success for her 10-year-olds students: "Orients the reader by establishing a situation and introducing a narrator and/or characters." A teacher in England might have as a criterion for narrative writing: "Can describe setting." In these instances, the criteria have been drawn from mandated curriculum/standards documents. However, if her students are subject to high-stakes tests, the teacher is likely to want access to the criteria that are applied in the tests themselves, rather than rely on an assurance that a test is *actually* aligned with criteria implicit in curriculum or standards documents.

- *Step 8:* In both cases, because assessment and testing are used for monitoring purposes of various kinds, the focus is not just on an individual child's learning and how this is to be reported to parents. The overriding purpose becomes the regulation and standardization of a teacher's practice in order to achieve political and policy goals that may be serving agendas other than the good of the individual child. Large sums of money are at stake whenever a new curriculum is introduced, with or without an accompanying standardized testing regime.

To repeat a point made earlier, a national curriculum or a system of state or national standards constitutes a huge pressure on teachers to conform and comply. Where teachers *do* end up serving the extrinsic master, the result is a subscription to a particular construction (discourse) of writing and writing assessment. For instance, Diane, the teacher in Wohlwend's study (2009), had to adopt, against her better judgment, a "skills mastery discourse" (p. 344) in her assessment because it was effectively mandated by government in the evaluation and ranking practices prescribed. Knowing that curriculums and systems of standards have a limited life-span and are the product of the volatile world of political policy is cold comfort. To safeguard her professional autonomy, develop her expertise and retain her ethical center and altruism, a teacher needs recourse to the second master.

CRITICAL READING TASK 12.3

Depending on where you live, access an example of a national or core standard, or set of curriculum outcomes related to writing. Read the text carefully and ask yourself the questions: "What kind of writing teacher is this text encouraging me to be?" "What aspects of my students' writing does this text require me to focus attention on when assessing?" "How sympathetic am I to the view of writing and the kinds of pedagogical practices this text is encouraging?"

Intrinsically Oriented Assessment Practice

As you know, this book is premised on the proposition that teachers who identify as writers are ideally placed to guide their students to also assume the identity of writers and to develop self-efficacy around writing. The first part of this book was dedicated to contributing to your knowledge of what writing is and to your own development as a writer. It was about the development of your professional content knowledge as a teacher who knows what it *means* to write. In contrast, the second part of this book has been focused on what it means to be a teacher of writing and, to use Shulman's (1986) term, is concerned with your pedagogical content knowledge (PCK). Pedagogical content knowledge (the *how* of teaching) is viewed as dependent on professional content knowledge (the *what* of learning).

The professional content knowledge that underpinned the first section of this book was not drawn from a curriculum document, a set of national stand-ards, or an educational assessment discourse. Rather, it was drawn from a number of disciplines which have something to teach us about writing, for example, applied linguistics, cognitive psychology, semiotics, cultural studies, rhetoric, literary criticism, sociocultural learning theory, to name a few. A teacher in possession of such expertise is well equipped to make autonomous decisions about the quality of a student's writing that is responsive to that student's needs, especially because the teacher will know what the production of an effective piece of writing entails.

In the current environment, the demands of high-stakes, one-size-fits-all, summative assessment are inescapable, even though "This mind-set is at odds with what we know about biodiversity of the student body and the needs of society" (Berninger & Winn, 2006, p. 109). Intrinsically oriented assessment practice, on the other hand, is primarily concerned with the individual student's learning. This kind of practice restores teacher autonomy by providing conditions for the exercise of professional judgment and the duty of care (Noddings, 1986). In this section, I discuss two (potentially) intrinsically oriented assessment tools, learning conversations and rubrics.

Learning Conversations

Peter Elbow (2000) makes the point that not all pieces of writing we assign are high stakes and that the kinds of evaluative response we make are likely to be affected by whether the writing task is high or low stakes. He suggests that we need to make it clear to students if we expect more writing than we intend to respond to and if so, to make it clear if we are doing so because we want them to develop a private writing habit. Here is his continuum of response:

- *Zero response* (lowest stakes)
- *Supportive response—no criticism* (e.g. "Your language is really lively.")
- *Descriptive or observational response* (e.g., "I notice you've chosen to write your narrative in the present tense.")
- *Minimal, nonverbal critical response* (e.g. using a wavy line beneath a sentence with incorrect syntax.)
- *Critical response, diagnosis, advice (highest stakes)* (e.g., "Your writing would be stronger with more concrete detail.") (2000, p. 356; the examples are added by me)

As discussed in Chapter 8, my use of the word "critique" in this book is not about criticism in the sense of identifying faultiness in something like a piece of writing. Rather, critique is the practice of commentary on the basis of evaluative criteria. Praise can be thought of as positive critique. The second and third bullets above illustrate positive critique since they indicate the presence of evaluative criteria.

In the writing classroom, a learning conversation can be thought of as a verbal interaction between two or more people where the primary purpose is the facilitation of learning through the exchange of expertise and the engagement in critique. In assessment terms, the purpose is formative. All parties to the conversation are viewed as having expertise in something and as having legitimate responses. As discussed in more detail in Chapter 8, they can be students engaging in paired or group conversations (response groups), or teacher-student conferences.

Rubrics

A rubric is a marking guide customized to a particular type of text which sets out a range of criterial categories, sometimes weighted, and generally incorporating a rating scale. By way of illustration, here is the rubric that has been used by the judging panel of the June Jordan Poetry prize. Since 2003, the prize has invited 9th and 10th grade teachers to submit poems for a competition and many teachers have incorporated the competition into their classroom programs (Jocson, 2009).

1. **Purpose:** There is a purpose to this poem. The poem is driven by ideas. Every line and stanza serves the same, governing purpose of the poem.
2. **Is it a poem?** The words speak some truth. The poem is dense and the writer uses a minimal number of words to achieve maximal impact.
3. **Subject:** Each line and stanza follows logically from the one before it. The poem is a complete dramatic event. It has a beginning, middle, and end. The poem creates and/or discovers connections among otherwise apparently unrelated phenomena.
4. **June Jordan's Craft Checklist:**
5. • Strong descriptive verbs used
    • Adjective use is limited
    • Singularity and vividness of diction
    • Clarity of each stanza, and overall
    • Specific details
    • Visual imagery
    • Defensible line breaks
    • Abstractions and generalities avoided
    • The poem makes music
    • The poem fits into a tradition of poetry
    • The poem is not predictable or cliché
    • Limited use of punctuation. (Jocson, 2009, p. 278)

As can be seen, this rubric contains four criterial categories. For each of these, students' poems are given a grade on a 10-point scale. Each category has an equal weighting; as a result, a poem can earn a possible grade of 40. The language of this rubric is remote from the CCSS. In discourse terms, we can link the language used back to the New Criticism school of literary criticism and even Ezra Pound's advice to writers (Pound, 1913). The language also suggests the emancipatory discourse of culturally responsive pedagogy. We see this discourse in the insistence on the primacy of ideas and the emphasis on "speaking one's truth." The rubric is customized, not only to a particular form of writing, but also to students who are disfavored and minoritized by the American schooling system.

While this particular rubric is designed for summative purposes (judging poems for a competition), it can be made available to students and used for formative assessment purposes and as the basis for a learning conversation. In particular, the "Craft Checklist" offers a range of useful and usable criteria for poetic excellence.

Rubrics are everywhere and address most genres, as any online search will show. However, while I generally endorse the practice of using rubrics for formative assessment, the fact is that they *can* be conscripted to serve the extrinsic master (see, e.g., Spence, 2010). However, students can be actively involved in the assessment process by having them generate criteria themselves and use their *own* criteria for self-evaluation of their drafts. Researchers Andrade, Du, and Wang (2008) found that when students did this, the quality of their writing improved.

I invite you to use the following criteria for evaluating rubrics and rubric use:

1. All rubrics in some ways *construct* the object assessed. For instance, implicit in the June Jordan rubric above is a particular version of what it means to write poems. In examining a rubric, think about its "construct validity," that is, the way it constructs the particular text-type to be assessed (be it a short story, a memoir, an opinion piece or a laboratory report). If your own professional judgment suggests that there is something unsatisfactory about the way a rubric constructs the target text-type, don't use it.

2. Could you come up with a better rubric if you developed one yourself, perhaps constructing it with your students on the basis of a critical discussion of a range of excellent examples of the target text-type? If so, this is a powerful option to consider as a learning strategy.

3. Is the use of the particular rubric likely to *blind* you to the qualities of a student's writing because of the way it focuses your attention? Spence (2010) illustrates this particular pitfall by showing how a teacher of a third-grade Hispanic student used the widely disseminated "Six Traits" rubric for assessing writing in a way that led her to overlook or devalue her personal knowledge of the student's progress. In this instance, the rubric had been conscripted for high-stakes extrinsic assessment purposes, so had become an authority that silenced the teacher's own judgment. The teacher termed this rubric an "enforcer" (p. 341).[6]

4. Where each criterial category has a weighting, does this weighting appear to put the emphasis on an aspect of writing that you deem to be of minor importance, for example, surface errors? Are there categories that you would want a rubric to include, such as a willingness to engage in drafting processes?

5. Are certain kinds of students disadvantaged in some way by the way this rubric has been devised?

6. Does this rubric allow you to provide some kind of positive critique for *all* students?

Serving the Intrinsic Master

How does intrinsically oriented assessment relate to the eight assessment steps discussed earlier in this chapter?

1. *Step 1:* Learning goals are established and agreed upon in relation to a target genre or writing purpose decided on, perhaps in negotiation with the students, and in accordance with the teacher's professional understanding of the skills and knowledge required to produce the target genre.

2. *Step 2:* Goal-related activities are designed by the teacher in accordance with her understanding as a writer herself of what works in developing the required skills and knowledge. There is a tendency towards *mastery goals* representing a "concern with developing competence and skills . . . to be evaluated against internal norms" (Urdan & Schoenfelder, 2006, p. 334).

3. *Step 3:* A teacher will base her decisions related to relevant, goal-related information on her knowledge of how a text-type is produced and her knowledge of her students' individual capabilities in relation to these goals. A decision is made in respect of *what* kind of information/data ("evidence") will allow for a determination of how well the student has attained the goals determined in Step 1.

4. *Step 4:* In relation to Step 3, the information she collects will be tailored to the kind of progress she has learned to expect from each student. For less able students, she may be more focused on information related to the student's ability to clearly sequence events. For a more able student, she may focus on how he or she has managed the issue of stance.

5. *Step 5:* While most rubrics allow for quantification, the decision on whether to use rubrics with numbered scales will be made on the basis of their formative assessment value. Where the rubric has been prescribed for use by an educational authority as a way of "unpacking" a state or national standard or curriculum level, the teacher may decide on a strategy of deferral. By that I mean deferring the use of the rubric until the moment of obligation when the system requires its use for summative assessment purposes. In this instance, both masters receive their due but at different times in the learning cycle.

6. *Step 6:* Criteria of evaluation of a text-type have their origin in real-world writing practices as experienced by the teacher herself. Where rubrics are used for formative assessment purposes, they have been carefully screened and perhaps modified to suit the needs of the students. Or else, they are co-constructed *with* the students.

7. *Step 7:* In the first instance, students receive feedback from teacher and peers on the basis of Step 6 criteria. Where there is an obligatory judgment to be made on the basis of a high-stakes test or rubric aligned with a state or national standard, then a strategy of deferral may be practiced (see Step 5). However, the teacher will want to ensure that her use of criteria for formative assessment

purposes does not disadvantage her students in relation to the high-stakes summative assessment regime. A way to do this is to ensure that her criteria include categories that are emphasized in the high-stakes assessment system. In this way, she serves both masters.

8. *Step 8:* Despite the reporting pressure that is generated by high-stakes assessment, the teacher reminds herself and her students that there is a life outside of school and that the skills her students have developed in her writing program will serve them well in their ongoing lives regardless of how they perform in a high-stakes test or examination.

RESEARCH AND EVALUATION TASK 12.4

Decide on a text-type that you engage your students with (or would like to). Conduct an Internet search and select a rubric that relates to your chosen text-type. Apply the six criteria discussed earlier in an evaluation of this rubric.

Notes

1. National Governors Association Center for Best Practices, Council of Chief State School Officers (2010a). The Common Core State Standards will be abbreviated to CCSS in this chapter.
2. Retrieved from http://www.corestandards.org/ELA-Literacy/W/5
3. Readers with an interest in age/grade equivalences across a range of English-speaking countries should visit www.oup.com/oxed/pdf/GradeEquivalents.pdf
4. DfE. (2013). 2013 Key Stage 2 tests: English grammar, punctuation and spelling test. Retrieved April 22, 2013 from https://www.education.gov.uk/schools/teaching andlearning/assessment/keystage2/b00208296/ks2–2013/english-tests/grammar-punctuation-spelling-test
5. In Appendix A of the CCSS (National Governors Association Center for Best Practices, Council of Chief State School Officers (2010b), we find the following: "The narrative category does not include all of the possible forms of creative writing, such as many types of poetry. The Standards leave the inclusion and evaluation of other such forms to teacher discretion" (p. 23).
6. The "Six Traits Scoring Rubric" was developed by the Oregon Department of Education and can be accessed in Spence, 2010, pp. 347–352. It has six criterial categories (Ideas and Content, Organization, Voice, Word Choice, Sentence Fluency and Conventions), each with six detailed descriptors ranged on a scale of 1–6.

Further Reading

Assessing Writing

*   Wohlwend, K. (2009). Dilemmas and discourses of learning to write: Assessment as a contested site. *Language Arts, 86*(5), 341–351.

- Calfee, R., & Miller, R. (2007). Best practices in writing assessment. In S. Graham, C. MacArthur, & J. Fitzgerald (Eds.), *Best practices in writing instruction* (pp. 265–286). New York, NY: Guilford.

The Impact of Standardized Assessment Regimes

- McCarthey, S. (2008). The impact of *No Child Left Behind* on teachers' writing instruction. *Written Communication, 25*(4), 462–505.

Formative Assessment of Writing

- Parr, J., & Timperley, H. (2010). Feedback to writing, assessment for teaching and learning and student progress. *Assessing Writing, 15*(2), 68–85.

Learning Conversations

- Dawson, C. (2009). Beyond checklists and rubrics: Engaging students in authentic conversations about their writing. *English Journal, 98*(5), 66–71.

Using Rubrics for Teaching Writing

- Spence, L. (2010). Discerning writing assessment: Insights into an Analytical Rubric. *Language Arts, 87*(5), 337–352.
- Andrade, H., Du, Y., & Wang, X. (2008). Putting rubrics to the test: The effect of a model, criteria generation, and rubric-referenced self-assessment on elementary school students' writing. *Educational measurement: Issues and practice, 27*(2), 3–13.

Teaching Writing in the Context of a Standards Regime

- Beach, R, Thein, A., & Webb, A. (2012). *Teaching to exceed the English Language Arts Common Core State Standards: A literacy practices approach for 6–12 classrooms.* New York, NY: Routledge.

BIBLIOGRAPHY

Afflerbach, P., Pearson, P., & Paris, S. (2008). Clarifying differences between reading skills and reading strategies. *The Reading Teacher, 61*(5), 364–373.

Allison, P. (2009). Be a blogger: Social networking in the classroom. In A. Herrington, K. Hodgson & C. Moran (Eds.), *Teaching the new writing: Technology, change, and assessment in the 21st-century classroom* (pp. 75–91). New York, NY: Teachers College Press.

Andrade, H., Du, Y., & Wang, X. (2008). Putting rubrics to the test: The effect of a model, criteria generation, and rubric-referenced self-assessment on elementary school students' writing. *Educational Measurement: Issues and Practice, 27*(2), 3–13.

Andrews, R. (Ed.). (1992). *Rebirth of rhetoric: Essays in language, culture and education.* London, UK: Routledge.

Andrews, R. (1995). *Teaching and learning argument.* London, UK: Cassell.

Andrews, R. (Ed.) (2004). *The impact of ICT on literacy education.* London, UK: RoutledgeFalmer.

Andrews, R. (2008a). *The case for a National Writing Project for teachers.* Reading, UK: CfBT Education Trust.

Andrews, R. (2008b). Shifting writing practice in DCSF (2008). In *Getting going: Generating, shaping and developing ideas in writing* (pp. 4–21). Nottingham, UK: Department for children, Schools and Families.

Andrews, R. (2011). *Re-framing literacy: Teaching and learning English and the language arts.* New York, NY: Routledge.

Andrews, R., & Smith, A. (2011). *Developing writers: Teaching and learning in the digital age.* Maidenhead, UK: Open University Press/McGraw-Hill.

Andrews, R., Torgerson, C., Beverton, S., Freeman, A., Locke, T., Low, G., Robinson, A., & Zhu, D. (2006). The effect of grammar teaching on writing development. *British Educational Research Journal, 32*(1), 39–55.

Andrews, R., Torgerson, C., Low, G., & McGuinn, N. (2009). Teaching argument writing to 7- to 14-year-olds: An International review of the evidence of successful practice. *Cambridge Journal of Education, 39*(3), 291–310.

Anon. (2012a). Writing systems. *Wikipedia* entry. Retrieved August 14, 2012, from http://en.wikipedia.org/wiki/Writing_system.

Baddeley, A. (2000). The episodic buffer: A new component of working memory. *Trends in Cognitive Science, 4*(11), 417–423.

Bakhtin, M. (1986). The problem with speech genres (V. McGee, Trans.). In C. Emerson & M. Holquist (Eds.), *Speech genres and other late essays: M. M. Bakhtin* (pp. 60–102). Austin, TX: University of Texas Press.

Ball, A., & Ellis, P. (2008). Identity and the writing of culturally and linguistically diverse students. In C. Bazerman (Ed.), *Handbook of research on writing: History, society, school, individual, text* (pp. 499–514). New York, NY: Erlbaum.

Bandura, A. (1982). Self-efficacy mechanism in human agency. *American Psychologist, 37*(2), 122–147.

Bandura, A. (1997). *Self-efficacy in changing societies.* New York, NY: Cambridge University Press.

Barnes, D. (1976). *From communication to curriculum.* Harmondsworth, UK: Penguin.

Barrett, S. (2013). Supporting student growth in syntactical fluency as writers: A paired learning approach (Master's thesis. The University of Waikato, Hamilton, New Zealand).

Beach, R., Thein, A., & Webb, A. (2012). *Teaching to exceed the English Language Arts Common Core State Standards: A literacy practices approach for 6–12 classrooms.* New York, NY: Routledge.

Bereiter, C. & Scardamalia, M. (1987). *The psychology of written composition.* Hillsdale, NJ: Erlbaum.

Berninger, V., Abbott, R., Jones, J., Wolf, B., Gould, L., Anderson-Youngstrom, M., Shimada, S., & Apel, K. (2006). Early development of language by hand: Composing, reading, listening, and speaking connections; three letter-writing modes; and fast mapping in spelling. *Developmental Neuropsychology, 29*(1), 61–92.

Berninger, V., & Winn, W. (2006). Implications of advancements in brain research and technology for writing development, writing instruction and educational evolution. In C. MacArthur, S. Graham, & J. Fitzgerald (Eds.), *Handbook of writing research* (pp. 96–114). New York, NY: Guilford.

Bilton, L., & Sivasubramaniam, S. (2009). An inquiry into expressive writing: A classroom-based study. *Language Teaching Research, 13*(3), 301–320.

Blau, S. (1988). Teacher development and the revolution in teaching. *English Journal, 77*(4), 30–35.

Bomer, R., & Maloch, B. (2011). Relating policy to research and practice: The Common Core Standards. *Language Arts, 89*(1), 38–43.

Boscolo, P. (2009). Engaging and motivating children to write. In R. Beard, D. Myhill, J. Riley, & M. Nystrand (Eds.), *The Sage handbook of writing development* (pp. 300–312). London, UK: Sage.

Boyd, B. (2009). *On the origin of stories: Evolution, cognition, and fiction.* Cambridge, MA: The Belknap Press of Harvard University Press.

Brinton, D., Snow, M. A., & Wesche, M. B. (1989). *Content-based second language instruction.* Boston, MA: Heinle & Heinle.

Brooks, C., & Warren, R. P. (1976). *Understanding poetry* (4th ed.). New York: Holt, Rinehart and Winston.

Bruning, R., Dempsey, M., Kauffman, D., McKim, C., & Zumbrunn, S. (2013). Examining dimensions of self-efficacy for writing. *Journal of Educational Psychology, 105*(1), 25–38.

Bruning, R., & Horn, C. (2000). Developing motivation to write. *Educational Psychologist, 35*(1), 25–37.

Burbules, N. (1997). Rhetorics of the Web: Hyperreading and critical literacy. In I. Snyder (Ed.), *Page to screen: Taking literacy into the electronic era* (pp. 102–122). St. Leonards, New South Wales, Australia: Allen & Unwin.

Burchenal, M. (2002). The natural laws of teaching: A study of one classroom. In E. Eisner, *The educational imagination: On the design and evaluation of school programs* (3rd ed.; pp. 293–308). Upper Saddle River, NJ: Merrill Prentice Hall.

Calfee, R., & Miller, R. (2007). Best practices in writing assessment. In S. Graham, C. MacArthur & J. Fitzgerald (Eds.), *Best practices in writing instruction* (pp. 265–286). New York, NY: Guilford.

Callaghan, M., Knapp, P., & Noble, G. (1993). Genre in practice. In B. Cope & M. Kalantzis (Eds.), *The powers of literacy: A genre approach to teaching writing* (pp. 179–202). Pittsburgh: University of Pittsburgh Press.

CCCC Committee on Assessment. (1995). Writing assessment: A position statement. *College composition and communication, 46*(3), 430–437.

Cloonan, A., Kalantzis, M., & Cope, B. (2010). Schemas for meaning-making and multimodal texts. In T. Locke (Ed.), *Beyond the Grammar Wars: A resource for teachers and students on developing language knowledge in the English/literacy classroom* (pp. 254–275). New York, NY: Routledge.

Cochran-Smith, M., Barnatt, J., & Friedman, A., & Pine, G. (2009). Inquiry on inquiry: Practitioner research and student learning. *Action in Teacher Education, 31*(2), 17–32.

Codd, J. (1997). Knowledge, qualifications and higher education: A critical view. In M. Olssen & K. Morris Matthews (Eds.), *Education policy in New Zealand: The 1990s and beyond* (pp. 130–144). Palmerston North, NZ: Dunmore Press.

Collom, J., & Noethe, S. (2005). *Poetry everywhere: Teaching poetry writing in school and in the community.* New York, NY: Teachers & Writers Collaborative.

Colquhoun, G. (1999). *The art of walking upright.* Wellington, New Zealand: Steele Roberts.

Cope, B., & Kalantzis, M. (1993). *The powers of literacy: A genre approach to teaching writing.* Pittsburgh, PA: University of Pittsburgh Press.

Cremin, T., & Baker, S. (2010). Exploring teacher-writer identities in the classroom: Conceptualising the struggle. *English Teaching: Practice and Critique, 9*(3), 8–25.

Cremin, T., & Myhill, D. (2012). *Writing voices: Creating communities of writers.* London, UK: Routledge.

Damasio, A. (2000), *The feeling of what happens: Body, emotion and the making of consciousness.* London, UK: Vintage.

Dawson, C. (2009). Beyond checklists and rubrics: Engaging students in authentic conversations about their writing. *English Journal, 98*(5), 66–71.

De La Paz, S., & Graham, S. (2002). Explicitly teaching strategies, skills, and knowledge: Writing instruction in middle school classrooms. *Journal of Educational Psychology, 94* (4), 687–69.

Department of Education (1983). *English: Forms 3–5, statement of aims.* Wellington, New Zealand: Department of Education.

DfE. (February, 2013). English: Programmes of study for Key Stages 1–2. Runcorn, UK: Department for Education.

DiPardo, A., Storms, B., & Selland, M. (2011). Seeing voices: Assessing writerly stance in the NWP analytic writing continuum. *Assessing Writing, 16,* 170–188.

Dix, S., & Cawkwell, C. (2011). The influence of peer group response: Building a teacher and student expertise in the writing classroom. *English Teaching: Practice and Critique, 10*(4), 41–57.

Dix, S., Cawkwell, G., & Locke, T. (2011). New Zealand's Literacy Strategy: a lengthening tail and wagging dogs. In A. Goodwyn & C. Fuller (Eds.), *The great literacy debate: A critical response to the Literacy Strategy and the Framework for English* (pp. 87–105). London, UK: Routledge.

Dixon, J. (1975). *Growth through English: Set in the perspective of the* seventies (3rd ed.). Huddersfield, UK: National Association for the Teaching of English.

Dyson, A. H. (1990). Talking up a writing community: The role of talk in learning to write. In S. Hynds & D. L. Rubin (Eds.), *Perspectives on talk & learning* (pp. 99–114). Urbana, IL: National Council of Teachers of English.

Dyson, A. H. (2004). Writing and the sea of voices: Oral language in, around, and about writing. In R. B. Ruddell & N. J. Unrau (Eds.), *Theoretical models and processes of reading* (pp. 146–162). Newark, DE: International Reading Association.

Eagleton, T. (2007). *How to read a poem.* Malden, MA: Blackwell.

Eco, U. (1979). *A theory of semiotics.* Bloomington, IN: Indiana University Press.

Education Northwest (2014). 6 + 1 Trait(r) Definitions. Retrieved March 10, 2014 from http://educationnorthwest.org/resource/503

Eggins, S., & Martin, J. (1997). Genres and registers of discourse. In T. van Dijk, (Ed.), *Discourse as structure and process* (pp. 230–56). London, UK: Sage.

Eisner, E. (2002). *The educational imagination: On the design and evaluation of school programs* (3rd ed.). Upper Saddle River, NJ: Merrill Prentice Hall.

Elbow, P. (1973). *Writing without teachers* (2nd ed.). New York, NY: Oxford University Press.

Elbow, P. (2000). *Everyone can write: Essays toward a hopeful theory of writing and teaching writing.* New York, NY: Oxford University Press.

Elley, W. (2004). New Zealand literacy standards in a global context: The uses and abuses of international literacy surveys. *English Teaching: Practice and Critique, 3*(1), 32–45.

Faigley, L. (1985). *Assessing writers' knowledge and processes of composing.* Norwood, NJ: Ablex.

Fairclough, N. (1992a). *Discourse and social change.* Cambridge, UK. Polity Press.

Fairclough, N. (Ed.). (1992b). *Critical Language Awareness.* London, UK: Longman.

Faulkner, W. (1963). *As I lay dying.* Harmondsworth, UK: Penguin Books.

Flower, L. (1979). Writer-based prose: A cognitive basis for problems in writing. *College English, 41*(1), 19–37.

Flower, L., & Hayes, J. (1980). The cognition of discovery: Defining a rhetorical problem. *College Composition and Communication, 31*(1), 21–32.

Flower, L., & Hayes, J. (1981). A cognitive process theory of writing. *College Composition and Communication, 32*(4), 365–387.

Forster, E.M. (1976). *Aspects of the novel* (O. Stallybrass, ed.). Harmondsworth, UK: Penguin.

Frank, C. (2003). Mapping our stories: Teachers' reflections on themselves as writers. *Language Arts, 80*(3), 185–195.

Fraser, D., Aitken, V., & Whyte, B. (2013). *Connecting curriculum, linking learning.* Wellington, New Zealand: NZCER Press.

Freedman, A., & Medway, P. (Eds.). (1994). *Learning and teaching genre.* Portsmouth, NH: Boynton/Cook.

Gabriel, B. (2008). History of writing technologies. In C. Bazerman (Ed.), *Handbook of research on writing: History, society, school, individual, text* (pp. 23–34). New York, NY: Erlbaum.

Galbraith, D. (2009a). Writing about what we know: Generating ideas in writing. In R. Beard, D. Myhill, J. Riley & M. Nystrand (Eds.), *The Sage handbook of writing development* (pp. 48–64). Los Angeles, CA: Sage.

Galbraith, D. (2009b) Writing as discovery. In V. Connelly, A. Barnett, J. Dockrell & A. Tolmie (Eds.), *Teaching and learning writing* (pp. 5–26). Leicester, UK: British Psychological Society (*British Journal of Educational Psychology* Monograph Series II, 6).

Gallagher, H., Penuel, W., Shields, P., & Bosetti, K. (January, 2008). *National evaluation of Writing Project professional development: Year 1 report.* Menlo Park, CA: Centre for Education Policy, SRI International.

Gardner, J. (2006). Assessment and learning: An introduction. In J. Gardner (Ed.), *Assessment and learning* (pp. 1–5). London, UK: Sage.

Gee, J. P. (1996). *Social linguistics and literacies: Ideology in discourse* (2nd ed.). London, UK: Taylor and Francis.

Gonzalez, N., & Moll, L. (2002). Cruzando el puente: Building bridges to funds of knowledge. *Educational Policy, 16*(4), 623–641.

Goodson, I. (1999). Representing teachers. In M. Hammersley (Ed.), *Researching school experience: Ethnographic studies of teaching and learning* (pp. 122–133). London, UK: Falmer Press.

Goodwyn, A., & Fuller, C. (Eds.). (2011). *The great literacy debate: A critical response to the Literacy Strategy and the Framework for English.* London, UK: Routledge.

Gordon, J. (2005). Teaching hypertext composition. *Technical Communication Quarterly, 14*(1), 49–72.

Graham, S., & Perrin, D. (2007). *Writing next: Effective strategies to improve writing of adolescents in middle and high schools —A report to Carnegie Corporation of New York.* Washington, DC: Alliance for Excellent Education.

Graves, D. (1983). *Writing: Teachers and children at work.* Portsmouth, NH: Heinemann.

Graves, D., & Hansen, J. (1983). The author's chair. *Language Arts, 60*(2), 177–183.

Halliday, M., & Hasan, R. (1985). *Language, context, and text: Aspects of language in a social-semiotic perspective.* Geelong, Australia: Deakin University.

Hargreaves, A., & Goodson, I. (1996). Teachers' professional lives: Aspirations and actualities. In I. Goodson & A. Hargreaves (Eds.), *Teachers' professional lives* (pp. 1–27). London, UK: Falmer Press.

Harlen, W. (2006). On the relationship between assessment for formative and summative purposes. In J. Gardner (Ed.), *Assessment and learning* (pp. 103–118). London, UK: Sage.

Hass, C. (1996). *Writing technology: Studies in the materiality of literacy.* Mahwah, NJ: Erlbaum.

Hayes, J. (1996). A new framework for understanding cognition and affect in writing. In C. Levy & S. Ransdell (Eds.), *The science of writing: Theories, methods, individual differences, and applications* (pp. 1–27). Mahwah, NJ: Erlbaum.

Hayes, J. (2006). New directions in writing theory. In C. MacArthur, S. Graham & J. Fitzgerald (Eds.), *Handbook of writing research* (pp. 28–40). New York, NY: Guilford.

Hemingway, E. (1962). *The first forty-nine stories* (new ed.). London, UK: Jonathan Cape.

Hillocks Jr, G. (2006). Research in writing, secondary school, 1984–2003. *L1 – Educational Studies in Language and Literature, 6*(2), 27–51.

Hodge, R., & Kress, G. (1988), *Social semiotics.* Cambridge, UK: Polity Press.

Honeyford, M. (2013). The simultaneity of experience: Cultural identity, magical realism and the artefactual in digital storytelling. *Literacy, 47*(1), 17–25.

Hoyle, E. (1982). The professionalization of teachers: A paradox. *British Journal of Educational Studies, 30*(2), 161–171.

Hoyle, E., & John, P. D. (1995). The idea of a profession. In E. Hoyle & P. D. John (Eds.), *Professional knowledge and professional practice* (pp. 1–15). London, UK: Cassell.

Hyland, K. (2002). *Teaching and researching writing*. London, UK: Longman.

Hymes, D. (1974). *Foundations in sociolinguistics*. Philadelphia, PA: University of Pennsylvania Press.

Ings, R. (2009). *Writing is primary*. London, UK: Esmée Fairbairn Foundation.

Ivanič, R. (1994). I is for interpersonal: Discoursal construction of writer identities and the teaching of writing. *Linguistics and Education, 6*(1), 3–15.

Ivanič, R. (1998). *Writing and identity: The discoursal construction of identity in academic writing*. Amsterdam, The Netherlands: Benjamins.

Ivanič, R. (2004). Discourses of writing and learning to write. *Language and Education, 18*(3), 220–245.

Janks, H. (1994). Developing Critical Language Awareness materials for a post-apartheid South Africa. *English in Aotearoa, 22,* 46–55.

Janks, H. (2010). *Literacy and power*. New York, NY: Routledge.

Jocson, K. (2009). Steering legacies: Pedagogy, literacy, and social justice in schools. *Urban Review, 41*(3), 269–285.

Kellogg, R. (1994). *The psychology of writing*. New York, NY: Oxford University Press.

Kincheloe, J., & McLaren, P. (1994). Rethinking critical theory and qualitative research. In N. Denzin & Y. Lincoln (Eds.). *Handbook of qualitative research* (pp. 138–157). Thousand Oaks, CA: Sage.

Kirby, D. L., & Kirby, D. (2010). Contemporary memoir: A 21st-century genre ideal for teens. *English Journal, 99*(4), 22–29.

Klassen, R., Tze, V., Betts, S., & Gordon. K. (2011). Teacher efficacy research 1998–2009: Signs of progress or unfulfilled promise. *Educational Psychological Review, 23,* 21–43.

Knapp, P., & Watkins, M. (2005). Genre, text, grammar: Technologies for teaching and assessing writing. Sydney, Australia: University of New South Wales Press.

Kolln, M. (1996). Rhetorical grammar: A modification lesson. *English Journal, 85*(7), 25–31.

Kress, G. (1997). Visual and verbal modes of representation in electronically mediated communication: The potentials of new forms of text. In I. Snyder (Ed.), *Page to screen: Taking literacy into the electronic era* (pp. 53–79). St. Leonards, New South Wales, Australia: Allen & Unwin.

Kress, G. (2010). A grammar for meaning-making. In T. Locke (Ed.), *Beyond the Grammar Wars: A resource for teachers and students on developing language knowledge in the English/literacy classroom* (pp. 233–253). New York, NY: Routledge.

Kress, G., & Van Leeuwen, T. (2001). *Multimodal discourse: The modes and media of contemporary communication*. London, UK: Arnold.

Kress, G., & Van Leeuwen, T. (2002). Colour as a semiotic mode: Notes for a grammar of colour. *Visual Communication, 1*(3), 343–368.

Lea, M. (2004). Academic literacies: A pedagogy for course design. *Studies in Higher Education, 29*(6), 739–756.

Lieberman, A., & Wood, D. (2003). *Inside the National Writing Project: Connecting network learning and classroom learning*. New York, NY: Teachers College Press.

Locke, T. (1997). Poetry and the internet. *English in Aotearoa, 33,* 36–48.

Locke, T. (2004a). *Critical discourse analysis*. London, UK: Continuum

Locke, T. (2004b). Reshaping classical professionalism in the aftermath of neo-liberal reform. *Literacy Learning: The Middle Years, 12*(1)/*English in Australia, 139,* 113–121.

Locke, T. (2009). Grammar and writing — The international debate. In R. Beard, D. Myhill, J. Riley & M. Nystrand (Eds.), *The Sage handbook of writing development* (pp. 182–193). London, UK: Sage.

Locke, T. (2010a). Minding the aesthetic: The place of the literary in education and research. *Waikato Journal of Education, 15*(3), 3–16.

Locke, T. (2010b). *Beyond the grammar wars: A resource for teachers and students on developing language knowledge in the English/literacy classroom.* New York, NY: Routledge.

Locke, T. (2011). If in doubt, reach for a story. In P-H van de Ven & B. Doecke (Eds.), *Literary praxis: A conversational inquiry into the teaching of literature* (pp. 109–122). Rotterdam, The Netherlands: Sense.

Locke, T. (2013). The effects of a high-school poetry competition: A case study. *Changing English: Studies in Culture and Education, 20*(3), 277–291.

Locke, T., & Kato, H. (2012). Poetry for the broken-hearted: How a marginal year 12 English class was turned on to writing. *English in Australia, 47*(1), 61–79.

Locke, T., with Riley, D. (2009). What happened to educational criticism? Engaging with a paradigm for observation. *Educational Action Research, 17*(4), 489–504.

Locke, T., Whitehead, D., & Dix, S. (2013). The impact of "Writing Project" professional development on teachers' self-efficacy as writers and teachers of writing. *English in Australia. 48*(2), 55–70.

Locke, T., Whitehead, D., Dix, S., & Cawkwell, G. (2011). New Zealand teachers respond to the "National Writing Project" experience. *Teacher Development, 15*(3), 273–291.

Luke, A. (1992). Reading and critical literacy: Redefining the "Great Debate." *Reading Forum New Zealand, 2,* 3–12.

Luria, A. (1973). *The working brain.* New York, NY: Basic Books.

Lytle, S., & Cochran-Smith, M. (1992). Teacher research as a way of knowing. *Harvard Educational Review, 62*(4), 447–474.

McCallister, C. (2008). "The author's chair" revisited. *Curriculum Inquiry, 38*(4), 455–471.

McCarty, M. (2006). How can I as a teacher encourage my students to become a community of writers? *Ontario Action Researcher.* Retrieved August 14, 2013 from http://oar.nipissingu.ca/PDFS/V913E.pdf.

McCarthey, S. (2008). The impact of *No Child Left Behind* on teachers' writing instruction. *Written Communication, 25*(4), 462–505.

Magnifico, A. (2010). Writing or whom? Cognition, motivation, and a writer's audience. *Educational Psychologist, 45*(3), 167–184.

Ministry of Education (1999, March). *Report of the Literacy Taskforce: Advice to the Government on achieving its goal that: "By 2005, every child turning nine will be able to read, write and do maths for success."* Wellington, New Zealand: Ministry of Education.

Moffett, J. (1989). *Bridges: From personal writing to the formal essay* (Occasional Paper #9). Berkeley, CA: National Center for the Study of Writing. Retrieved from http://www.nwp.org/cs/public/print/resource/704.

Moll, L., Amanti, C., Neff, D., & Gonzalez, N. (1992). Funds of knowledge for teaching: Using a qualitative approach to connect homes & classroom. *Theory into Practice, 32*(2), 132–140.

Morgan, W. (1997). *Critical literacy in the classroom: The art of the possible.* London, UK: Routledge.

Morgan, W., Gilbert, P., Lankshear, C., Werner, S., & Williams, L. (1996). *Critical literacy: Readings and resources.* Norwood, South Australia: AATE.

Myhill, D., Fisher, R., Jones, S., & Lines, H. (2008), *Effective ways of teaching complex expression in writing. A literature review of evidence from the secondary school phase* (Research Report No. DCSF-RR032). London, UK: The Department for Children, Schools and Families (DCSF).

Muller, H. (1967). *The uses of English: Guidelines for the teaching of English from the Anglo-American conference at Dartmouth College.* New York, NY: Holt, Rinehart and Winston

National Adult Literacy Database. (n.d.). Background information on the International Adult Literacy Survey (IALS). Retrieved August 14 from

National Commission on Writing in America's Schools & Colleges (2003). *The neglected "R": The need for a writing revolution.* New York, NY: College Entrance Examination Board.

National Governors Association Center for Best Practices, Council of Chief State School Officers (2010a). *Common core state standards for English language arts & literacy in history/social studies, science, and technical subjects.* Washington, DC: Author.

National Governors Association Center for Best Practices, Council of Chief State School Officers (2010b). *Common core state standards for English language arts & literacy in history/social studies, science, and technical subjects: Appendix A: Research supporting key elements of the standards; glossary of key terms.* Washington, DC: Author. Retrieved from http://www.corestandards.org/assets/Appendix_A.pdf.

Noddings, N. (1986). Fidelity in teaching, teacher education, and research for teaching. *Harvard Educational Review, 56*(4), 496–510.

Northwest Regional Educational Laboratory. (2010). *6 + 1 trait(c)definitions.* Retrieved August 15, 2013, from http://www.thetraits.org/definitions.php.

Nystrand, M. (2006). The social and historical context of writing research. In C. MacArthur, S. Graham & J. Fitzgerald (Eds.), *Handbook of writing research* (pp. 11–27). New York, NY: Guilford.

O'Connor, J. (2004). *Wordplaygrounds: Reading, writing, performing poetry in the English classroom.* Urbana, IL: NCTE (National Council of Teachers of English).

Olson, C. (1973). Human universe. In D. Allen & W. Tallman (Eds.), *Poetics of the New American Poetry* (pp. 161–174). New York, NY: Grove Press.

Olson, D. (2009). The history of writing. In R. Beard, D. Myhill, J. Riley, & M. Nystrand (Eds.), *The Sage handbook of writing development* (pp. 6–16). Los Angeles, CA: Sage.

O'Neill, C., & Lambert, A. (1991). *Drama structures: A practical handbook for teachers.* London, UK: Heinemann.

Ong, W. (1982). *Orality and literacy: The technologizing of the word.* London, UK: Methuen.

Parr, J., & Timperley, H. (2010). Feedback to writing, assessment for teaching and learning and student progress. *Assessing Writing, 15*(2), 68–85.

Penrod, D. (2007). *Using blogs to enhance literacy: The next powerful step in 21st-century learning.* Lanham, MD: Rowman & Littlefield.

Pinker, S. (1995). *The language instinct: The new science of language and mind.* London, UK: Penguin.

Pound, E. (1913). A few don'ts by an imagiste. *Poetry: A Magazine of Verse,* [non-paginated].

Prior, P. (2006). A sociocultural theory of writing. In C. MacArthur, S. Graham & J. Fitzgerald (Eds.), *Handbook of writing research* (pp. 54–66). New York, NY: Guilford.

Pritchard, R. (1987). Effects on student writing of teacher training in the National Writing Project model. *Written Communication, 4*(1), 51–67.

Pritchard, R., & Honeycutt, R. (2007). Best practices in implementing a process approach to teaching writing. In S. Graham, C. MacArthur & J. Fitzgerald (Eds.), *Best practices in writing instruction* (pp. 28–49). New York, NY: Guilford.

Raban, B. (1990). Using the "craft" knowledge of teacher as a basis for curriculum development: A review of the National Writing Project in Berkshire. *Cambridge Journal of Education, 20*(1), 57–72.

Rubin, D. (2011). The disheartened teacher: Living in the age of standardization, high-stakes assessments, and *No Child Left Behind* (NCLB). *Changing English: Studies in Culture and Education, 18*(4), 407–416.

Rohman, G (1965). Pre-writing: The stage of discovery in the writing process, *College Composition and Communication, 16*(2), 106–112.

Sachs, J. (1997). Reclaiming the agenda of teacher professionalism: An Australian experience. *Journal of Education for Teaching, 23,* 263–275.

Saddler, B., & Graham, S. (2005). The effects of peer-assisted sentence-combining instruction on the writing performance of more and less skilled young writers. *Journal of Educational Psychology, 97*(1), 43–54.

Salomon, G. (1988). Artificial intelligence in reverse: Computer tools that become cognitive. *Journal of Educational Computing Research, 4*(2), 123–140.

Scanlan, P., & Carruthers, A. (1990). Report on the New Zealand Writing Project: An informal evaluation. *English in Aotearoa, 11,* 14–18.

Schmandt-Besserat, D., & Erard, M. (2008). Origins and forms of writing. In C. Bazerman (Ed.), *Handbook of research on writing: History, society, school, individual, text* (pp. 7–22). New York, NY: Erlbaum.

Schunk, D., & Swartz, C. (1993). Goals and progress feedback: Effects on self-efficacy and writing achievement. *Contemporary Educational Psychology, 18*(2), 337–354.

Searle, C. (Ed.) (1972). *Fire words.* London, UK: Jonathan Cape.

Seglem, R. (2009). Creating a circle of learning: Teachers taking ownership through professional communities. *Voices from the Middle, 16*(4), 32–37.

Shepherd, M. (2006). Using a learning journal to improve professional practice: A journey of personal and professional self-discovery, *Reflective Practice, 7*(3), 333–348.

Shulman, L. S. (1986). Those who understand: Knowledge growth in teaching. *Educational Researcher, 15*(2), 4–14.

Silverman, D. (2006). *Interpreting qualitative data: Methods for analyzing talk, text and interaction* (3rd ed.). Los Angeles, CA: Sage.

Skillings, J., & Ferrell, R. (2000). Student-generated rubrics: Bringing students into the assessment process. *The Reading Teacher, 53*(6), 452–455.

Snyder, I. (1993). The impact of computers on students' writing: A comparative study of the effects of pens and word processors on writing context, process and product. *Australian Journal of Education, 37*(1), 5–25.

Snyder, I. (1994). Writing with wordprocessors: The computer's influence on the classroom context. *Journal of Curriculum Studies, 26*(2), 143–162.

Snyder, I. (1997). Beyond the hype: Reassessing hypertext. In I. Snyder (Ed.), *Page to screen: Taking literacy into the electronic era* (pp. 125–143). St. Leonards, New South Wales, Australia: Allen & Unwin.

Spence, L. (2009). Inquiry based writing workshop. *Teacher Librarian, 37*(1), 23–27.

Spence, L. (2010). Discerning writing assessment: Insights into an Analytical Rubric. *Language Arts, 87*(5), 337–352.

Sperling, M., & Woodlief, L (1997). Two classrooms, two writing communities: Urban and Suburban tenth-graders learning to write. *Research in the Teaching of English, 31*(2), 205–239.

Stannard, J., & Huxford, L. (2007) *The literacy game: The story of the National Literacy Strategy.* London, UK: Routledge.

Sturgess, J., & Locke, T. (2009). Beyond *Shrek*: Fairy tale magic in the multicultural classroom. *Cambridge Journal of Education, 39*(3), 379–402.

Subramaniam, K. (2010). Integrating writing frames into inquiry-based instruction. *Science Educator, 19*(2), 31–34.

Sullivan, A. M. (2000). Notes from a marine biologist's daughter: On the art and science of attention. *Harvard Educational Review, 70*(2), 211–227.

Sylvester, R., & Greenidge, W. (2009). Digital storytelling: Extending the potential for struggling writers. *The Reading Teacher, 63*(4), 284–295.

Taylor, A. (2004). *Footprints in Teams, thumbprints in blood: Poems by Apirana Taylor.* [CD]. Paekakariki, New Zealand: Author.

Teale, W., & Sulzby, E. (Eds.), (1986). *Emergent literacy: Writing and reading.* Norwood, NJ: Ablex.

Tolchinsky, L. (2003). *The cradle of culture and what children know about writing and numbers before being taught.* Mahwah, NJ: Erlbaum.

Tolchinsky, L. (2006). The emergence of writing. In C. MacArthur, S. Graham, & J. Fitzgerald (Eds.), *Handbook of writing research* (pp. 83–95). New York, NY: Guilford.

Tschannen-Moran, M., Hoy, A., & Hoy, W. (1998). Teacher efficacy: Its meaning and measure. *Review of Educational Research, 68*(2), 202–248.

Urdan, T., & Schoenfelder, E. (2006). Classroom effects on student motivation: Goal structures, social relationships, and competence beliefs. *Journal of School Psychology, 44*(5), 331–349.

Vanderburg, R. M. (2006). Reviewing research on teaching writing based on Vygotsky's theories: What we can learn. *Reading & Writing Quarterly, 22*(4), 375–393.

van Gelderen, A. (2006). What we know without knowing it: Sense and nonsense in respect of linguistic reflection for students in elementary and secondary education. *English Teaching: Practice and Critique, 5*(1), 44–54.

Vasudevan, L., Schultz, K., & Bateman, J. (2010). Rethinking composing in a digital age: Authoring literate identities through multimodal storytelling. *Written Communication, 27*(4), 441–468.

Vygotsky, L. S. (1978). *Thought and language.* Cambridge, MA: Massachusetts Institute of Technology Press.

Weaver, C., Bush, J., with Anderson, J., & Bills, P. (2006). Grammar intertwined throughout the writing process: An "inch wide and a mile deep." *English Teaching: Practice and Critique, 5*(1), 77–101.

Wells, G. (1995). Language and the inquiry-oriented curriculum. *Curriculum Inquiry, 25*(3), 233–269.

Wendt, A., Whaitiri, R., & Sullivan, R. (Eds.). (2003). *Whetu moana: Contemporary Polynesian poems in English.* Auckland, New Zealand: Auckland University Press.

Wenger, E. (1998). *Communities of practice: Learning, meaning, and identity.* New York, NY: Cambridge University Press.

Wheeler, R., & Swords, R., (2006). *Code-switching: Teaching standard English in urban classrooms (theory and research into practice).* Urbana, IL: National Council of Teachers of English.

White, C. (2000). Strategies are not enough: The importance of classroom culture in the teaching of writing. *Education 3–13, 28*(1), 16–21.

White, E. J., & Peters, M.A. (Eds.) (2011). *Bakhtinian pedagogy: Opportunities and challenges for research, policy and practice in education across the globe.* New York, NY: Peter Lang.

Whitney, A. (2008). Teacher transformation in the National Writing Project. *Research in the Teaching of English, 43*(2), 144–187.

Whitney, A. (2009). Writer, teacher, person: Tensions between personal and professional writing in a National Writing Project summer institute. *English Education, 41*(3), 235–258.

Wohlwend, K. (2009). Dilemmas and discourses of learning to write: Assessment as a contested site. *Language Arts, 86*(5), 341–351.

Wood, D., & Lieberman, A. (2000). Teachers as authors: The National Writing Project's approach to professional development. *International Journal of Leadership in Education, 3*(3), 255–273.

Wrigley, S., & Smith, J. (October, 2010). Making room for writing: The NATE Writing Project. *EnglishDramaMedia,* pp. 13–19.

Zehm, S., & Kottler, J. (1993). *On being a teacher: The human dimension.* Thousand Oaks, CA: Corwin.

Zimmerman, B., & Risemberg, R. (1997). Becoming a self-regulated writer: A social-cognitive perspective. *Journal of Contemporary Educational Psychology, 22*(1), 70–101.

INDEX